Decorate your Home with NEEDLECRAFT

Decorate your Home with NEEDLECRAFT

67 Original step-by-step projects

Martini Nel

HUTCHINSON AUSTRALIA

Hutchinson Australia
an imprint of
Random Century Australia Pty Ltd
20 Alfred Street, Milsons Point NSW 2061

Sydney Melbourne London
Auckland Johannesburg
and agencies throughout the world

First published by Random Century Australia 1991

National Library of Australia
Cataloguing-in-Publication Data

Nel, Martini.
Decorate your home with needlecraft.

ISBN 0 09 182644 6

1. Needlework. I. Title.

746.4

Cover design by Christie and Eckermann, Sydney
Typeset by Savage Type Pty Ltd, Brisbane
Printed by Colorcraft Ltd, Hong Kong
Production by David Ell Press Pty Ltd, Sydney

Contents

Introduction

Needlework can be a wonderfully creative and relaxing pastime. There is much more to sewing than just dressmaking. Ideas abound for making unusual accessories to add individual character to your home. The choice between making a simple or intricate project is entirely up to you! Experiment with different fabrics, colours and designs to create unique craft articles reflecting your personality. Your family, relatives and friends will be delighted to receive handmade gifts. It could be a key ring made in a few minutes, or a quilt which will definitely become an heirloom – the fact that you made it yourself will make the recipient feel very special.

School holidays can be transformed into enjoyable, productive times when children discover how easy and what fun it is to make some of the novelty items for their own rooms or as gifts. So be shrewd and allow them to page through this book!

Four techniques for creative needlework are explained and used: patchwork, appliqué, candlewicking and quilting. Patchwork is the sewing together of scraps of fabric to form a pattern; appliqué is the stitching of one piece of fabric onto another and quilting is the stitching together of two pieces of fabric with a thick padding or lining between them. Candlewicking is a special kind of embroidery.

Until you have mastered the technique, it is wise to begin by making something small and then you can tackle something larger. Be as inventive as you please – adapt the patterns and techniques, improvise and enjoy decorating either your own home or those of your friends with decorative needlework accessories.

Materials

It is essential to have the correct basic equipment at hand before embarking on any needlework project. The following items are indispensable: good quality fabric, matching thread, a pair of sharp scissors, needles, pins and a sewing machine (if you intend using the machine method). There are additional, though expensive devices to facilitate and simplify the work, but do not buy them unless you are really going to use them. For instance, do not buy a rotary cutter and cutting board if you intend making only one or two cushions, but if you decide to make a bed quilt, such as the log cabin quilt for a nursery (p. 96), or the seminole quilt for a teenager's room (p. 89), it will save time when cutting out the pattern pieces.

Fabric

It is essential to choose the correct fabric for your project. Keep in mind the purpose of the accessory you intend making. For example, although towelling fabric is particularly suitable for bathroom accessories, it will not do for sewing small patches together to make a patchwork cushion. Silk and satin tend to fray and would therefore be impractical for an accessory that requires frequent washing.

Most fabrics are suitable for machine-sewn appliqué. You can use fabrics that are normally too thick to fold, since seam allowances are not folded over. Take care when choosing fabrics for patchwork, however. Cotton is easy to fold, cut and stitch, making it an excellent choice. Blends of cotton and polyester are also suitable. Choose similar fabrics for a specific accessory, since the patches may react differently to washing and general wear and tear.

Consider the following when choosing a fabric:

- It should not fray too easily;
- It should not stretch;
- It should be colourfast and shrink-resistant;
- It should not be too thick for a needle to pass through easily.

If you are uncertain whether the fabric is colourfast or shrink-resistant, it is best to wash and iron each piece beforehand. This simple precaution will prevent all your hard work being destroyed after the first wash. Always remember to prewash unbleached calico in hot water, to preshrink it and remove all the starch. Add fabric softener to the final rinse.

The following fabrics are best avoided for patchwork:

- Those with very large, distinct designs;
- Those with stripes, except when the stripes are necessary to create a special effect;
- Those with patterns running in one direction.

Fabrics with stripes or regular border patterns are striking when used to form a border. Strips of fabric with border patterns can be bought by the metre.

When decorating a room, the existing colour scheme is an important consideration. Clever use of colour can even make architectural flaws less apparent. Warm colours such as red, orange or yellow make a room appear warmer. A very sunny room will appear cooler if colours such as blue or green are used. A combination of cool and warm colours works well.

In the nursery (p. 95), the three primary colours are predominant (blue, yellow and red), alternating with green, a secondary colour. Bright colours, and particularly the three primary colours, are suitable for a child's room.

The texture of the fabric also influences the colour. Satin and glazed cotton reflect light, whereas rough fabrics absorb light. For example, although the colour scheme of the dining room (p. 47) is white, the different fabric textures provide variety.

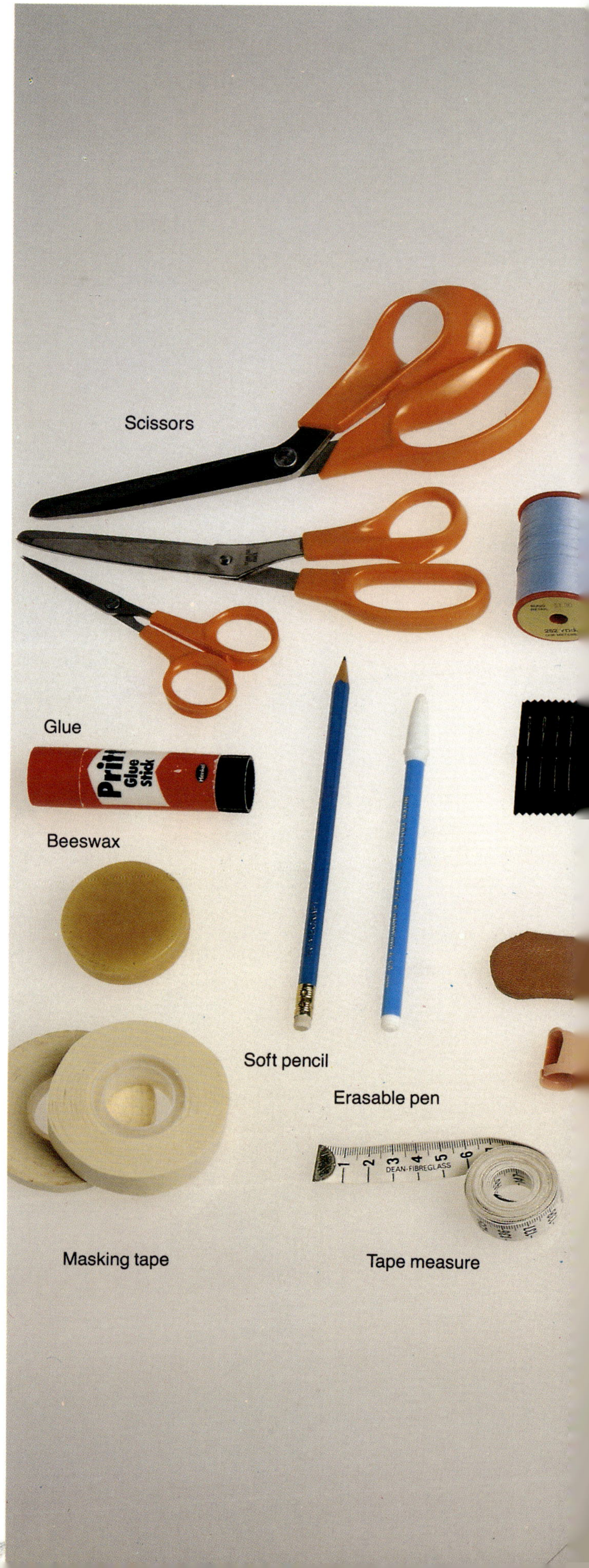

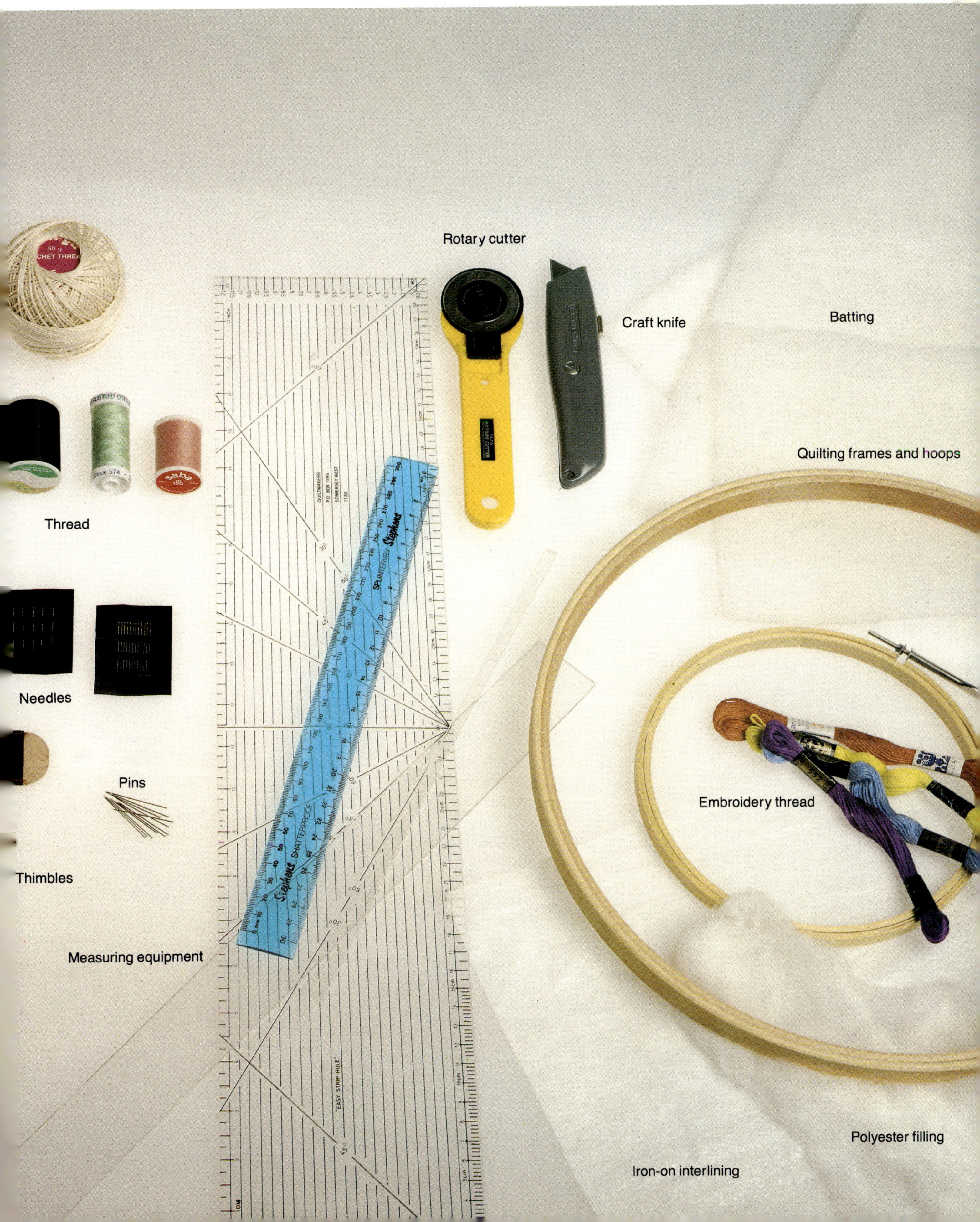
Rotary cutter
Craft knife
Batting
Quilting frames and hoops
Thread
Needles
Pins
Thimbles
Embroidery thread
Measuring equipment
Polyester filling
Iron-on interlining

The background colour of a bed quilt is very important. A light-coloured fabric contrasts well with a dark background and vice versa. Explore fabrics with a fine pattern or dots for a quilt with fairly large squares to create a more interesting effect.

Needles

Make sure the correct needles are at hand for your specific project – this will prevent intense frustration!

Use sharp-pointed needles (no thicker than no. 8) for sewing patches together. Thin needles pass through several layers of fabric more easily.

A needle with a large eye – chenille no. 18-24 – is best for candlewicking, since the thread used for candlewicking is quite thick.

Shorter, medium-sized needles (also called "betweens") with a sufficiently large eye – no. 7-10 – are best for quilting. Initially the small needles may feel strange, but you will soon get used to them.

Pins

Use long, smooth, rustproof pins. They should be thin enough not to make holes in the fabric, especially if you are working with organdie or voile.

Thread

The correct thread for a specific technique and accessory is essential. Use the following:

- Mercerised cotton thread that blends into the colour scheme for joining patches;
- Inexpensive tacking thread in a contrasting colour – but do be careful not to use very dark tacking thread on light fabric as it may leave marks;
- Special quilting thread imported from America is best for quilting. It is very strong and resists knotting. Ordinary mercerised cotton run through a cake of beeswax is a good substitute. Buttonhole-silk or mercerised saddle-stitch thread may also be used although it is slightly thicker. Select the colour of quilting thread very carefully. Use either the same colour as the accessory, a contrasting colour, or even different colours to blend in with the background for a special effect.
- Use embroidery thread to embroider detail on an appliquéd motif.

Scissors

It is preferable to have three different pairs of scissors:

- Invest in a good pair of long-bladed needlework scissors. Use them only for cutting fabric and keep them away from your children (and your husband)!
- An inexpensive pair is fine for cutting templates and paper.
- A small pair of sharp-pointed scissors is very handy for snipping off cotton threads.

Thimble

There are many kinds of thimbles. You will need two, especially for quilting: one for the middle finger of your right hand and one for the index finger of your left hand.

If you are not used to working with an ordinary thimble, try using a leather thimble (cut off the finger of an old leather glove if you cannot find a leather thimble).

If you have long nails, a special thimble with an opening at the head is available.

Rotary cutter

A rotary cutter is very handy for cutting strips of fabric as it enables one to cut through several layers at once. The larger rotary cutter is best as it can cut through more layers at a time and does not become blunt as quickly.

Cutting board

A cutting board is essential for protecting your work surface when using a rotary cutter. Never test the rotary cutter on any other surface such as glass or wood, as it may damage the blade as well as the surface.

Measuring equipment

You will need several rulers:

- An ordinary ruler;
- A special long ruler (60 cm), available at specialist shops;
- Long plastic strips of different widths can be cut by a plastics dealer if unobtainable. Widths of 2, 3, 5, 7 and 10 cm are generally used;
- A 6 mm wide quilter's quarter for cutting seam allowances is also obtainable.

Small blade or craft knife

A small blade or craft knife is used for cutting out cardboard templates.

Soft pencil

A soft pencil is necessary for tracing the outlines of a template onto the fabric.

Erasable pen

A special blue erasable pen is available and is especially handy for marking out quilting patterns. Do not iron over the pen marks and rinse the article in cold water, or the ink may stain it. First test the pen on a piece of fabric to check that it does not run and washes out completely.

Masking tape

Different widths of masking tape are used for marking quilt patterns. The narrowest masking tape (6 mm wide) is particularly suitable for marking the straight lines for echo (contour) and outline quilting (p. 29).

Use a broader masking tape, e.g. 2.5 cm wide, when you mark patterns for filling-in quilting (p. 29). The widest masking tape (5 cm) is suitable for cutting out motifs, e.g. leaves or hearts. The motif is stuck onto the background and quilting stitches are made around it. The tape is removed and used again.

Cardboard

Use cardboard or thin, hard plastic (e.g. old X-ray film) to make templates. Fine sandpaper is also very effective because it does not slide on the fabric.

Glue

A glue stick (Pritt) is needed to paste paper on cardboard and for some appliqué methods.

Quilting frames and hoops

An embroidery or quilting frame may be used for both small and larger projects. When quilting a large accessory one simply moves the frame or hoop to the next section to be worked on. An embroidery or quilting frame is essential for candlewicking, since the fabric must be held securely.

Rectangular frames come in different sizes. A very large frame is suitable for group quilting projects, but is unwieldy and difficult to move around. A smaller frame is made in the same way. It is easier to handle and suitable for one person to use.

Beeswax

Thread for quilting is run through beeswax to prevent breaking or tangling.

Iron-on interlining

In some appliqué methods interlinings are ironed onto the wrong side of the fabric panel to strengthen it.

Batting

Batting of varying thickness and quality is available.

- Thick, soft batting is suitable for quilts and cushions, but is more difficult to use than the thinner type;
- Thin, stiff batting is suitable for wall hangings;
- Thin, soft batting is used for jackets. This batting should not be too stiff, as it may otherwise spoil the appearance of the article.

Polyester filling

This kind of filling is fully washable and therefore suitable for stuffing cushions, pincushions and toys.

Techniques

The practice of patching skins and later fabric to make coverings and other home accessories has existed for centuries. Patchwork, as we know it today, originated in America. The British settlers in America had many problems to contend with: long and severe winters, an isolated existence and worst of all, poverty.
Fabric was very scarce. Clothes were not easily discarded, instead they were adjusted and used again and again. When they were too old and worn to wear, the remnants were used to make quilts.
"Crazy" quilts were the first kind of quilting. They consisted of various sized scraps patched together. Such quilts were actually too large and unwieldy to handle with ease. Later, smaller squares were sewn together to make a larger quilt. This was more manageable. Initially the fabric squares were very simple but eventually more complicated patterns were designed.
So-called quilting bees were formed – women got together to do patchwork. This was an important social activity in isolated communities. Children were taught needlework from a very early age, and tradition required a bride to possess 12 quilts, as well as a bridal quilt decorated with doves, hearts and roses.
Patchwork is not confined to quilts and cushions. You can make patchwork, appliqué and quilted accessories for every room in your home. This technique is eminently suitable for large or small domestic items. Patchwork garments are very popular too.
The same pattern can often be used for different techniques, e.g. an appliqué pattern for quilting or candlewicking. Patterns can also be adjusted to obtain a completely different effect – there is great scope for experimenting.

Patchwork

Single-seam method (American block patchwork)

The single-seam method is the most versatile patchwork method. Anything from a quilt, cushion, wall hanging to clothes can be made with this method.

Decide on the project you want to tackle, and the block pattern you wish to use.

Trace the templates onto paper, cut them out carefully and paste them onto cardboard or stiff plastic (X-ray film). Write down the name of each template and the quantity needed for the pattern. Also write down the number of sections the pattern consists of – this way you will notice immediately if one is missing.

Consider the colour choice and combination carefully – this can determine the success of your project. If you are uncertain, draw the pattern a few times and use different colour combinations.

Now place the first template on the wrong side of the fabric. Leave a seam allowance of at least 5 or 6 mm around each template, but use the fabric economically.

Trace the outlines accurately onto the fabric using a soft pencil, and be especially careful at the corners. Continue in this way until all the pattern pieces have been traced (fig. 1).

Cut out the pattern pieces.

Arrange the fabric pieces until you are satisfied with the effect. Do not omit this step, or you may find that you are not happy with the end product!

Patchwork may be done by hand or machine; this is a matter of personal preference.

Hand method

Place two patches with right sides together. Pin the fabric layers exactly at the corners (A and B in fig. 2). Place another pin through the stitching line and make sure that both stitching lines correspond exactly.

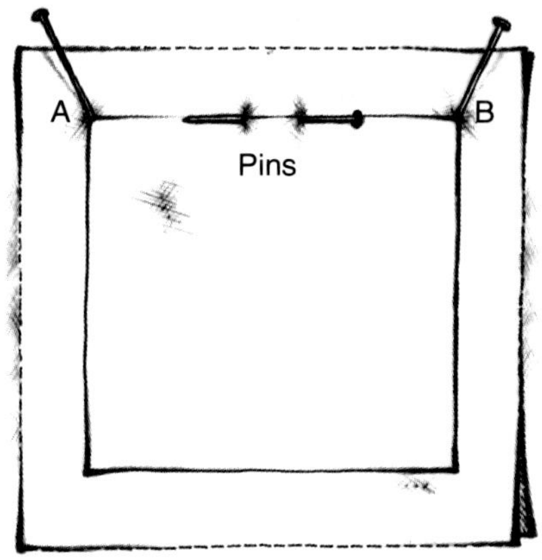

Figure 2

Begin with a double stitch and continue with small running stitches from corner to corner, ending with another double stitch. Press the seam flat with your finger. The seam is not folded open, it is pressed towards the darkest fabric, so that it does not show through on the other side.

Decide on the easiest sequence beforehand and sew all the patches together according to the specific pattern.

If the pattern piece has a slight curve, leave a slightly smaller seam allowance (approximately 4 mm) than for straight-sided pieces. First find the centre of the curve, place the two patches on top of each other, right sides together, and pin through both layers of fabric in the centre. Then pin the fabric at both corners. Sew as for straight lines.

Machine method

Place two patches on top of each other, right sides together as for the hand method. Pin at each corner, making sure the pins penetrate both layers of fabric. Place another pin through the stitching line making sure they correspond exactly. Join as many patches in this way as needed.

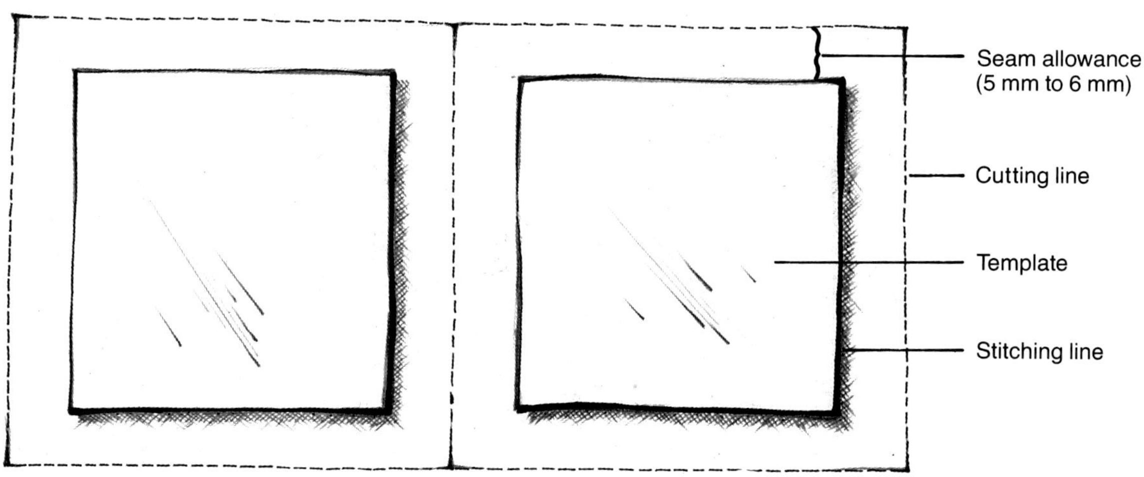

Figure 1

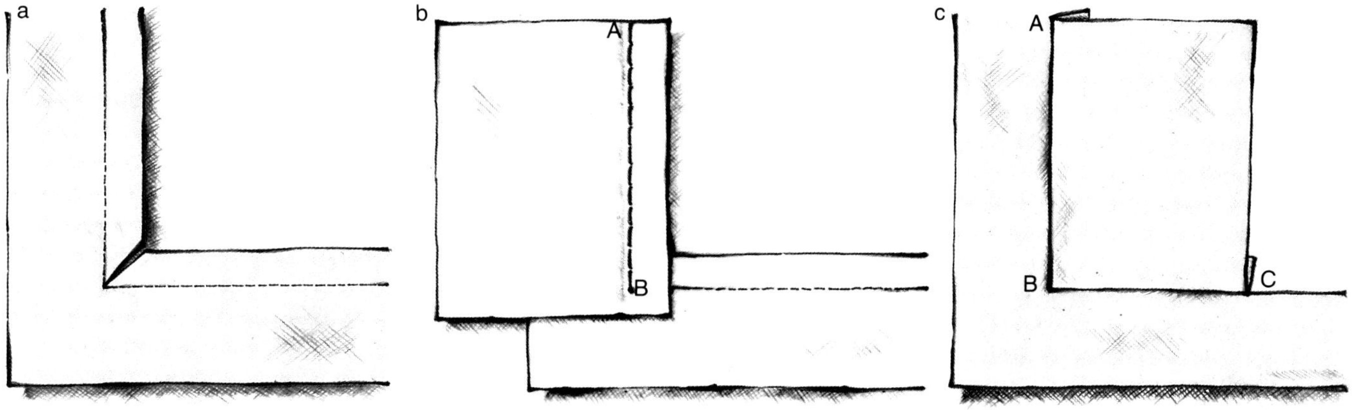

Figure 3

Sew, using medium stitch length and tension. Do not use double stitching at the beginning or end, as this may cause the stitches to pull too tightly and creases may form. Leave a thread of about 5 mm at either end of each row of stitches to prevent the stitching from unravelling. Do not cut the thread after stitching a patch. Make a "chain" of patches and do all the cutting at the same time – this saves time. Join all the patches according to the pattern.

The setting of pattern pieces into corners or angles is discussed briefly because it occurs so often. To set a patch into a corner, snip the corner (fig. 3a). Then sew one side of the patch to the corner (from A to B in fig. 3b). Fold in the seam allowance of the patch, and sew the second side of the patch (from B to C in fig. 3c).

Log cabin method

This patchwork method works on the same principle as the log cabins the American settlers built. Narrow strips of fabric surround a central block, and each strip overlaps the previous one. The strips are usually stitched onto backing fabric or paper, and it is a good method to do on a machine. It is also one of the easiest patchwork methods. The use of colour plays an important role – each completed block consists of a lighter and a darker section. Sometimes prints and plain fabrics are alternated in these half sections.

There are several variations of the log cabin method. For example, by placing the central block in a corner and stitching the strips to two sides, a fan effect from one corner is achieved. Or the central block is positioned so that one section of the pattern is twice as large as the other. The strips in the larger section are double the width of the smaller one. In this way a log cabin pattern is achieved in which the proportions between the two sections are 2:1. Figure 4 is an example of the commonest method, with three light and three dark colours, and one main colour.

The width of the strips is a matter of choice. A seam allowance of 5 mm is usually left on either side. You may cut the strips first, but do not subdivide them yet. Cut a square of fabric the size of the completed log cabin block from unbleached calico or thin paper (which is removed afterwards).

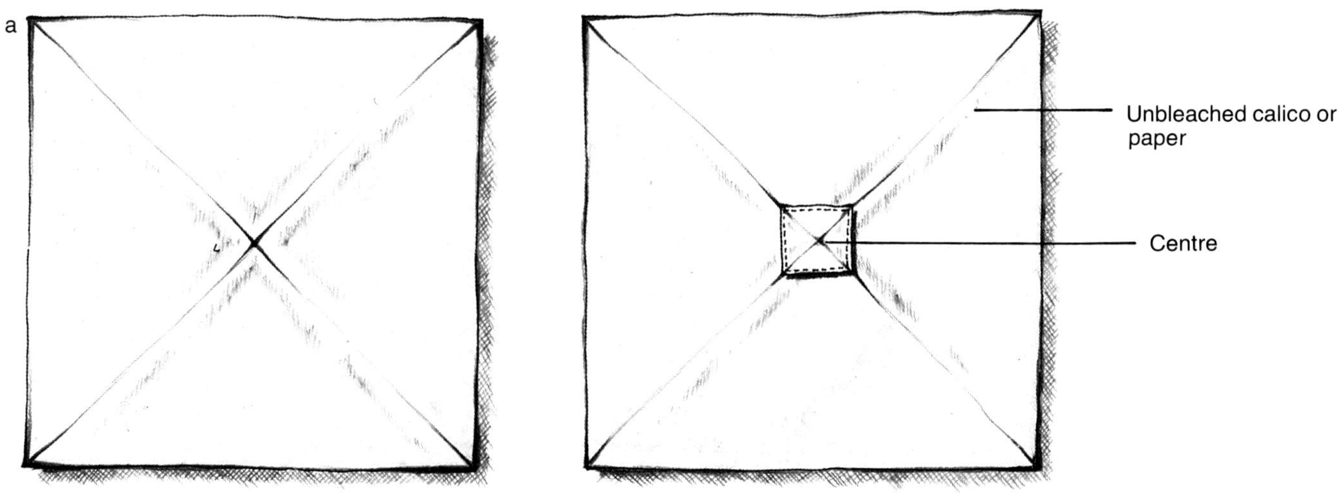

Figure 4

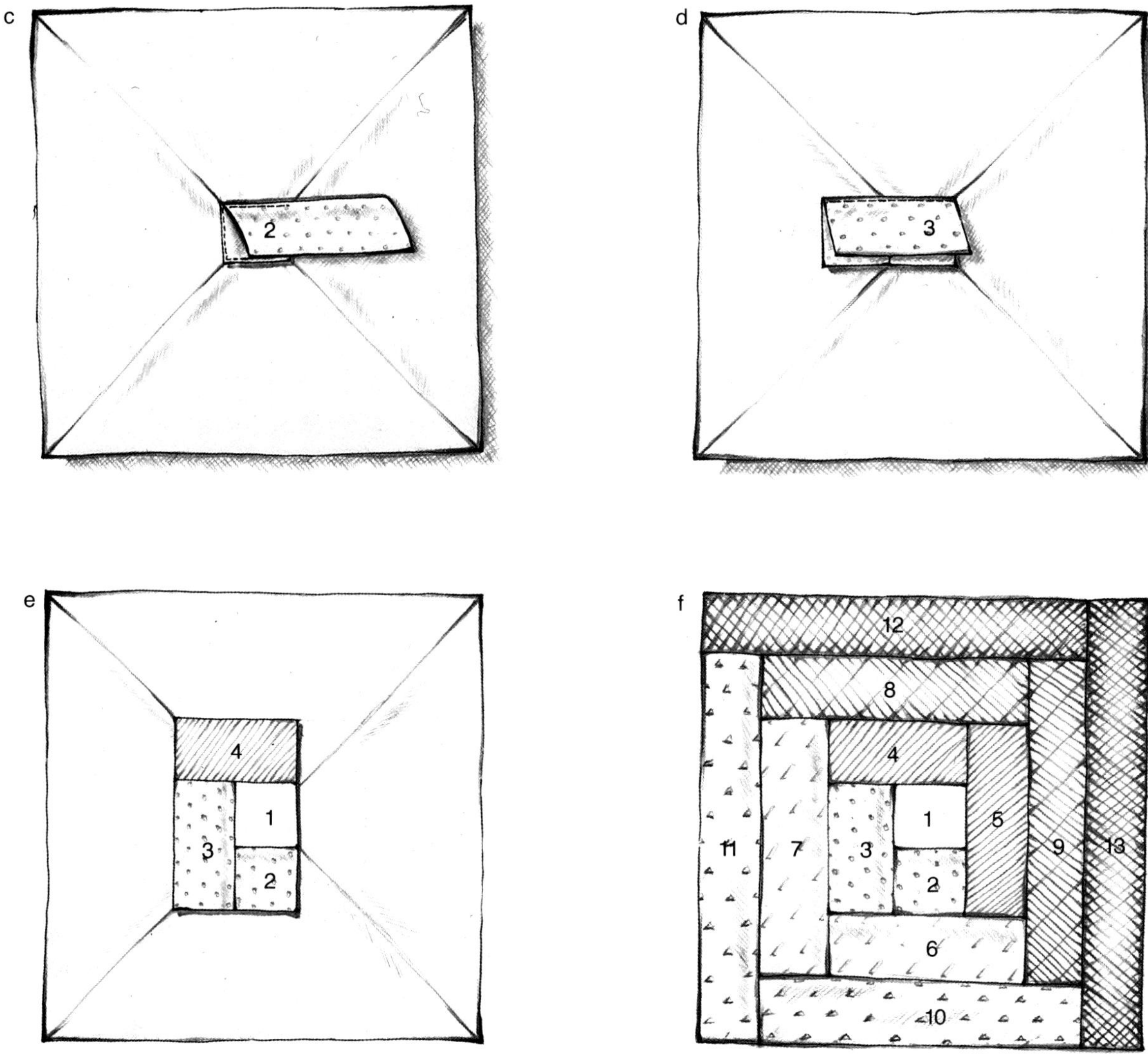

Figure 4

Decide in advance on the order in which you will use the different fabrics. Number them to avoid using the wrong piece, e.g. no. 1 light, no. 2 light, etc. You may use a main colour for the centre block. Cut a centre block with edges as long as the width of the strips.

Establish the centre of the centre block and of the unbleached calico or paper by folding it twice diagonally (fig. 4a). The fold lines will help you to sew straight. Place the two centres on top of one another with right sides up. Tack the small block onto the unbleached calico or paper (fig. 4b).

Begin with the first light-coloured fabric. Place the strip of fabric on the centre block with right sides together, and pin it to one side. Join, using small running stitches. Begin and end with double stitching, or stitch with ordinary straight machine stitches (fig. 4c). Cut the excess fabric to correspond exactly with the edge of the centre block. Fold the strip, smooth it flat with your nail, and pin. Remember always to turn the fabric in the same direction (anticlockwise), so that the section where the following strip is to be sewn is at the top of the block.

Then take the same light-coloured fabric, place over the previous two blocks with right sides together, and stitch. Trim the excess fabric again (fig. 4d). Fold the strip and smooth flat.

Sew a strip of the first dark-coloured fabric (fig. 4e).

Follow the diagram and complete the block (fig. 4f). The last strip of the outer edge may also be stitched to the backing material. The stitching line serves as a guide when the panels are stitched together. When all panels have been completed, stitch them together. Since the effect is achieved by the arrangement of panels, it is best to try a few variations before joining them (fig. 5a and b).

Inlay method (English patchwork)

This method consists of tacking paper patches without seam allowances to cut-out fabric patches with seam allowances and then joining them with tiny oversewing stitches. Each fabric patch is placed on a separate paper patch. To save time, trace the template onto paper and make photostats. Or place a few layers of paper on top of one another and cut out simultaneously (you need only to trace the templates on the top sheet of paper).

Centre and pin the backing paper to the wrong side of the fabric patch (fig. 6a).

Begin at one side of a patch. Make a knot in the thread and fold the fabric seam allowance over the backing paper. Begin about 1 cm from the corner and use large tacking stitches through both layers of fabric and paper (fig. 6b).

Fold the fabric over the second side of the backing paper. Tack through all the layers (fig. 6c).

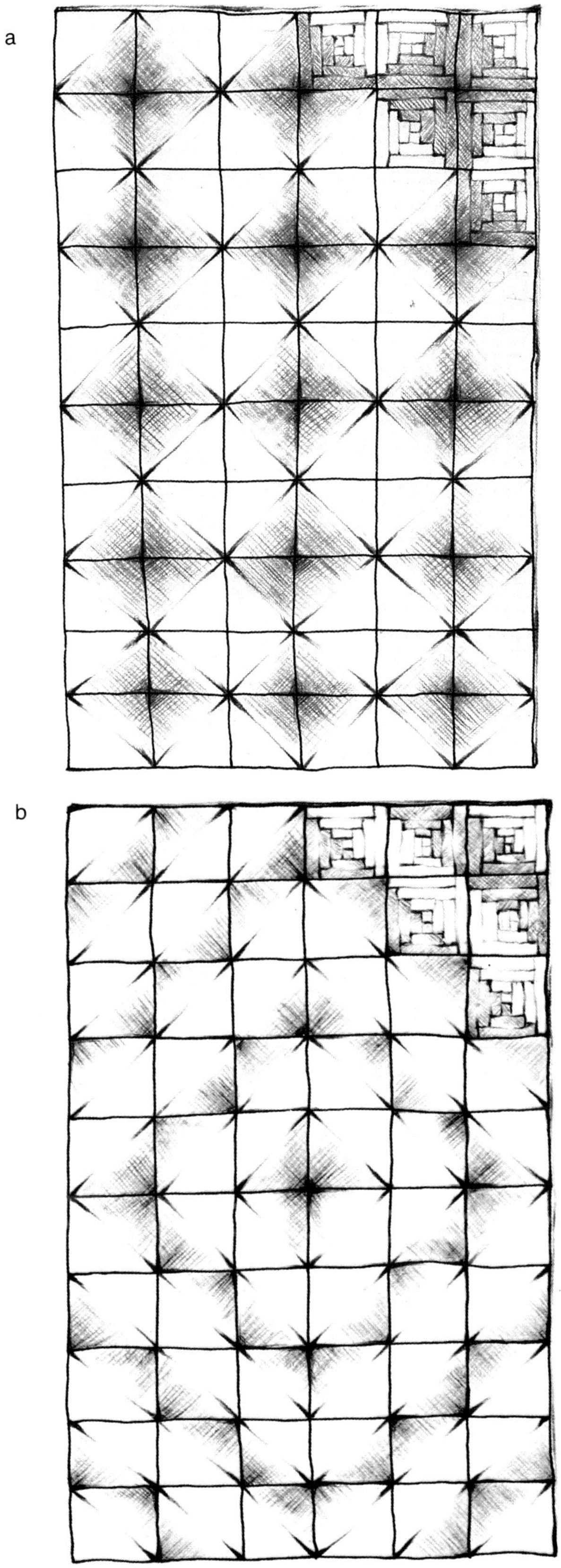

Figure 5

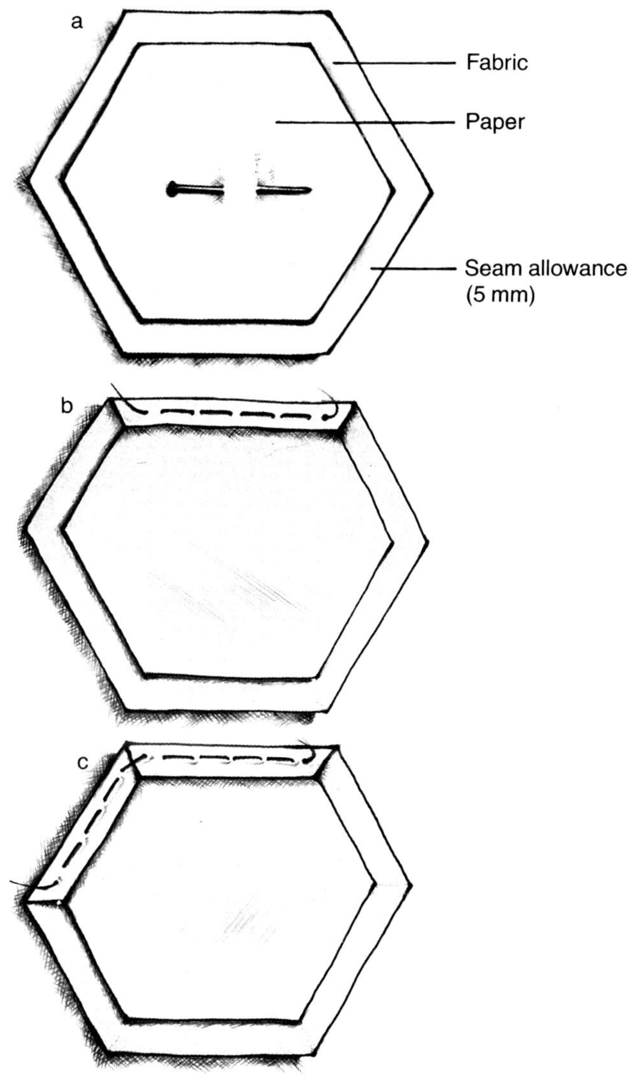

Figure 6

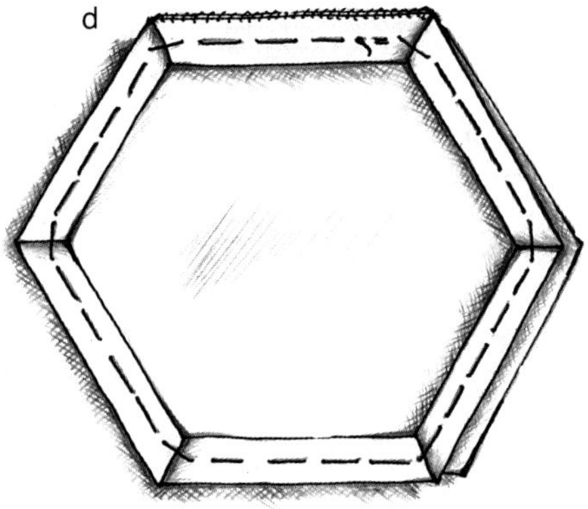

Figure 6

Complete all the sides in the same way. When all patches are complete, join them as follows:

Place two patches with right sides together and join with small oversewing stitches (fig. 6d). Begin about 3 mm from the corner with a double stitch and sew three tiny oversewing stitches back towards the corner. Make sure the corners match perfectly. Do not sew too far from the edge, as this may result in a thick ridge. Continue with oversewing stitches to the next corner. Make three back stitches again and end with a double stitch. Cut the thread. Join all the patches in this way following the pattern.

Do not sew through the backing paper, as it will be difficult to remove afterwards. Leave it in as long as possible to prevent the edges of fabric cut on the bias from stretching.

Seminole

This patchwork method originated from the Seminole Indians in Florida. The technique they developed enables one to make tiny fabric patches. Seminole strips were originally sewn onto garments, but nowadays they are often used to make patchwork quilts because it is such a quick and easy method. Fabric strips are sewn together, cut in sections and then joined again in long or diagonal strips.

The fabric strips may be any width or length and may consist of two or more colours. They are stitched together with the same seam allowance throughout. The seam allowance is usually 6 mm or the width of the presser foot of a sewing machine.

The strips are cut through the width and then rejoined. It is very important to measure, cut and stitch the strips carefully. Always follow the length- or crosswise grain of the fabric. Figures 7a and b illustrate the different ways of cutting seminole strips. Use them on garments, in quilts and as borders for quilts. You may even use them on smaller items such as a tea cosy or traycloth (p. 52).

Clamshell patchwork

This patchwork method is more difficult than most others because of the curved lines. Cotton fabric is best for this method. Clamshell patchwork is very effective when appliquéd on garments. It is not necessary however, to make a complete garment or article using this method – just a small area of clamshell patchwork is sufficient to make it look special.

Method 1

Using a template, trace the required number of patches onto iron-on interlining. Cut them out without seam allowances. Cut the same number of patches from fabric, with seam allowances.

Iron each interlining piece onto the wrong side of a fabric patch (fig. 8a).

Fold the top seam allowance over to the wrong side of the fabric and secure with tacking stitches. Make neat little pleats to smooth the curves (fig. 8b).

Do not tack the two concave curves, as they will be covered by the next row.

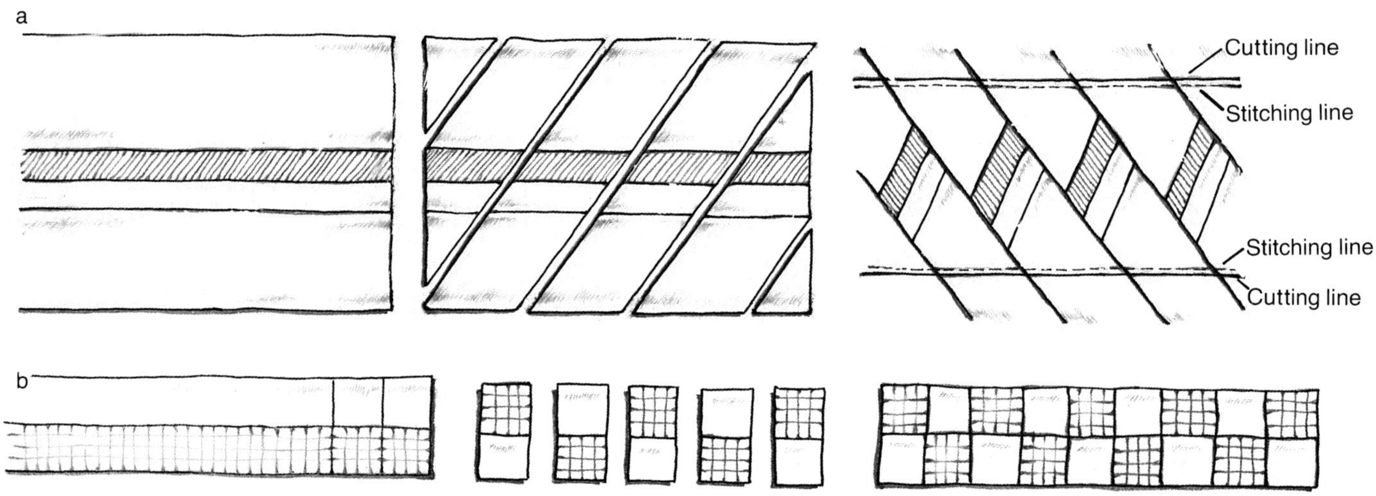

Figure 7

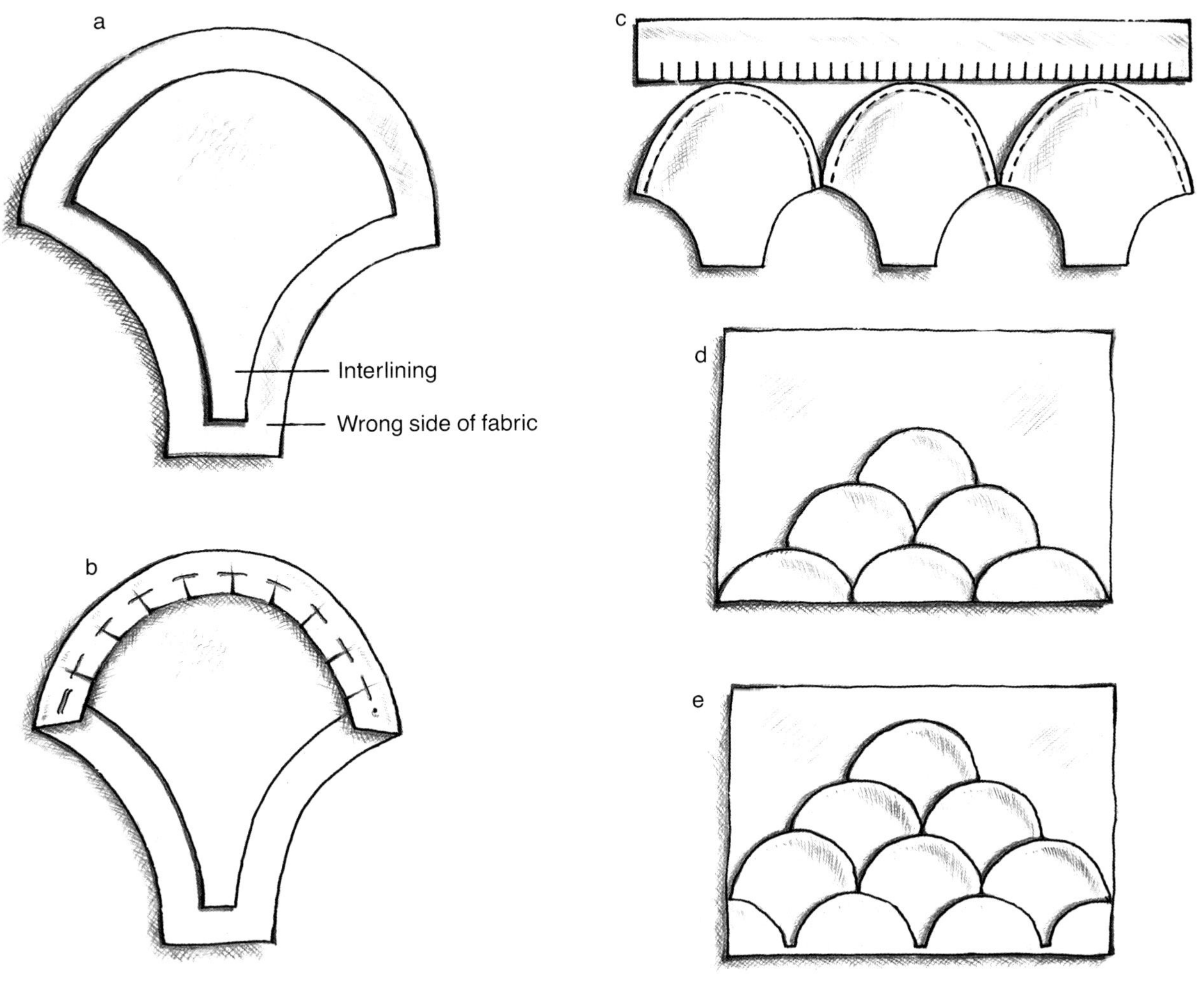

Figure 8

Method 2

Paste the original template onto stiff cardboard. Trace the pattern onto the right side of the fabric, using an erasable pen. Add the seam allowance and cut out.

Use these outlines as a guide and fold the seam allowance over to the wrong side of the fabric. Make neat little tucks in the seam allowance to keep curves smooth and tack. Do not tack the two concave curves – they will be covered by the next row.

Use a ruler as a guide to arrange the completed clamshell motifs in a straight line (fig. 8c). Place them directly onto the background fabric. Alternatively, first join the rows and then sew them onto the background fabric.

Begin at the top and sew downwards. The second row overlaps the seam allowances of the first row. Use hem or slip-hemming stitches. Repeat the process. The last row may end flush with a seam, e.g. on a garment. The whole pointed section is then folded in, leaving only a half-moon visible, or the concave curves of the last row may be tacked, so that it ends with a pretty point (fig. 8d and e).

Folded-star technique

For this technique small pieces of fabric are folded to form triangles, and then sewn onto the background fabric in a star shape. The folded triangles may also be used to decorate jackets, pockets and other garments. Arrange them to form a motif or alternate in rows.

If you wish to make a round object, start with a round piece of background fabric. This fabric is always cut slightly larger than the required size of the completed article.

Cut a square to the required size from the background fabric. Mark the centre by folding the square twice diagonally. If you have a white background and the first star point is red, cut another smaller red patch and place it in the centre so that the white does not show through.

Cut four squares from the first fabric. Fold each one in half diagonally. Fold the (two) corners in towards the centre to form a triangle (fig. 9a). The folds must be made very accurately.

Place the triangle on the background fabric with the point

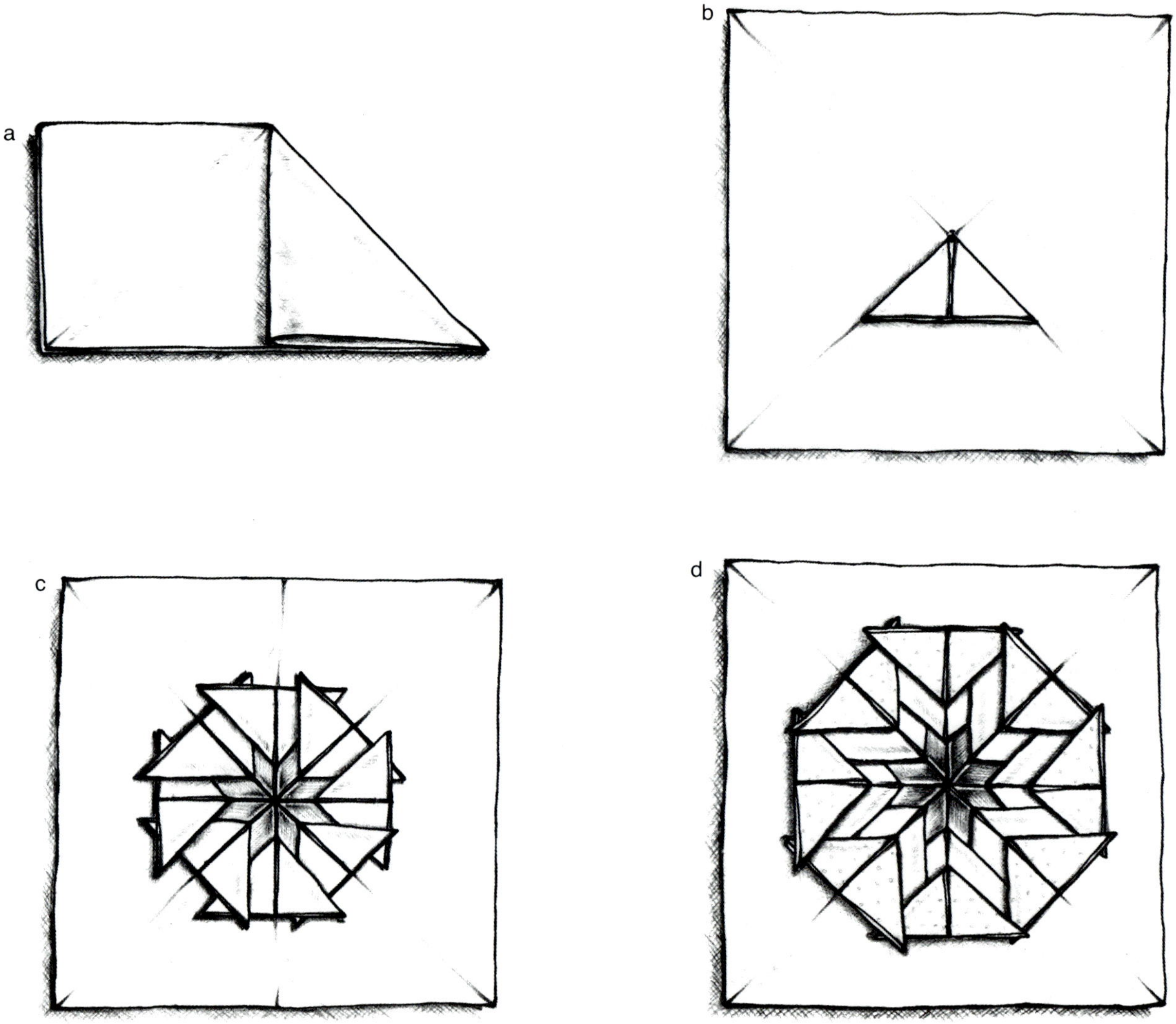

Figure 9

in the centre (fig. 9b). Sew the point down firmly. Make sure the base of the triangle is neatly closed and tack it to the raw edge. Secure the other triangles in the same way, making sure the points meet in the centre.

For the second row you will need eight squares of the same size in a different colour. Fold as before. Place the triangles over the previous triangles with their centres exactly on top of one another (fig. 9c). Make sure the short sides of the triangles overlap evenly. Secure the points and tack close to the raw edge of the triangle bases.

Use eight fabric patches for the third row. Place them exactly over the previous star points (fig. 9d). The folded star is now complete and ready for finishing.

If you wish to make a pot holder with the folded star, use an underlayer of fabric and stitch bias binding all round the edge. Fold the bias binding over to the back and secure with hem stitching.

To make Christmas decorations, use the same method as above, but use smaller squares. You could use red and green fabric and bias binding. Make a loop using crochet cotton and your Christmas decoration is complete!

Hint: If you wish to use ribbon for your star points, cut it in lengths twice the width of the ribbon and form a star point simply by folding the two points towards the centre.

Cathedral window technique

The cathedral window method creates a lovely effect but is time-consuming and can only be done by hand.

For this patchwork method, fabric squares are folded to a quarter of their original size. (The fabric should therefore be easy to fold.) The squares are sewn together and decorated with contrasting square fabric patches. The end result consists of several layers of fabric, without the need for additional

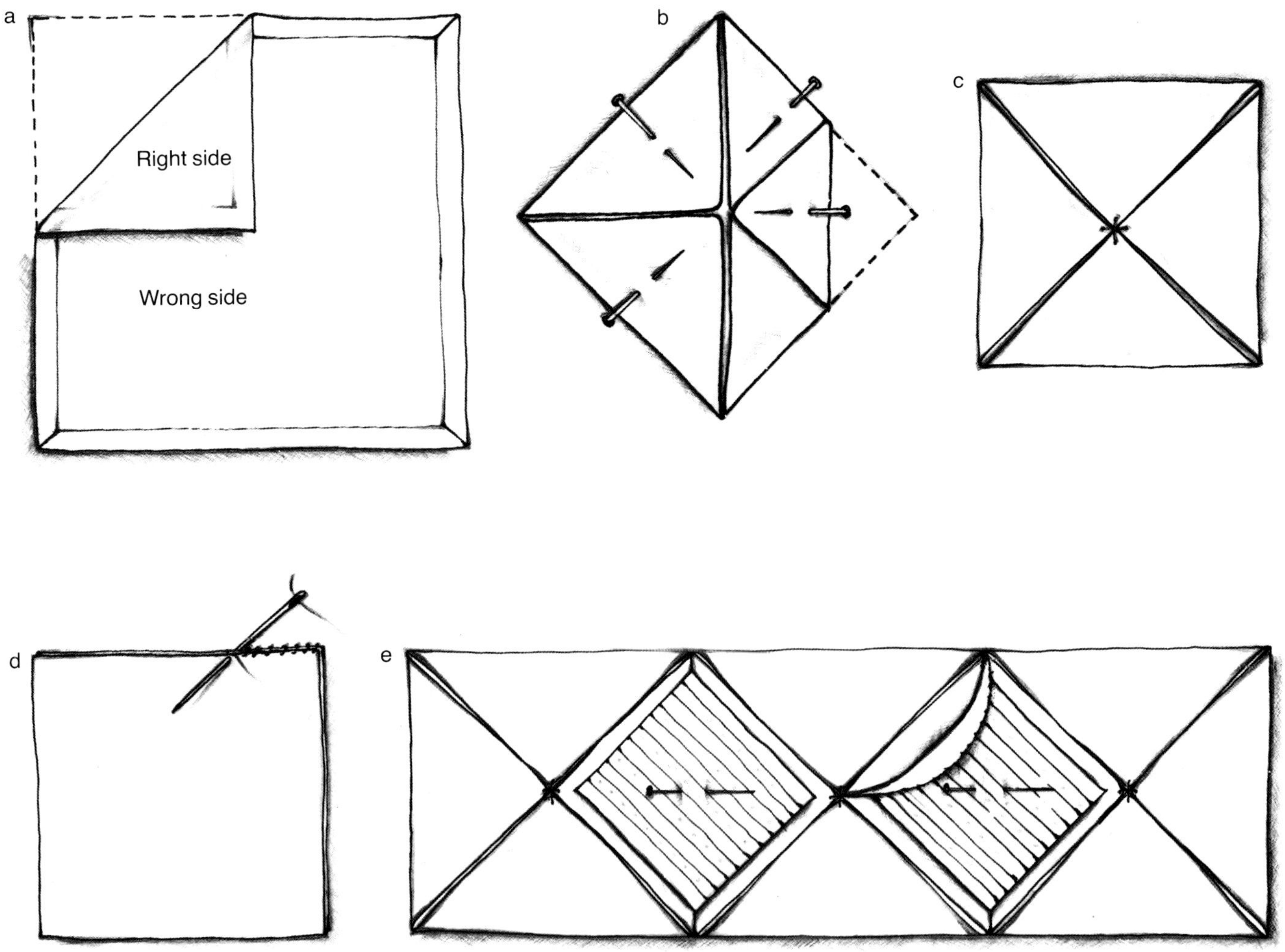

Figure 10

linings or interlinings – an ideal bed covering which is warm yet light. No finishing is necessary to tidy the back.

The large squares must be cut out very accurately. They must be four times the size of the completed square, with a seam allowance of 5 mm all round. If the sides of the completed square have to be 7 cm, you will start with a square with sides measuring 7 cm x 2 = 14 cm + 1 cm seam allowance = 15 cm.

Cut the large squares to the required size. Fold each one twice diagonally to establish the centre and make a mark.

Fold the seam allowance over the outer edge to the wrong side of the fabric and secure with tacking stitches.

Fold the corners to the centre (wrong sides together) and pin neatly (fig. 10a). Then fold the corners to the centre again and pin neatly. Remove the first pins (fig. 10b).

Secure the corners of the square in the centre with two or three cross stitches. Be careful to sew through all the fabric layers. Remove all the pins (fig. 10c).

Make another square in the same way. Place the two squares with folded sides against each other and secure with tiny top-sewing stitches (fig. 10d). Make sure the start and endings are neat. Join all the blocks in this way.

When joined, the blocks form a diamond shape. Measure the size of the diamond. Cut a square 5 mm smaller all round from a contrasting fabric, and pin the square to the diamond shape (fig. 10e).

The raw edge of the small square is covered by folding back the folded edge of the large square, making it form a curve. Pin and sew the layers together, using small slip-hemming stitches. Secure the corners with two or three stitches. Repeat for the other three sides. Continue in this way until the article is complete (fig. 10e).

There will be triangles (half diamonds) at the sides of the article. Either leave it like that, or fill in the gaps with a square folded diagonally to form a triangle. Fold back the edges and sew as before.

Appliqué

Appliqué consists of sewing small fabric shapes onto a background fabric to form a motif. It can be done by hand or machine: both methods are discussed briefly. Any simple picture or photograph can serve as an appliqué design. Colouring books often contain delightful motifs for appliquéd accessories. The motifs may be enlarged on graph paper or on a photostat machine.

Each section of an appliqué pattern is used as a template. Remember, however, to place the wrong side of the template (in other words, the side on which you have written) onto the wrong side of the fabric, otherwise you will get a mirror image of the original pattern!

The order in which the pieces are sewn down is also important. It is wise to reassemble the sections after cutting them out and to number them before you start sewing (fig. 11a). The lowermost pieces are secured first and the other pieces are positioned on top. For the cat in figure 11 for example, the body is sewn down first and then the head. Do not fold the seam allowance of the lowermost piece over where it is overlapped by a second piece (fig. 11b).

It is important to cut the background fabric slightly larger than the required size of the finished product, since appliqué causes the fabric to "shrink" slightly.

b

a

Figure 11

Hand method

Enlarge the design if necessary. Place iron-on interlining (shiny side up) over the design and trace each piece. Cut them out. Then cut each piece from the fabric with a seam allowance of 6 mm. Iron the interlining onto the wrong side of the fabric. (Iron-on interlining strengthens the article and prevents loosely-woven fabric from pulling. It also makes the fabric stiffer and therefore more difficult to quilt through.) Fold the seam allowance over to the wrong side and clip to about 1 mm from the seam line at curves and corners.

Sew the design onto the background fabric using slip-hemming or blind stitching. Take care when sewing – the stitches should not show. The thread should match the motif. Embroidery stitches may also be used to secure motifs, e.g. blanket stitch.

If you wish, leave the interlining out and just fold the seam allowance over. This is called the folding-over method and is ideal when you want to sew quilting stitches on the appliquéd motif, since the fabric layers are not so thick. Trace the pattern or design very lightly onto the right side of the fabric, preferably with an erasable pen. Fold the seams over to the wrong side along the pen line and secure the fabric piece.

If the template has been cut from thickish cardboard, you can even iron the fabric piece right side up over the template. A clear line will indicate where to fold the seam allowance over.

Machine method

Enlarge the design if necessary and trace the pattern onto the shiny side of the iron-on interlining. No seam allowances are necessary, except where one section is overlapped by another. Cut out the pattern pieces and iron onto the different fabrics. Cut out the fabric panels. Tack the first pattern piece in position on the background fabric. Then stitch onto the background fabric using tiny zigzag or satin stitches. Place the next pattern piece in position; tack and stitch. Repeat until all the pieces have been secured. Remember to put the same colour thread on the top and in the bobbin of your machine. First test the stitch size and width on a piece of fabric before stitching the pattern pieces.

It is not always necessary to use interlining: tack each pattern piece onto the background fabric and put thin paper under the background fabric before you start stitching. Stitch through all the layers and remove the paper once you have finished.

If you wish to attach appliqué designs to pullovers or other garments, use the double iron-on interlining technique. Trace the design onto the shiny side of the iron-on interlining. Do not leave seam allowances, except where one section is overlapped by another. Cut out the pattern pieces.

Iron onto the wrong side of the fabric. Cut out the fabric pattern pieces and tack them onto iron-on interlining again. Secure with tiny satin stitches. Neatly trim the interlining close to the stitching and appliqué the motif onto the garment by hand or by machine, using a slightly larger satin stitch.

Hint: Pattern pieces may be padded slightly with batting for a three-dimensional effect.

Hawaiian appliqué

This form of appliqué originated in Hawaii, where American missionaries taught the Hawaiians to make garments. They also taught them various other needlework techniques, such as quilting.

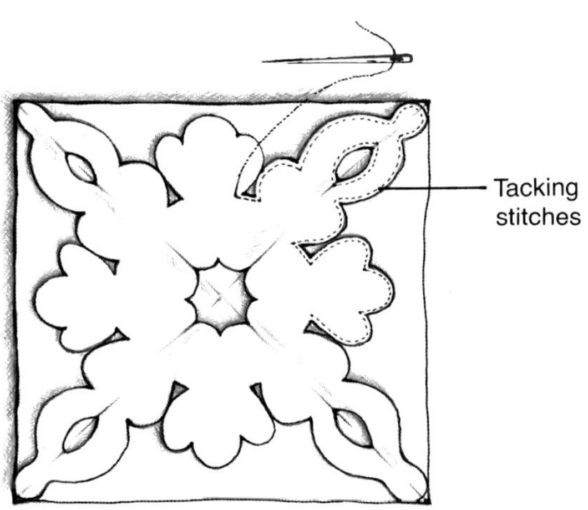

Figure 12

The designs are created by folding paper, usually into eighths, as well as sixths, quarters or halves, and then cutting them out. When opened up, the folds on the paper serve as a pattern for cutting the fabric. The design should preferably not be too small, since the edges are folded in as seam allowances. Two contrasting fabrics are normally used, one for the (appliqué) pattern and the other for the background fabric.

The design is tacked onto the background fabric (approximately 1 cm from the edge). A small seam allowance of about 4 or 5 mm is folded in and secured with tiny hem stitches (fig. 12). Alternatively, use an embroidery stitch, e.g. buttonhole stitch.

The background fabric is tacked onto batting and an underlayer and the outline quilting technique is applied. The whole background is filled in with parallel lines, 1 cm apart, after the first row of quilting stitches.

Stained-glass appliqué

The stained-glass method creates the illusion of stained-glass windows. It is time-consuming but the end result makes it worthwhile. Real stained-glass patterns can be adjusted for stained-glass appliqué, since patterns for this form of needlework are not easily obtainable. The pattern pieces should not be too small, however, as it complicates matters.

A plain cotton fabric is generally used. Chintz is a good choice. A bold colour scheme can be very striking, as the colours are separated by black bias binding. Make your own bias strips (6 mm wide), or buy ready-made cotton bias binding and fold it in half.

Enlarge the pattern you wish to use and trace it onto tracing paper. Then trace the pattern onto tracing paper again using a black pen to mark the outlines clearly. Colour the picture with crayons matching the fabric you intend using to ensure that the colour combination is just right. Number the pattern pieces the same on both traced patterns. Cut out all the pattern pieces from the tracing paper not coloured in; these are your templates.

Cut the background fabric to the required size. Trace the entire design onto it. Use a light-box and pencil, or dressmaker's carbon paper. Number all the pattern pieces on the background fabric to correspond with the traced pattern pieces.

Trace the outlines of the templates onto the appliqué fabric, or simply pin the paper templates to save time. Cut out the pattern pieces. Do not add seam allowances, since the bias binding performs this function.

Paste all the fabric pieces onto the background fabric with a glue stick. Otherwise, tack the pieces, but this is time-consuming. Position the bias binding over the raw edge of each fabric piece. Pin it and tack into place. Sew the bias binding with tiny hemming or blind stitching. Make sure the edges of the fabric pieces do not slip out under the bias binding. Where one piece runs into another, both edges are tucked under one strip of bias binding.

To simplify the shaping of the curves, first sew the inside of

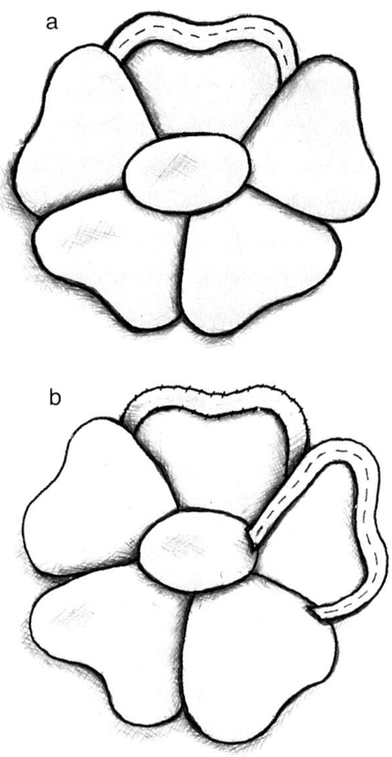

Figure 13

the curve and then the outside (fig. 13a). Both ends of each strip of bias binding must be covered by the next one so that the raw edges do not show (fig. 13b). Therefore, begin at the furthest point of the design. Otherwise, leave an opening, continue sewing and later tuck the end of the bias binding in and secure.

Complete the article as above and neatly press with a warm iron. You can now begin quilting.

Place the bottom layer down first, then the batting and lastly the stained-glass appliquéd fabric. Tack all layers firmly. Do not use black tacking thread on a light-coloured background as it may leave marks. Use black thread and quilt right round both sides of the bias binding.

You are now ready for the final step, e.g. making a cushion or wall hanging.

Shadow appliqué

Trace the pattern with a black pen onto paper. Cut the background fabric to the required size and place it over the pattern. Trace the pattern onto the fabric with an erasable pen.

Trace the pattern pieces you wish to appliqué onto the shiny side of iron-on interlining, cut out and iron onto the wrong side of the fabric to be appliquéd. Cut the fabric pieces without a seam allowance. Put some glue on the wrong side of the fabric panels. Paste them in place onto the background fabric.

Place a piece of transparent fabric, such as chiffon, organdie or voile, of the same size as the background fabric, on top of the design. Tack. Be careful not to catch the fine fabric. Begin with a knot on the wrong side and quilt tiny stitches on the inner edges of the fabric panels of the whole appliqué design. You are ready to embroider.

Cut a layer of batting and backing fabric the same size as the background fabric and place the design on top of it. Tack. Quilt all round the outer edge of the appliqué design. Add the finishing touches.

Mola or San Blas appliqué

Mola or San Blas appliqué originated from the Cuna Indians who live on the San Blas Islands near the coast of Panama. Mola appliqué consists of a combination of appliqué methods and embroidery. Three to six layers of brightly coloured fabric are tacked together. A motif is drawn on it – usually birds, wild animals or plants – based on life on the island.

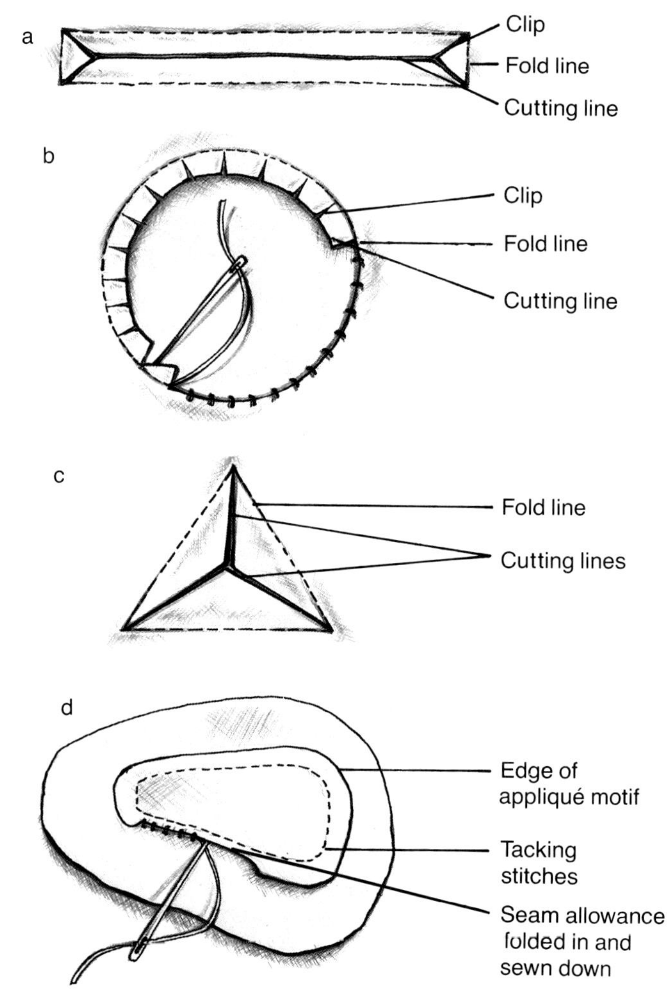

Figure 14

These layers are carefully cut away, one by one or sometimes two layers at a time, to reveal the brightly coloured fabric underneath. The edges of the cut-out fabric are turned back each time with the point of the needle and secured with tiny hemming or embroidery stitches. Clip the fabric close to the fold lines; it will be easier to turn the edges back. The background around the motifs is filled by cutting circles, notches and small snips in some of the fabric layers (fig. 14a to c); by adding appliqué spots or other shapes (fig. 14d), and embroidery stitching.

Mola appliqué can be used effectively on garments, e.g. pockets, collars, shoulder insets and dress hems. Cushions, wall hangings, handbags and belts are also ideally suited for this method.

Thickly woven light-weight fabric that does not fray, e.g. cotton, is perfect for this technique. Mola appliqué can be enhanced with embroidery stitches such as stem stitch, chain stitch, herringbone stitch and French knots.

Candlewicking

Candlewicking originated from the aristocracy in America. Traditionally, only cream or beige thread on cream or beige fabric was used.

The original candlewicking stitch was a tacking stitch that was cut through to form small tassels. After washing and shrinking, the tassels become more fluffy. Candlewicking accessories were never ironed.

Over the years American women began substituting French knots for the tassels. Nowadays a variety of embroidery stitches are used, of which French knots, stem stitch, back-stitch, satin stitch, padded satin stitch and couching stitch are the most popular (fig. 15a to m). There are no rules for using any particular stitch – it is entirely up to you.

Coloured and lustre yarn can greatly enhance any article.

a Daisy stitch

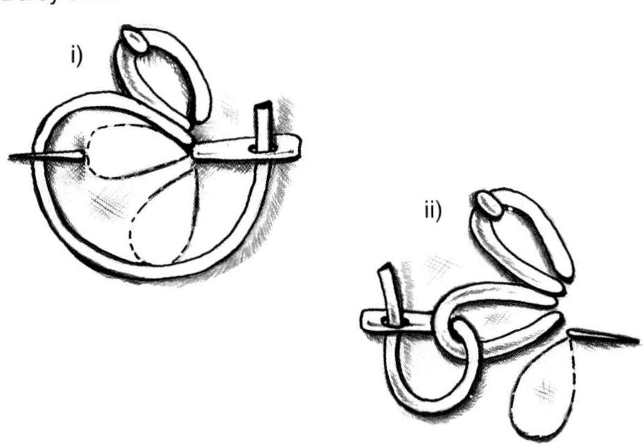

b Back stitch

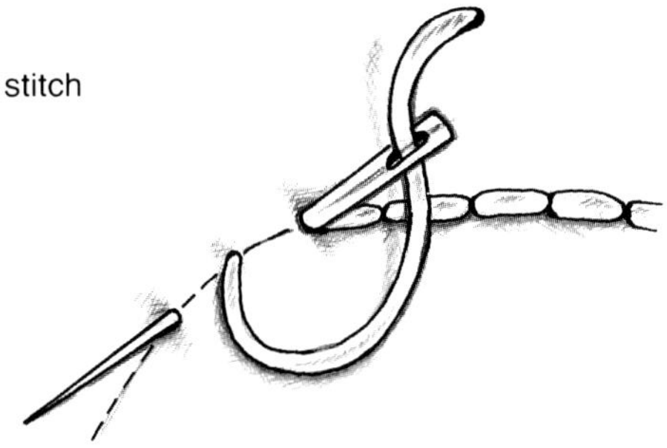

c Couching stitch

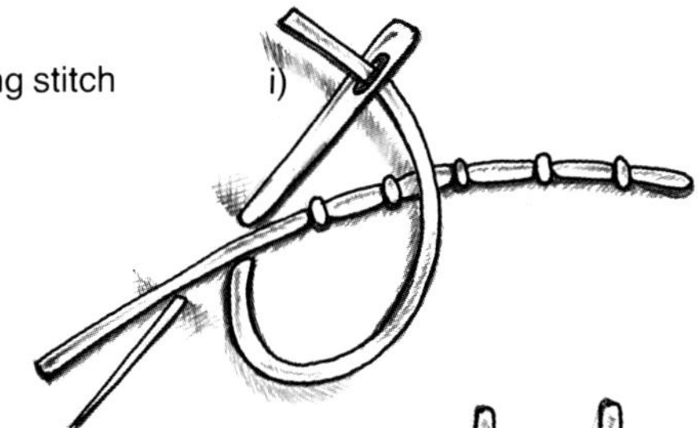

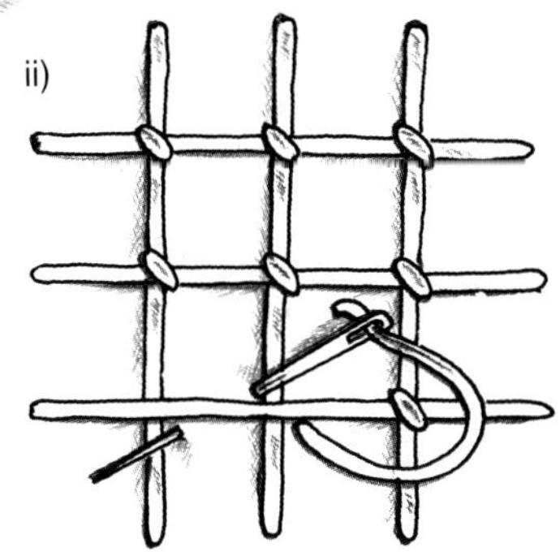

d Blanket stitch

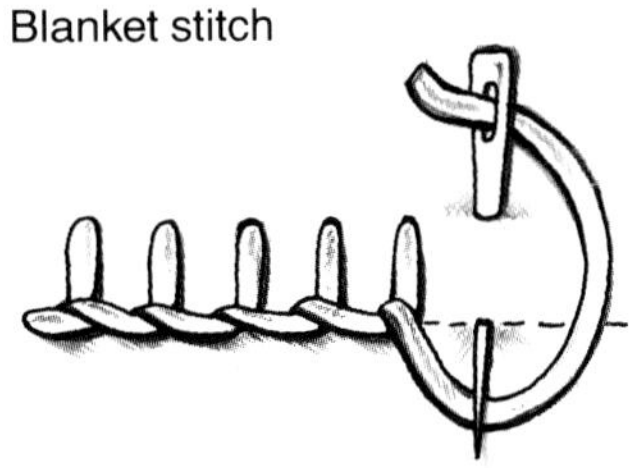

e Stem stitch

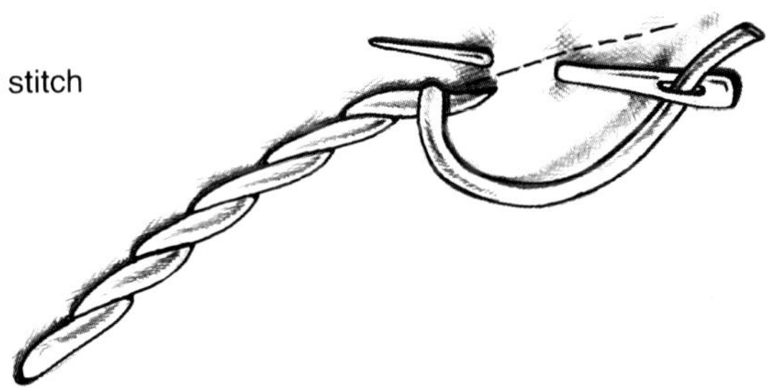

f Satin stitch

Figure 15

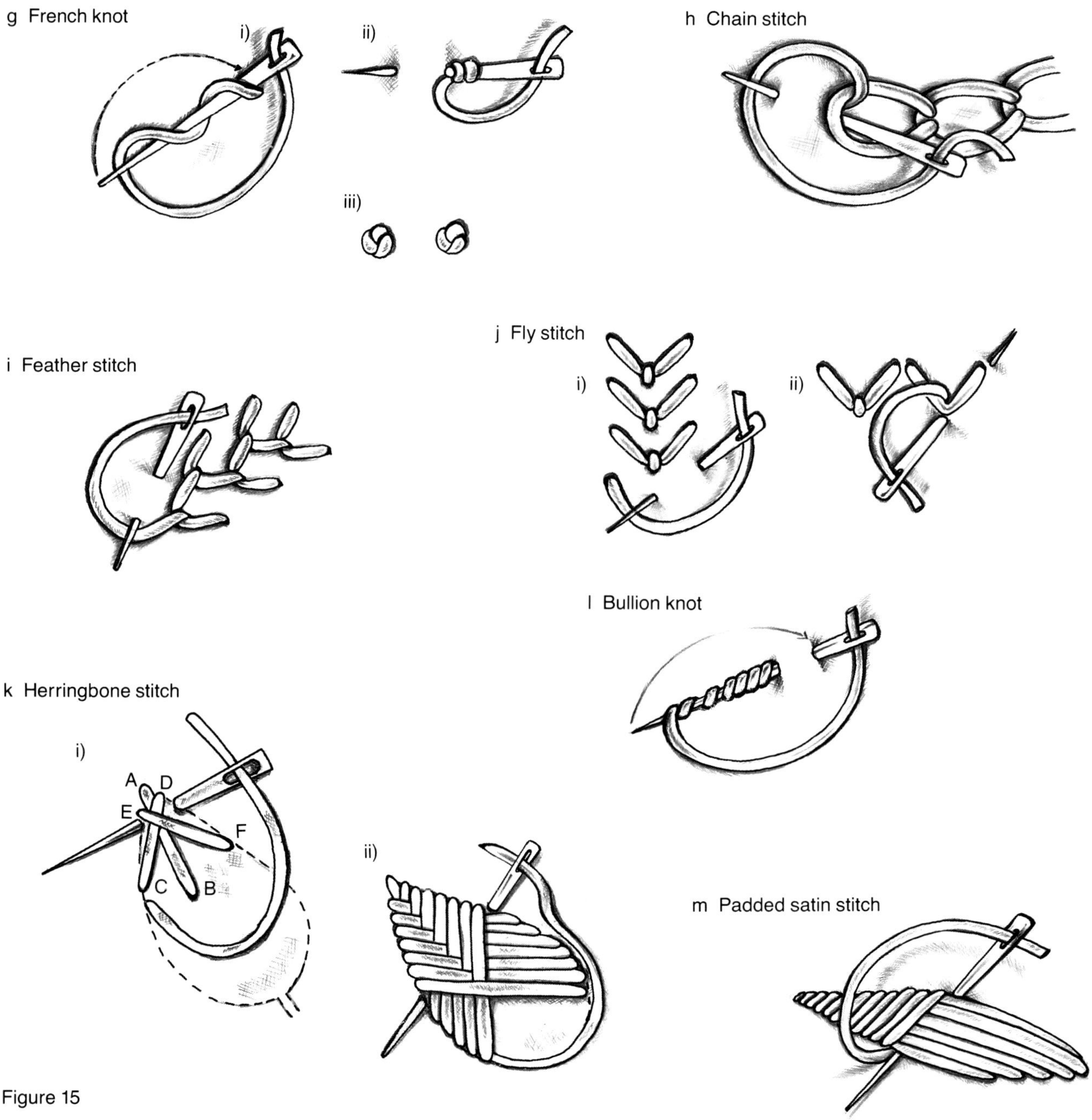

Figure 15

No. 5 and no. 8 crochet yarn or cotton knit are generally used. Use a finer thread for a more delicate effect, or thicker thread for a chunky effect.

Usually 100% unbleached calico is used for candlewicking, although a blend of polyester and cotton is also suitable. Furthermore use a sharp-pointed embroidery needle with a large eye.

Trace the design onto the fabric with an erasable pen. Stretch the fabric on a large embroidery frame; this will help you to keep the tiny stitches even. Begin on the wrong side with a knot and end by working the thread through the back of one or two stitches so that it does not show on the right side.

By embroidering the same pattern in different stitches a completely different effect can be achieved, thus providing variation.

Candlewicking is not confined to cushions and quilts; use this technique to decorate collars and pockets of jackets and other garments. It also looks striking on handbags, picture frames and potpourri containers.

Quilting

Quilting consists of sewing or stitching through two or more (usually three) layers of fabric. Old blankets and flannel used to serve as interlinings for quilts but nowadays special batting of varying thicknesses is available.

A quilted article usually consists of a top layer, a layer of batting, and a backing layer. Quilting is versatile: either quilt an ordinary piece of fabric or combine the technique with any of the patchwork methods. Motifs with straight lines work as well as motifs with curved lines, so there is a wide choice of designs. Quilts, wall hangings, jackets and pockets are just some of the possibilities for quilting.

Trace the quilting pattern onto the fabric in one of the following ways:

- Use an erasable pen (one that washes out – not the kind that disappears by itself after a while). Rinse the fabric in cold water immediately afterwards, and do not iron before the marks have been washed out.
- The pattern can be traced using a soft pencil.
- Leftover pieces of soap can be used to trace designs onto dark fabric.
- Masking tape is suitable for indicating straight lines. Various widths are available – from 6 mm to approximately 8 cm. The same piece of masking tape can be used more than once. If you wish, cut tiny patterns, e.g. leaves, from masking tape, paste them on the fabric and quilt around the tape.
- To trace a pattern, use either a light-box or glass-topped table with a light underneath. Use a window to trace smaller articles. Paste the pattern onto the glass with adhesive tape or Prestik, hold the fabric on top and trace the pattern.
- Dressmaker's carbon paper is also suitable. Just make sure that there is sufficient contrast between the paper and the colour of the fabric so that the pattern shows clearly.

A patchwork article must be prepared before quilting: cut off any loose threads and excess seam width. Iron carefully on the wrong side. Remember to iron the seams in the direction of the darker fabric; it should not show through.

Quilting techniques

Various quilting techniques exist for finishing an article.

Outline quilting
This is the most popular method for patchwork and appliqué. Sew 4 to 6 mm away from the seam edge of the pattern piece. No additional marking is required, as the seam line is followed (fig. 16).

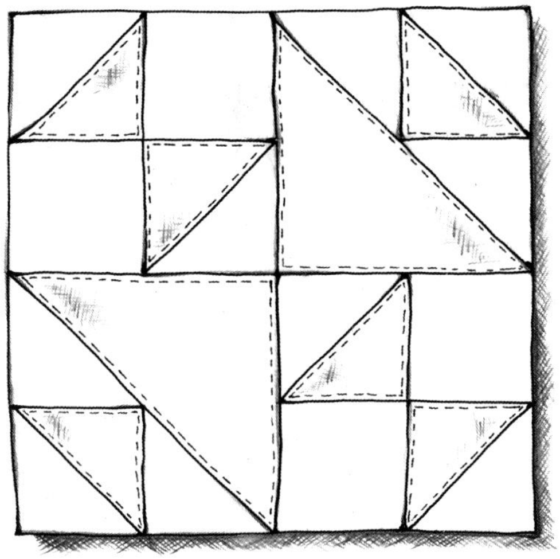

Figure 16

In-the-ditch quilting
This method consists of quilting in the seam lines of patchwork and appliqué articles. It provides a puffed effect and is particularly suitable when squares are joined.

Echo or contour quilting
This quilting method forms a contour outside the lines of the patched motif, e.g. a star (fig. 17). It consists of regular lines which follow the star until all the space is filled up. The lines are spaced between 6 mm and 1 cm apart.

Figure 17

Filling-in quilting
Incorrectly quilted cotton batting is inclined to form lumps after washing. For this reason it is better to use the filling-in method on surfaces with large open areas. Straight or curved lines, or a combination of these lines, are equally attractive (fig. 18).

Figure 18

Figure 19

Figure 20

Motif quilting
Motif quilting is very effective on open spaces. Specific motifs, e.g. hearts and flowers (fig. 19) can be used.

Border quilting
This method forms a border frame around an article. It usually consists of repetitive patterns (e.g. the border pattern in fig. 20).

Stipple quilting
Stipple quilting consists of tiny stitches sewn closely together on patchwork or appliqué (e.g. the stamen of the flower in fig. 20).

Knots
A flat knot can be used to hold the three layers together so that no quilting stitches show. Insert the needle from the right side through all the layers of fabric and leave a thread of ± 7 cm. Make a back stitch (fig. 21a) and leave another piece of thread at the other end (fig. 21b). Make a double knot (fig. 21c) and cut the thread 2,5 cm from the fabric. The two threads serve as decoration.

When you wish to quilt a pattern onto an article, it is better to transfer your pattern onto the background fabric before tacking on the batting and backing. The pattern will be reproduced more accurately.

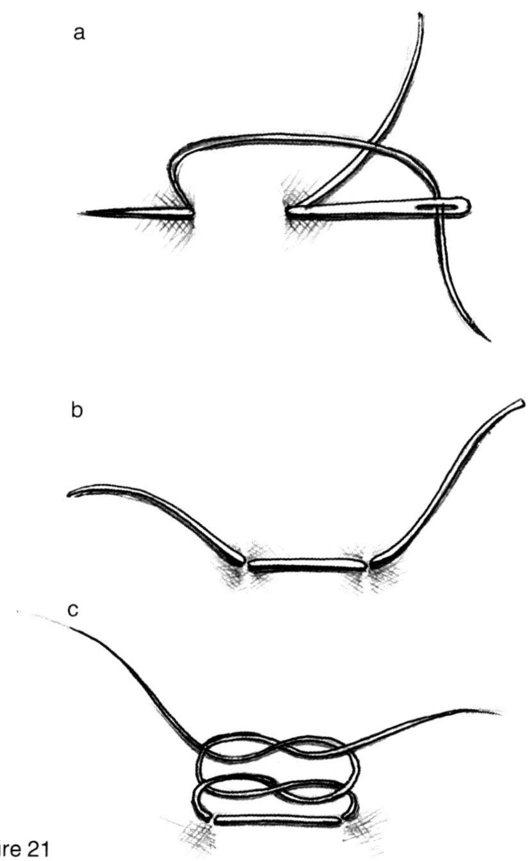

Figure 21

Cut pieces of batting and unbleached calico (or any other suitable plain fabric) slightly larger than required. Make sure there are no creases in the fabric. Arrange the layers as follows: backing (unbleached calico) with wrong side facing upwards, batting and top layer with wrong side facing downwards (fig. 22a). Pin the three layers neatly together.

Then tack together firmly with tacking thread, making sure the fabric does not fold or crease while you work. Always begin in the centre and work outwards (fig. 22b). A large article, e.g. a wall hanging or quilt, must be firmly secured so that it does not shift or bulge. The tacking threads should not be more than 10 cm apart. The more you tack, the neater the end product.

It is now ready for quilting. Large quilting frames are convenient, especially when more than one person is working on an article. One big disadvantage, though, is that it takes up a lot of space. An embroidery frame or quilting hoop is less unwieldy. Some people prefer quilting without a frame.

You will find that thimbles are indispensable when quilting – one for your right middle finger and one for the index finger of your left hand – especially when working on a large article requiring a lot of quilting.

To strengthen the quilting thread and to prevent it from knotting, run it through a cake of beeswax.

Begin in the centre of the article and work outwards. Make a small knot and pass the needle through from underneath the fabric. Pull the knot through the unbleached calico (backing fabric), leaving it in the batting (fig. 23a). Then sew small tacking stitches through all three layers.

The size of the stitches is up to you: you can sew stitches as small as ten stitches per 2 cm, although six stitches per 2 cm is a good guideline. The stitches must be regular and even and must show on the other side. Insert the needle through the layers from the top. Hold one hand underneath the fabric and feel with your index finger (the one with the thimble) whether the needle has penetrated all the layers, then bring the needle to the top again. Initially you will probably do only one stitch at a time but with practice you will be able to sew three or four stitches before pulling the thread through.

To finish, insert the needle from the back. Make a small knot in the thread close to the fabric before sewing the last stitch. Sew another stitch through the fabric and batting only, leaving the knot in the batting (fig. 23b and c). Pull the thread through to the bottom and cut the quilting thread against the fabric. You can finish with two back stitches but this will show where you ended off.

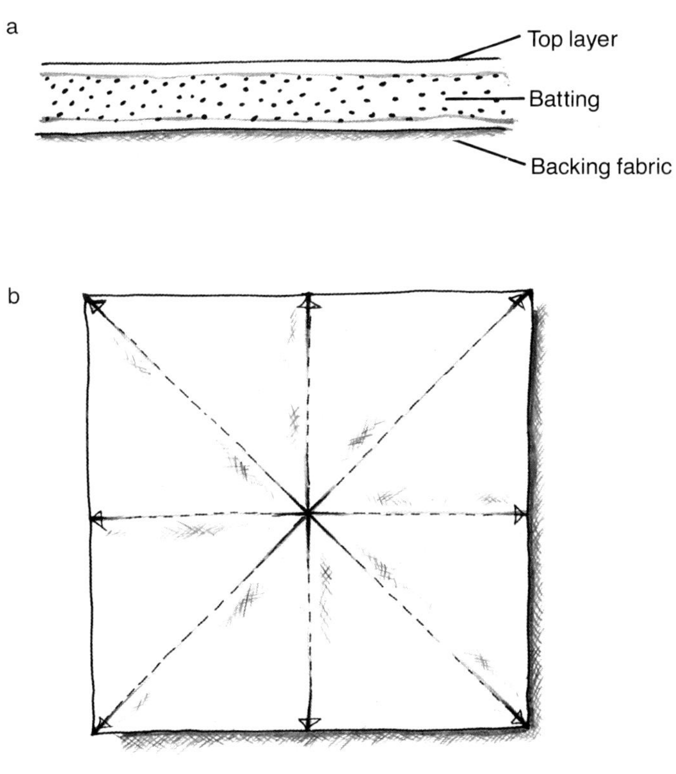

Figure 22

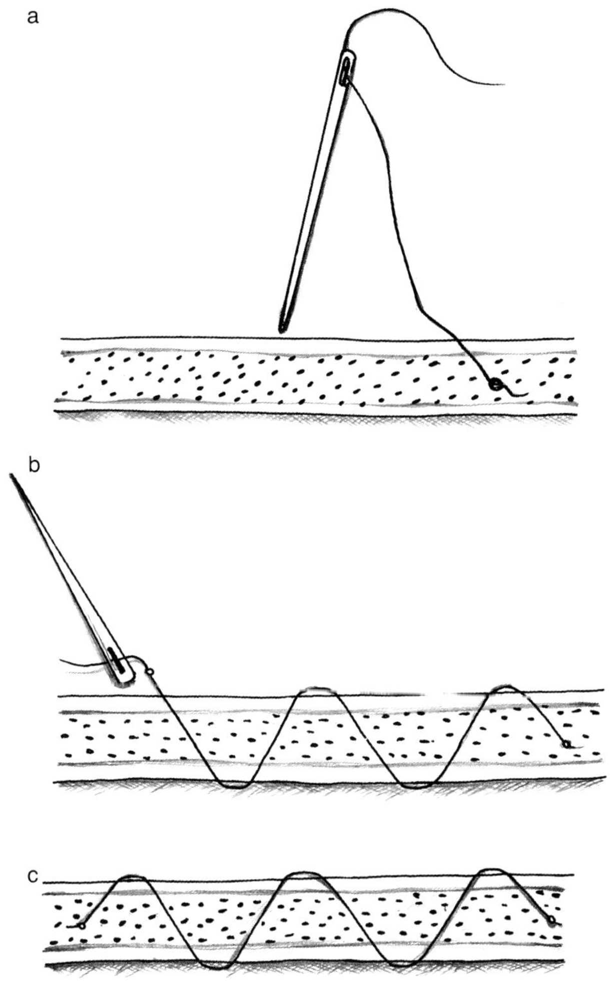

Figure 23

Machine quilting

Machine quilting usually consists of straight lines running parallel with lines crossing to form a square, or stitched diagonally to form a "diamond". Keep in mind that a machine-quilted article may shrink slightly.

Iron the article first, as for the hand-quilting method. Mark the stitching lines with an erasable pen on the top layer before tacking it firmly to the batting and underlayer.

Stitch the centre line first and then the lines to the right of it. Begin each stitching line at the top. Hold the work flat on either side of the machine foot, do not push forwards or backwards. Stitch slowly without pulling the fabric. Turn the work around immediately after completing one half. Begin again alongside the centre and sew towards the right. Be especially careful not to allow the first row of stitches to pucker.

Quilting is much quicker by machine than by hand but it does not have the same effect as the hand quilting method. Preferably use this method only for smaller articles such as place mats, and the hand method for something special like a patchwork quilt.

Quilt as you go method

This method is particularly suitable for a quilt consisting of blocks, such as the blue quilt for a guest room (p. 82). Completing the top layer of a quilt, tacking it onto the batting and backing fabric and then quilting the whole article is often quite difficult. A large quilt confines you to your workroom. If you work piecemeal, you can utilise spare moments, for example while waiting for the children at school.

Complete all the squares for the top layer. Cut off any threads and iron them. If you wish to frame each square individually, do it at this stage. Trace all the quilting patterns onto the fabric. Leave the quilting of the outer edge until the whole quilt has been sewn together.

For each block, cut the backing fabric and batting about 2.5 cm larger than the top layer. Make provision for additional batting and underlayer if you intend sewing a strip around the edge of the whole quilt, so that it does not have to be joined. Tack the backing fabric, batting and top layer of each block together as illustrated in fig. 22a and b (p. 31). Quilt the individual squares.

Cut the batting for each block exactly the same size as the top layer without the seam allowance. Sew the blocks of the top layers with right sides together forming strips, then join them.

Secure the batting with neat oversewing stitches. Be careful not to let a thick ridge form or to let it pull too tightly.

Cut the seam allowances of the backing fabric smaller if necessary. Where the backing fabric of one block is joined to another, work as follows: Fold one block's seam allowance over to the inside. Place it over the other block where the seam allowance is not folded back. Join with small hemming stitches (fig. 24).

Complete the quilt in this way. If you wish to have an additional border, do it now. Place the right sides of the edge and the quilt together and stitch. Finish the edge as usual (p. 39).

Trapunto quilting

Trapunto (or padded) quilting and Italian (or corded quilting) are usually combined. It is traditionally sewn only in white or cream, although nowadays coloured fabric is used also.

Trace a design onto fabric with dressmaker's carbon paper or an erasable pen. Cut a piece of muslin or loosely woven fabric of the same size and tack it onto the back. Sew small tacking stitches around the design, or use your machine. Carefully pull the fibres of the muslin apart with a large blunt-pointed needle to form a small hole. Fill the design with pieces of polyester filling by pushing it through with the needle. Alternatively, snip a hole in the fabric and sew it up afterwards (fig. 25a and b).

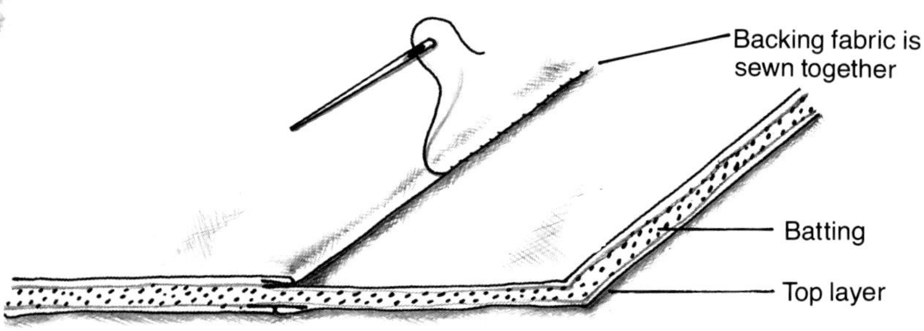

Figure 24

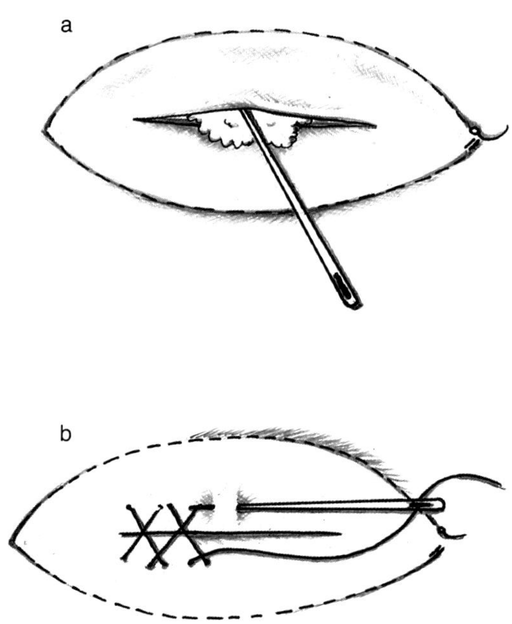

Figure 25

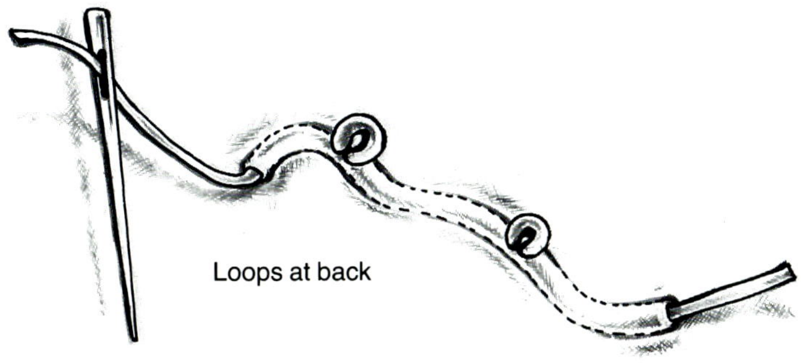

Figure 26

Where two lines run parallel, they can be sewn with thick wool or cotton yarn according to the Italian (corded) quilting method. Use a blunt-pointed needle and sew from the back. Feed the needle between the top layer and the muslin. Pull the wool or yarn to the back through the muslin at equal distances. Pass the needle back through the same hole, but leave a small loop of wool at the back. (These loops prevent the article from pulling to one side should the wool or yarn shrink or pull when washed or worn.) End by leaving a 1 cm piece of wool dangling (fig. 26).

Shadow trapunto and shadow Italian quilting are worked in the same way, but use coloured padding and wool so that they show through the white or cream fabric.

General finishing

A neat finish is essential to do justice to the beautiful patchwork or appliqué articles that so many hours of painstaking labour have been spent on. Without the right finish the impact will be lost. Using the proper methods will simplify the task and ensure a professional look.

Borders

Sometimes an article needs a border to finish it, e.g. a cushion, especially one consisting of patchwork or appliqué squares. It is best to use a colour used in the article. With a soft pencil, mark four strips as wide as the border is to be, plus a seam allowance on either side. Each strip must be as long as the side of the cushion plus twice the width of the strip. Cut the strips. First secure the top and bottom strips and then the two side strips (fig. 27). Use the folding-over method to join the strips. Place each strip over the top layer with right sides facing and raw edges together. Stitch and fold back.

For a larger article, e.g. a quilt or wall hanging, use strips for the border. Experiment to get an interesting effect, e.g. strips made by joining small squares and triangles (fig. 28a, b and c). Consider appliquéing motifs on the border strips (fig. 28d), or try a double border by joining another four strips in the same way as the first four.

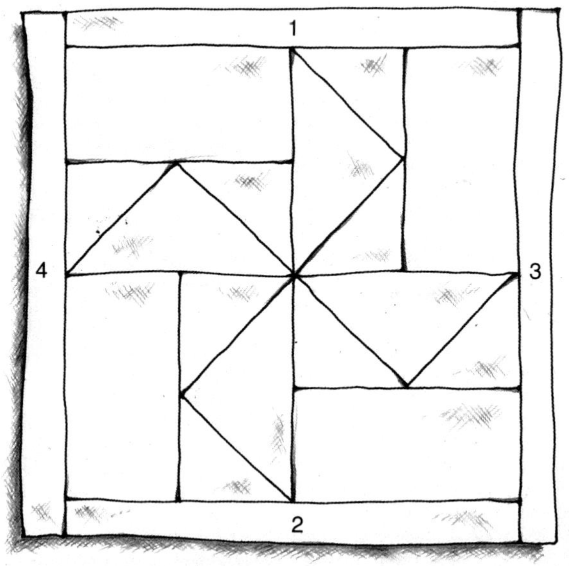

Figure 27

Figure 28

Figure 28

The border strips can also be joined by mitring the corners. Cut four strips, each the length of the article plus twice the width of the strip. For example, if the side of the article is 30 cm and the border strip is 5 cm wide, the total length of each strip will be 40 cm. Stitch the strips to the article so that the ends extend equally for the corners (fig. 29a). Place the article with the stitched border flat with wrong side facing upwards. Lift the inner corners of the strips up so that the right sides of the strips meet at the corner. Pin the strips at a 45 degree angle. Secure. Trim excess fabric (fig. 29b).

Alternatively, place the article with the right side facing upwards (fig. 30a) and fold one strip at the corner at an angle of 45 degrees. Sew it on top with small slip-hemming stitches (fig. 30b).

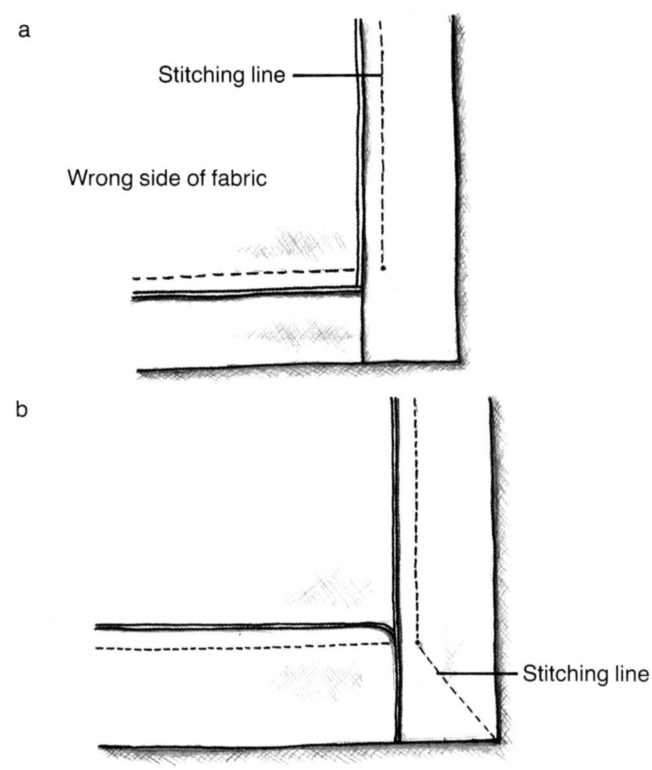

Figure 29

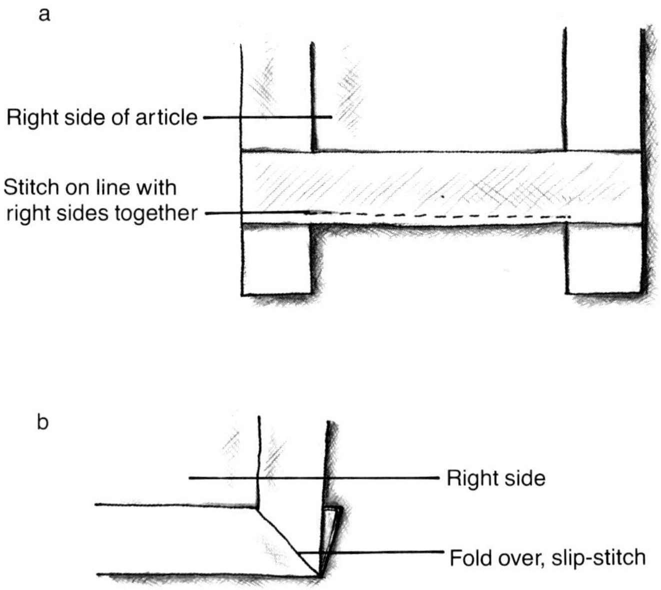

Figure 30

Laying out the blocks

The blocks for a quilt can be arranged in a variety of different ways.

Strip layout without sashing

The blocks are simply joined together without sashes around each block, and therefore the patterns flow into one another.

Lay the blocks out alongside each other and join them one by one to form a long strip.

After all the blocks have been joined, the strips are joined one by one (fig. 31).

Figure 31

Strip layout with sashes between blocks

This is a very popular method. Because each block is framed by a strip of fabric, the patterns on the individual blocks stand out more clearly.

Lay the patterned blocks side by side as you want them in the quilt. Cut strips of fabric to the required width to form the sashes.

Alternate blocks and strips of fabric in the first row and join. Repeat the process with every row (fig. 32a).

Cut strips of fabric as long as the rows of blocks. Attach the first row of blocks to the strip of fabric (fig. 32b). Stitch the second row of blocks to the other side of the strip of fabric. Add a strip of fabric between each row of blocks until they form a unit. Join a strip of fabric to the top and bottom ends of the large piece of work. Join a strip of fabric to each side. All the blocks will have a frame around them.

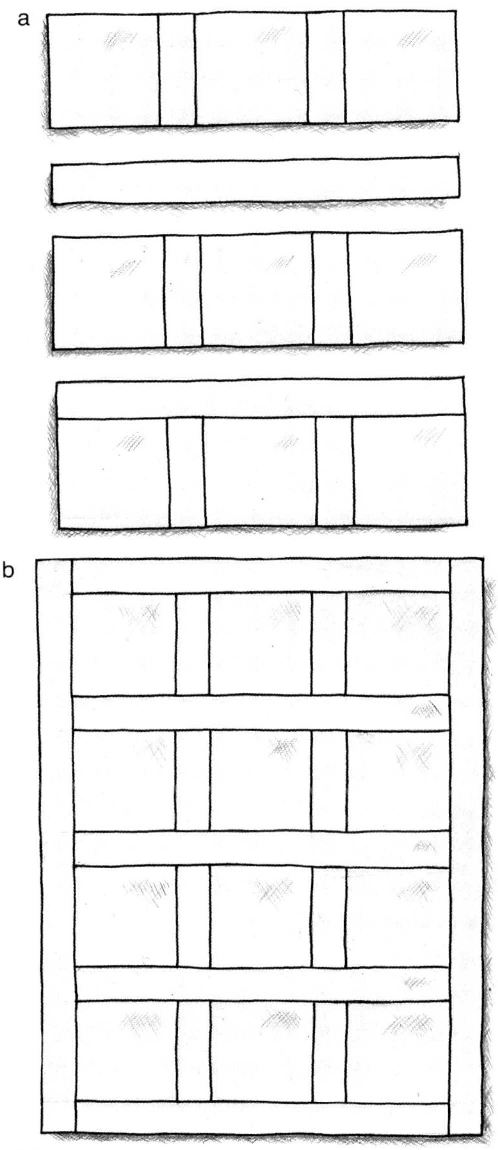

Figure 32

Figure 33

a

b

Figure 34

Diagonal layout

Arrange the blocks diagonally and join. Use plain fabric for the triangles around the edges and quilt them (fig. 33).

Medallion layout

If you have made one special block and wish to use it in a larger article, let it form the centrepiece. Position it either horizontally or diagonally. If you decide to position it diagonally, join four triangles to form a square. Then sew the border strips around the square (fig. 34a and b).

Finishing of cushions

Cushions are handy and wonderfully versatile articles to make. There are many possibilities – use patchwork or appliqué techniques, or make a cushion with an unusual shape and decorate it with ribbon and lace, such as the cushions for the main bedroom (p. 71). Cushion covers decorated with candlewicking, such as the one for grandmother's room (p. 75) are sure to invite compliments!

Plan the effect you wish to achieve, and complete the front panel first. If you wish to add a frill, do it before you sew the front and back panels together.

Use either a ready-made frill, or make one yourself. To make a frill, cut a strip about 6 cm wide, one and a half times to twice the circumference of the cushion, and hem it with your sewing machine. Alternatively, cut a strip about 12 cm wide and one and a half times to twice the circumference of the cushion, then fold the fabric in half with wrong sides facing. Stitch large tacking stitches 1 cm from the raw edge or open side. Divide the frill into four equal sections and mark with pins (fig. 35a). Gather evenly.

To gather evenly without breaking the thread, divide the frill into four equal sections first. Stitch each quarter separately, using tacking stitches. If the thread breaks during the gathering process, it will be easier to stitch it again.

Join the two ends of the frill. Place the frill on the fabric, right sides together. Shape the corners by pulling the gathers slightly tighter and make a small flat pleat to prevent the frill from pulling askew. Tack (fig. 35b) and machine stitch.

A double, overlapping back panel – as in an ordinary pillowcase – works well for a cushion cover. For example, if the cushion is 40 cm long and 25 cm wide, make two strips of 40 cm long and 25 cm wide. Sew a hem in each strip on the side that is going to overlap. Place the two sections of the back panel with right sides together over the right side of the decorated front panel. Pin the front and back panels neatly together. With the decorated panel facing upwards, stitch on the row of stitching where you joined the frill (fig. 35c).

Finish the seam with zigzag stitching, turn the work right side out and the cushion cover is complete. Either buy a loose cushion or make one yourself. When you want to wash the cover, just remove the cushion. Sew a small button or press stud at the back to prevent the overlapping parts from gaping – this is not essential though. Another method is to cut a piece of fabric the same size as the decorated front panel, and join them, right sides together. Leave an opening on one side, turn the cover right side out and stuff with polyester filling or sponge-rubber chips. This kind of cushion is more difficult to wash and dry however, than one with a loose cover.

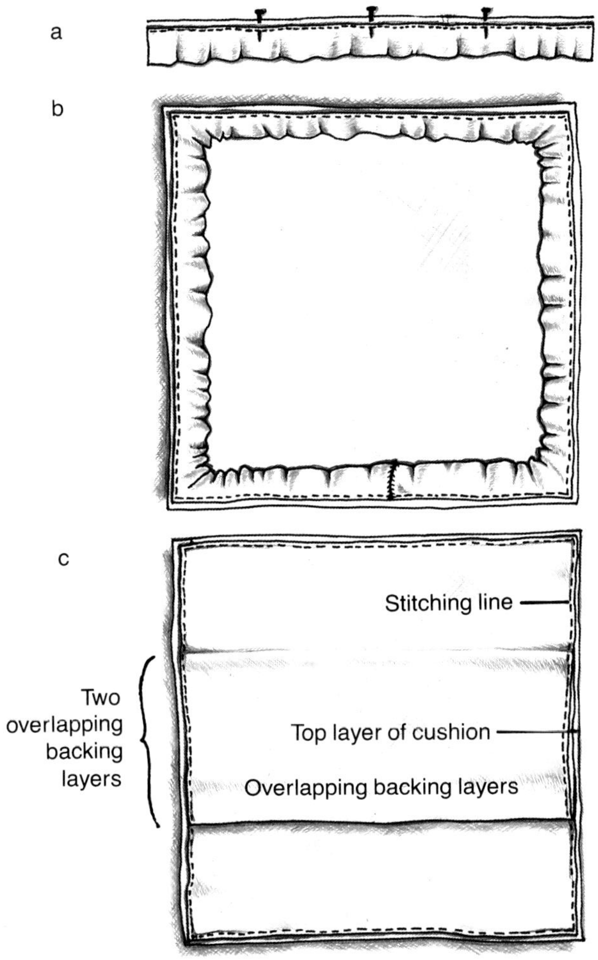

Figure 35

Finishing of other articles

There are various methods for finishing the edges of articles such as wall hangings and quilts.

Folded-over edge (to the back) or hemming

If you do not want a prominent additional border strip, make a folded-over edge. Cut the edges of the article 3 to 4 cm larger than the batting and unbleached calico of the backing layer. Fold the edge over as for a hem and stitch with small hemming stitches (fig. 36).

To shape the corners neatly, fold the seam allowance diagonally across the corner of the quilt. Cut the points off and fold the sides on either side towards each other to form a mitred corner (45 degree angle). Secure the two folded edges with tiny stitches.

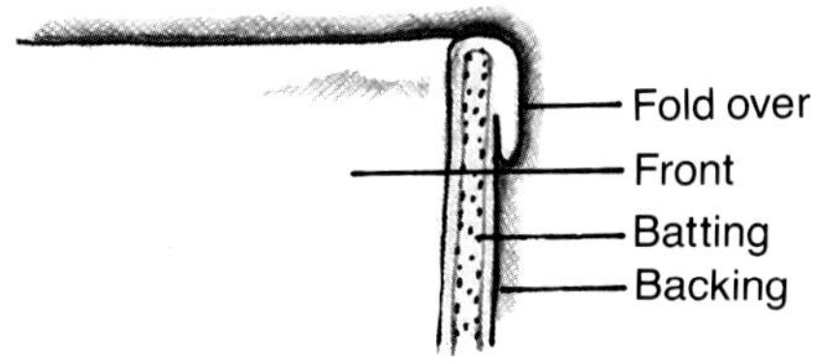

Figure 36

Folded-closed edge

Cut front and back panels the same size, and a panel of batting 1 to 2 cm smaller. Fold the edges of the front and back panels to the inside between the layers, and secure with small stitches (fig. 37).

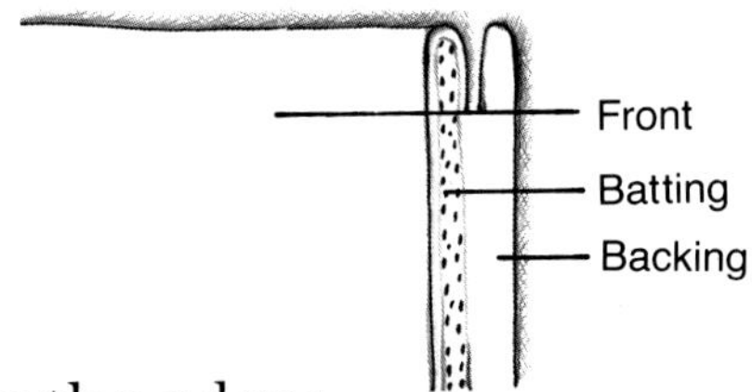

Figure 37

Binding the edges

Binding is used for articles with rounded corners, or else straight strips are also suitable. Trim the top layer, batting and unbleached calico neatly. Cut the strips to the required width. Place the strip on the article with right sides together and sew 1 cm from the side of the article through all the layers. Turn the raw edge of the binding in about 1 cm and fold back. Secure with small hemming stitches. Make sure the first machine stitches do not show (fig. 38).

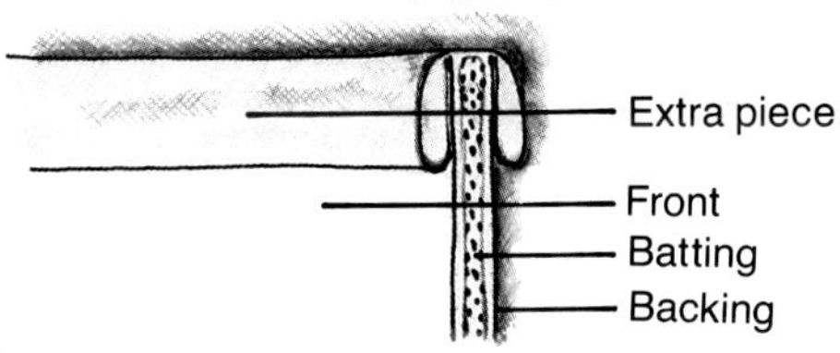

Figure 38

Folded-over edge (to the front)

If you use an attractive fabric for the back that matches the front, the back section can be cut 3 to 4 cm larger than the batting and the front section. Fold it forward and secure with small hemming stitches (fig. 39).

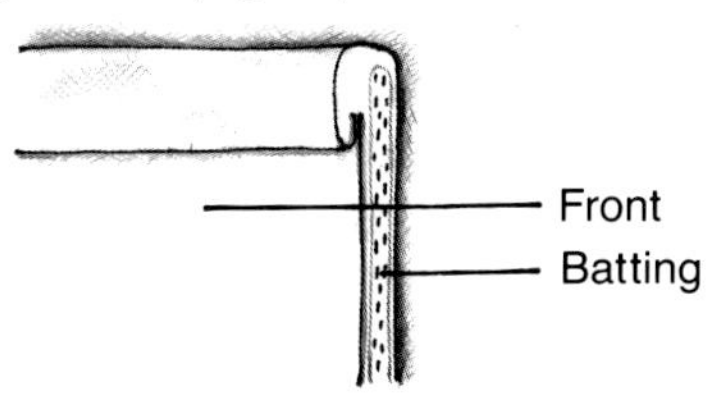

Figure 39

How to make bias binding

Method 1

Decide how broad you want the bias strip to be, e.g. 3 cm. A strip of cardboard or a ruler of exactly the required width will help you to work accurately.

Take a rectangular piece of fabric, cut on the selvedge thread of the fabric, and draw parallel diagonal lines at a 45 degree angle on the fabric. A quiltmaker's rule, a ruler marked with a 45 degree angle, will simplify this step: Place the mark on the rectangle and draw the lines.

Draw as many lines as possible on the fabric rectangle to form a parallelogram (fig. 40a). Cut the parallelogram out. Pin the parallelogram with right sides together at points C and E, and again at points B and F. Secure between the two points (fig. 40b). Iron the seam open and start cutting on the lines at point E. This will form one long bias strip.

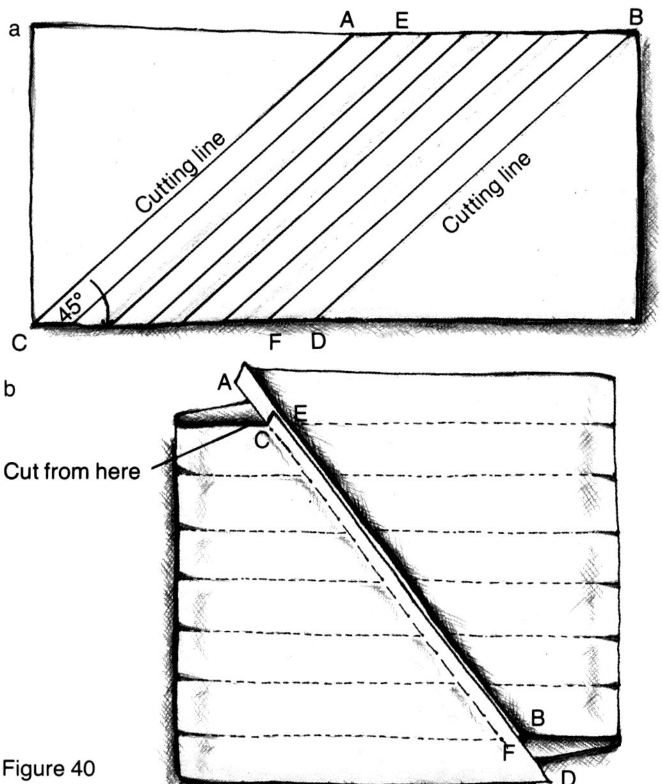

Figure 40

Method 2

Cut a square on the selvedge thread of the fabric and mark the centre of the top and bottom edges with a dot. Mark the centre of the two side edges with a star. Cut the square in half diagonally (fig. 41a). Place the two edges marked with dots right sides together and stitch (fig. 41b). Iron the seam open and draw straight lines (fig. 41c) as wide as you want the bias strip to be, e.g. 3 cm apart. Join the two edges marked with stars so that one strip protrudes. Iron the seam open and cut on the line to form one long bias strip (fig. 41d and e).

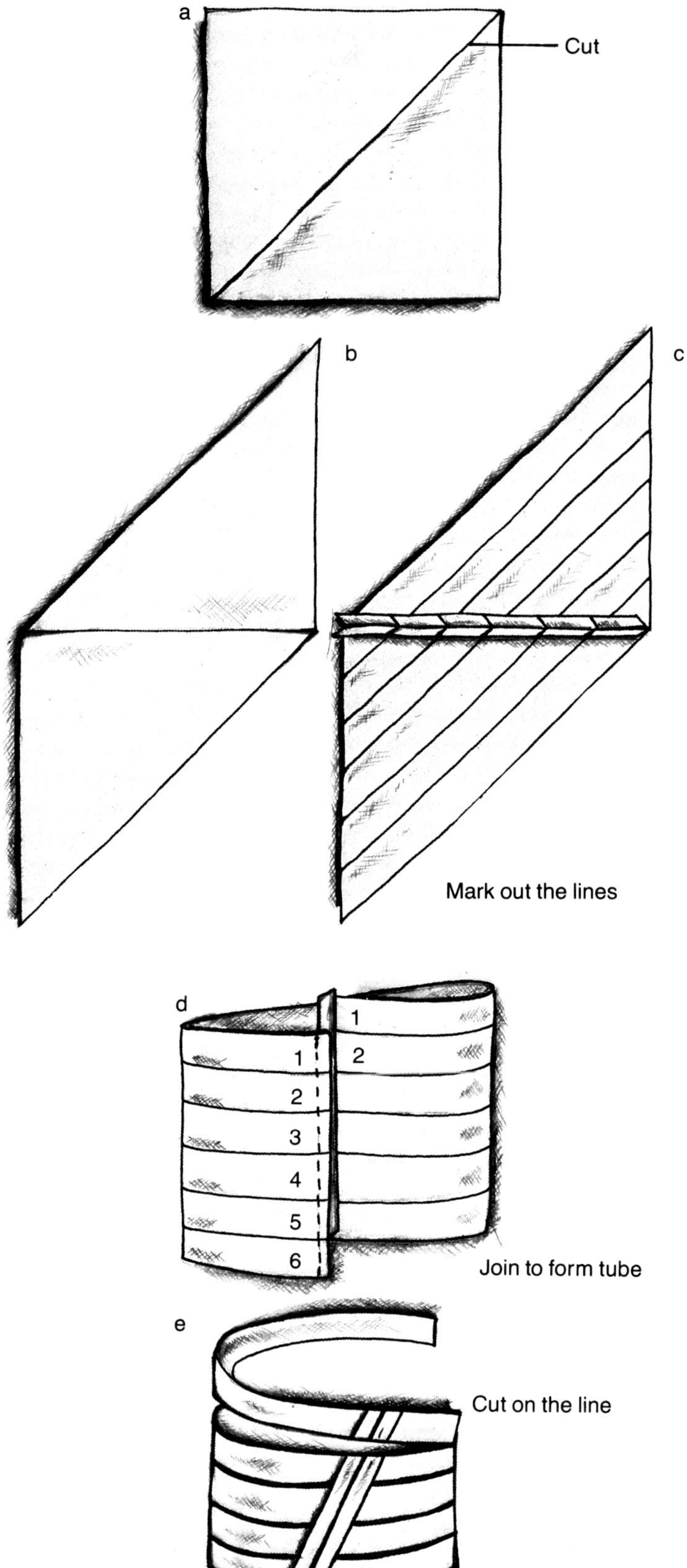

Figure 41

Projects

Living room

Stained-glass appliqué is a special appliqué technique that creates an illusion of stained-glass windows. The cushion, wall hanging and lampshade described here will brighten your living room without the need for floral or patterned fabric. Unlike patchwork and ordinary appliqué, stained-glass appliqué is not necessarily a country cottage style, which makes it suitable for virtually any interior decorating style – from antique to the modern look.

Stained-glass wall hanging

Techniques: stained-glass appliqué; general

Materials
70 cm x 60 cm background fabric
30 cm x 1.2 m wine-red fabric for the edging and loops
sufficient remnants of plain fabric
70 cm x 60 cm batting
70 cm x 60 cm backing fabric
15 m black bias binding
black thread
light-coloured thread
pattern (p. 113)

Enlarge the pattern and follow the instructions for stained-glass appliqué (p. 25) to complete the pattern. Then cut a border, 7 cm wide, from the wine-red fabric and paste it around the completed motif. If preferred, divide the border into small squares of different colours. Finish the bias binding border around the edge.

Place the top layer over the batting and underlayer, and tack, using the light-coloured thread. Quilt both sides very near the bias binding.

Cut a 90 cm long and 10 cm wide strip of fabric. Fold it in half, along the length with wrong sides together. Fold the bias binding open and position it over the length of the fabric with right sides together. Stitch both sides of the bias binding to the strip of fabric. Fold the bias binding back and secure with small stitches. Divide the strip into five sections and fold each one in half for the loops. Take a piece of bias binding, fold it open and with right sides together, stitch around the edge of the whole wall hanging. With raw edges together, place the loops on the stitching of the bias binding at the back of the wall hanging. Stitch the loops along the previous stitching. Fold the bias binding to the back and stitch with tiny stitches. Fold the loops to the top and secure carefully once more.

Stained-glass cushion cover

Techniques: stained-glass appliqué; general

Materials (per cushion)
40 cm x 1 m background fabric
40 cm x 40 cm backing fabric
40 cm x 40 cm batting
± 6 m black bias binding
± 2 m piping
black thread
light-coloured thread
pattern (p. 114)

Enlarge the pattern and follow the instructions for stained-glass appliqué (p. 25). Place the completed top layer over the batting and backing fabric, tack with light-coloured thread and quilt on both sides of the bias binding. Stitch the piping onto the right side of the cover. Follow the instructions for adding a frill (p. 38).

Cut two 25 cm x 40 cm pieces of fabric for the back of the cover. Hem each one on one long side. Place the two sections with right sides to the bottom of the right side of the work to form a pillowcase. Stitch all round, finish and turn right side out.

Stained-glass lampshade

Techniques: stained-glass appliqué; pasting; general

Materials (size of the lampshade will determine the quantity)
newspaper
1 wire lampshade
parchment
background fabric
remnants of plain fabric
black bias binding
black thread
1 roll of cotton tape
glue (Bostik)
pattern (p. 114)

Make a pattern of the shape of the lampshade by wrapping newspaper around it and cutting along the outer edges of the wire. Cut this pattern from the parchment. Also cut the pattern from the background fabric, this time leaving a seam allowance of 2 to 3 cm all round.

Apply the motif to the background fabric, using the method for stained-glass appliqué (p. 25). The lampshade is not placed over batting and backing fabric before quilting. Sew through the single layer if you want the quilt stitches to show.

Wrap the cotton tape around the two wire circles. Glue the parchment to the tape (use clothes pegs to keep it in position until the glue has dried). Stretch the fabric over the parchment. Fold in the seam allowance at the seam of the back to cover the raw edge. Glue. Fold the bottom and top seam allowance around the wire and tuck it between the wire and the parchment with a sharp object. If the seam allowance is too large, trim it a little. Paste a strip of bias binding round the top and bottom edges of the lampshade.

Dining room

What could be more romantic than dinner by candlelight with someone special? And if you have made the tablecloth, serviette rings, serviettes and other accessories yourself, the occasion will be even more special. The tablecloth and other accessories are equally suitable for a romantic dinner or for a formal dinner with your boss. Your choice of flowers and tableware will help to create the right atmosphere. This tablecloth with accessories would also make an ideal wedding present.

Table mats

Techniques: folded-star patchwork; general

Materials (per table mat with a diameter of 30 cm)
four 12 cm x 12 cm squares – fabric 1
eight 12 cm x 12 cm squares – fabric 2
eight 12 cm x 12 cm squares – fabric 3
three 32 cm diameter circles in white fabric
two 32 cm diameter circles in batting
1.5 m lace
matching thread

Find the centre of the fabric circle by folding it in half twice. Follow the instructions for the folded-star method (p. 21) until you get to the finishing. Continue as follows:

Using a compass or saucer trace a 21 cm diameter circle round the folded star using an erasable pen. This is the stitching line. Add a seam allowance of 1 cm all round and cut the raw edge of the star. Take one white circle and cut out a 20 cm diameter circle in the centre. Place the white circle and the star right sides together, matching the inner edge of the white circle with the outer edge of the folded star. (This means that the outer edge of the white circle is folded back to the centre of the folded star.) Stitch 1 cm from the edge, then fold the white circle back so that the right side is facing upwards. Trim the seam allowance of the inner circle about 6 mm from the stitching line. The top section is now complete.

Attach a lace frill with tacking stitches (p. 38). Place the two circles of batting at the bottom, then the remaining circle of white fabric, and the folded star motif right on top with right side facing down. Stitch all round through all the layers, but leave an opening to enable you to turn the work right side out. Stitch the edges of the opening together with tiny stitches.

Tablecloth

Techniques: folded-star patchwork; general

Materials
1.5 m x 1.5 m fabric for the tablecloth
1.2 m x 1 m fabric or 12 m ribbon, 5 cm wide, for the star points
6.25 m bias binding
matching thread

Follow the instructions for the folded-star method (p. 21) and cut 112 squares measuring 10 cm x 10 cm for the star points. Since ribbon does not require as much folding, it saves time and is not as thick as fabric star points. The ribbon is cut in lengths of 10 cm. Sew the first layer of star points all round the edge of the tablecloth with no space between the points. Sew the second layer over the first layer so that they overlap exactly in the middle. Stitch the bias binding to the edge, right sides together, about 6 mm from the edge. Fold the bias binding over to the back and secure with small hemming stitches.

Serviette ring

Techniques: folded-star patchwork; general

Materials (for one serviette ring)
15 cm x 8 cm fabric
36 cm x 2 cm ribbon or 36 cm x 4 cm fabric
34 cm bias binding
matching thread

Cut two fabric strips, each measuring 15 cm x 4 cm, for the serviette ring. Cut the ribbon in lengths of 4 cm or cut nine fabric squares, each measuring 4 cm x 4 cm. Fold the fabric according to the folded-star method (p. 21). Sew half the star points close together along the length of one fabric strip. Then sew the remaining star points along the length of the same fabric strip, making sure the star points are not directly opposite each other.

Place the other fabric strip on the strip with the star points, right sides together. Stitch the two short sides together. Turn the work right side out. Stitch bias binding to both sides of the edge of the strip with right sides together. Fold over the bias binding. Tuck in the ends of the bias binding. Fold the bias binding back again and stitch down with hemming stitches. Fold the serviette ring closed and stitch the short sides, using small oversewing stitches.

Serviettes

Techniques: general

Materials (for one serviette)
35 cm x 35 cm fabric
1.5 m lace
matching thread

Hem the square piece of fabric for the serviette with a narrow handkerchief hem. Use the special hemming foot if your machine has one.

Stitch the lace all round on the right side of the fabric. Make a small tuck at each corner of the serviette to prevent the lace from bulging.

Place-card holder

Techniques: pasting; general

Materials
30 cm x 5 cm thin, firm cardboard
60 cm x 8 cm fabric
9 cm x 5 cm batting
45 cm piping
carpet adhesive tape
cold glue

Cut the following: three cardboard rectangles measuring 9 cm x 5 cm; four fabric rectangles measuring 12 cm x 8 cm; one fabric rectangle measuring 8 cm x 4 cm, and one batting rectangle measuring 9 cm x 5 cm.

Cut a window, 2 cm x 6 cm, in one of the cardboard rectangles. Glue the batting to the cardboard. Cut out the batting at the window. Place one of the larger fabric rectangles on top of the batting. Fold the fabric over to the back and paste the outer edges to the back of the cardboard with carpet adhesive tape.

Make a slit in the window section of the fabric. Clip the fabric to about 1 mm from the edge of the cardboard. Fold the fabric back and glue. Paste the piping neatly all round the edges.

Place a second cardboard rectangle over one of the larger fabric rectangles. Fold the seam allowance of the fabric over to the back and paste it down with carpet adhesive tape. Paste 8 cm x 4 cm fabric rectangles on the back over the raw edge and cardboard. Paste the two covered cardboard sections, wrong sides together, at the two short sides with the bottom sections together. Hold together with clothes pegs until the glue has dried.

Stitch together the long sides and one short side of the remaining two fabric rectangles, right sides together, 1 cm from the side. Trim the excess seam allowances and turn right side out. Insert the last cardboard rectangle into the holder. Secure it to the back of the holder with small oversewing stitches. This will serve as a stand for the place-card holder.

Tea-time retreat

After hours of work there is nothing as refreshing as a cup of tea. Make your favourite place for having tea bright and cheerful. This tea cosy with its seminole inset will keep your tea hot. You need not even remove the cosy when pouring the tea – it has openings for the spout and handle.

Traycloth

Techniques: seminole patchwork; single-seam patchwork method; general

Materials
34 cm x 42 cm unbleached calico
30 cm x 1.5 m light printed fabric
6.4 cm x 1.15 m dark printed fabric
3.2 cm x 1.15 m plain pink fabric
1.3 m narrow satin ribbon
2.5 m lace
34 cm x 42 cm batting
matching thread

Cut two strips of dark printed fabric and one strip of plain pink fabric 3.2 cm wide. Stitch the dark printed fabric strips to either side of the pink strip, leaving a seam allowance of 6 mm. Cut the long strip into short strips of 3.2 cm each (fig. 42a). Join them as shown in fig. 42b to form two strips consisting of eight rows and two strips consisting of nine row of patches.

Cut a 25.2 cm x 16.8 cm rectangle, plus a seam allowance of 6 mm all round (= 26.4 cm x 18 cm) from the light fabric. Place the two strips of nine rows on each side of the long sides of the left rectangle, right sides together. Stitch and fold open. Then place the two strips consisting of eight rows of patches

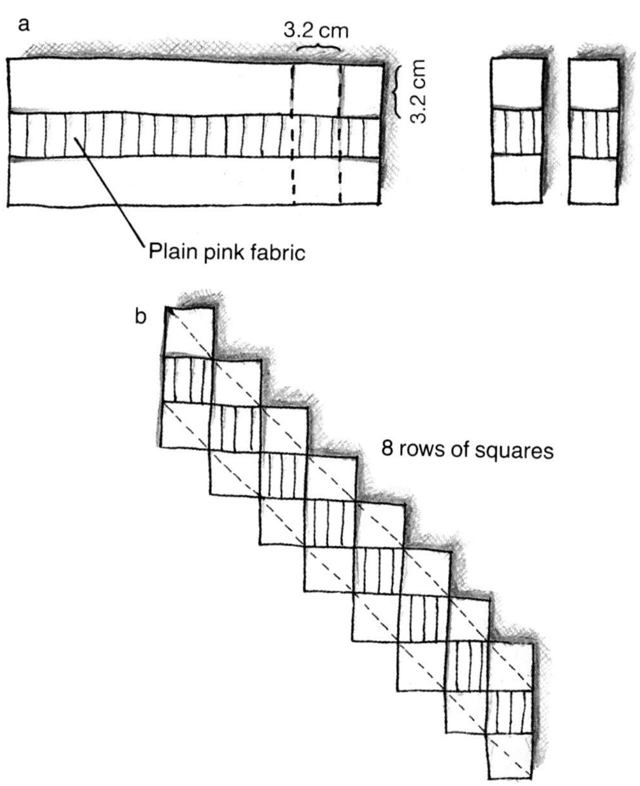

Figure 42

on either side of the short sides, right sides together. Stitch and fold open. To complete the large rectangle, fit the remaining dark fabric squares in the corners. Trim any excess fabric.

Cut two 34 cm x 5.5 cm strips and two 42 cm x 5.5 cm from the light fabric. Stitch narrow satin ribbon to one long side of each strip, 2 cm from the edge. First place the two strips next to the short sides of the rectangle, right sides together, stitch and fold open. Then place two long strips next to the long sides of the rectangle, right sides together, stitch and fold open. Follow the instructions for the mitred corner method (p. 36) at the corners.

Thread the lace through and stitch (p. 38). Put the batting in place, then the completed rectangle and unbleached calico with right sides together. Stitch 6 mm from the edge all round, but leave a gap to enable you to turn the work right side out. Slipstitch the opening.

Tea cosy

Techniques: seminole patchwork; general

Materials
80 cm x 3.2 cm plain pink fabric
two 80 cm x 3.2 cm strips of dark printed fabric
25 cm x 1.5 m light printed fabric
two circles, each with a diameter of 18 cm, of light printed fabric
25 cm x 65 cm batting
one circle batting, diameter 18 cm
1.25 m cord
60 cm bias binding
matching thread
pattern (p. 116)

Stitch the dark printed fabric strips to both sides of the plain pink strip, leaving seam allowances of 6 mm. Cut the long strip into smaller strips, 3.2 cm wide (fig. 42a). Join the strips as for the traycloth to form two strips consisting of 11 pink squares.

Cut the pattern pieces from the light printed fabric and the batting. Place the batting circle between the two fabric circles (with right sides facing outwards). Sew together all round.

Place the seminole strips with right sides together on the pattern pieces, respectively, and stitch. Fold open and place the pattern pieces, right sides together, on the seminole strips. Stitch and fold open. Lay the batting down first, then the seminole panel and the lining panel with right sides together. Stitch the sides and loose edges, but leave the base open. Repeat for the other side of the cosy. Turn the cosy right side out.

Sew the bias binding to the wrong side with two rows of stitching and leave a gap at the ends for threading the cord. Using tacking stitches, sew through all three layers 1 cm from the bottom. Gather slightly. Divide the circles in half and match the two panels exactly. Stitch to the wrong side. Trim all excess fabric and batting and finish neatly with zigzag stitches. Thread the cord through the bias binding casing and tie a bow.

Place the clock on the quilting frame. Pull tight and thread a piece of elastic through the bias binding casing. Make a hole in the centre of the cardboard circle with a sharp-pointed pair of scissors and push it into the frame from behind. Paste the numbers in position, place the watch mechanism behind and the hands in front.

Clock

Techniques: hand-method appliqué; quilting; general

Materials
50 cm x 50 cm unbleached calico
30 cm x 1.5 m printed fabric
50 cm x 50 cm backing fabric
50 cm x 50 cm thin batting
2 m lace
2 m wide bias binding
75 cm elastic
1 quilting frame with a diameter of 35 cm
1 circle of cardboard with a diameter of 35 cm
1 clock mechanism with hands and numbers
iron-on interlining
matching thread
pattern (p. 118)

Cut circles with diameters of 50 cm in the unbleached calico, backing fabric and batting respectively. Trace the 12 hearts onto the shiny side of the iron-on interlining. Cut them out. Iron the hearts onto the wrong side of the printed fabric. Cut out, leaving a seam allowance of 6 mm. Trace the pattern onto the unbleached calico with an erasable pen. Appliqué the hearts in position, using the hand method (p. 24). Place the top layer over the batting and backing fabric and tack. Quilt from about 5 mm from the centre to the points of the hearts and use outline quilting stitches round the hearts (p. 29). Quilt a motif round them.

Make a small hole in the centre through all three layers with a sharp-pointed pair of scissors for the clock mechanism. Cut a 12 cm x 2 m strip of printed fabric for the frill. Fold the fabric in half. Place a 2 m piece of lace on the fabric with edges together, and tack. Place the frill and raw edges of the clock right sides together and stitch. Place the bias binding and raw edges of frill together and stitch. Fold the bias binding over to the back and stitch. Leave the two ends open to form a casing for the elastic.

Knitting needle holder

Techniques: machine quilting; general

Materials
40 cm x 50 cm fabric for the top layer
45 cm x 50 cm backing fabric
45 cm x 50 cm batting
46 cm x 36 cm lining (pink)
46 cm x 30 cm printed fabric
46 cm x 10 cm fabric for the flap
1.6 m narrow ribbon
matching thread

Place the backing fabric, batting and top layer on top of one another and machine quilt in diagonal lines about 2 cm apart. Divide the ribbon into two equal parts. Place the pieces 15 cm from the top and 15 cm from the bottom respectively over the length of the top layer. Sew together 4 cm from the one side to 18 cm from the other side, leaving sufficient ribbon at both ends to make a bow.

Take the 46 cm x 30 cm piece of printed fabric and mark the centre of the 30 cm side on the left. Draw a line from this point to the top right-hand corner and cut along this line. Fold back a small seam in the diagonal side of the largest piece of fabric and stitch.

Place the diagonal fabric strip on the lining with the right side facing up. Stitch the pockets to hold the knitting needles. Begin with stitching 1 cm apart and end with stitching 2 cm apart. If your knitting needles are very thick, make the stitching lines further apart.

Fold the fabric forming the flap in half over the length with wrong sides together and place on the top end of the lining.

Place the lining over the machine-quilted fabric with wrong sides together. Fold the seam allowances over the lining to the inside. Fold over to form a small hem and secure with tiny hemming stitches.

Fold the knitting needle holder into three and tie the bows.

WHALE NATION
Futon
CREAM TEAS

Kitchen

A kitchen can be a cosy place where people enjoy being together – drinking tea, or having a pleasant conversation while a meal is being prepared. Unfortunately, kitchen cupboards cannot be moved around like the furniture in other rooms. The best way to brighten up a kitchen therefore is to change the accessories. Decide on a suitable colour scheme, e.g. yellow with appliquéd motifs in brown and green. The yellow fabric looks sunny and bright and the cottage, sheep and tree motifs add a country feeling. Electrical appliances can be kept under bright covers. A message board is invaluable in a kitchen, especially for your grocery list. Decorate preserved fruit and vegetable bottles with colourful fabric caps. Next time you are invited to a kitchen tea, or if a friend has a birthday, find out beforehand what the colour scheme of her kitchen is and make her a special matching accessory.

Cover for a mixer

Techniques: machine appliqué; quilting; general

Materials
50 cm x 1.1 m fabric
fabric scraps
50 cm x 90 cm batting
50 cm x 90 cm backing fabric
matching machine and quilting thread
iron-on interlining
pattern (p. 117)

From each layer (top layer, batting and backing fabric), cut a long 15 cm x 90 cm strip and two 30 cm x 40 cm rectangles with a seam allowance of 1 cm all round. Enlarge the pattern if necessary and trace it onto the shiny side of the iron-on interlining. Iron it onto the assorted fabric scraps and cut out. Tack the pieces in position on the fabric rectangle. Machine appliqué the motifs (p. 25). Stitch the fence using machine stitch.

Cut off the two top corners of the rectangles to form a curve. (Use a saucer to draw the curve before cutting.) Pin the two rectangles to both sides of the long strip with right sides together. Stitch. Place the batting on the backing fabric. Pin the rectangles, right sides together, onto either side of the strip. The batting will show on the outside. Machine stitch it carefully; do not let the batting catch on the machine foot.

Place the two completed sections together with right sides together. Stitch together at the bottom. Leave an opening of about 20 cm to enable you to turn the work right side out. Trim the excess seam allowance. Turn right side out and stitch the opening, using small stitches. Quilt the motif.

Use the same basic method to make covers for cooldrink machines, toasters or any other kitchen appliances. Measure the height, width and depth. Measure at the broadest parts and take handles into account. Add 2.5 cm to all measurements. Of this 6 mm is for the seam allowance all round, and the remainder to allow the cover to fit loosely over the appliance.

Make a pattern by drawing a rectangle as high and wide as the appliance on some paper. Cut the two top corners to form a curve, using a round object such as a glass to guide you. This pattern is for the front and back of the appliance cover. Cut two of each from the different fabric pieces.

The strip joining the front to the back is a rectangle as wide as the depth measurement of the appliance, and the length is the measurements of the front and back panels from one point at the base to the other point at the base.

The same appliqué pattern used for the mixer cover, can be rearranged to fit the appliance covers.

Place mats

Techniques: machine appliqué; quilting; general

Materials (per place mat measuring 44 cm x 34 cm)
48 cm x 38 cm yellow fabric for the background
35 cm x 25 cm printed fabric for the sheep's body
10 cm x 15 cm plain cream fabric for the sheep's head
10 cm x 12 cm plain brown fabric for the sheep's feet
48 cm x 38 cm batting
48 cm x 38 cm backing fabric
48 cm x 38 cm iron-on interlining
matching machine, quilting and embroidery thread
pattern (p. 116)

Enlarge the pattern and trace onto the shiny side of the iron-on interlining. Iron onto the wrong side of the different fabric pieces and cut out.

Appliqué the motif onto the background fabric, using the machine appliqué method (p. 25).

Place the top layer over the batting and backing fabric. Tack the three layers onto one another and use outline quilting for the sheep. Quilt curls onto the sheep with contrasting thread to form the wool.

Trim about 2 cm all round the batting and backing fabric. Turn the yellow fabric over to make a small hem. Stitch with tiny hemming stitches. Quilt all round the edge about 1 cm from the side.

Pot holder

Techniques: machine appliqué; quilting; general

Materials (for one 20 cm x 20 cm pot holder)
20 cm x 20 cm yellow fabric
20 cm x 20 cm backing fabric
20 cm x 20 cm batting
scraps of fabric for the sheep motif
1 m bias binding
matching machine, quilting and embroidery thread
iron-on interlining
pattern (p. 118)

Trace the pattern onto the shiny side of the iron-on interlining. Iron it onto the wrong sides of the different fabric pieces and cut out. Tack the motifs into position on the yellow fabric.

Appliqué the motif onto the background fabric, using the machine appliqué method (p. 25).

Place the yellow fabric with right sides facing up over the batting and backing fabric. Quilt the motif. With right sides together, stitch bias binding all round and fold over to the back. Make a small loop of the remaining bias binding and sew to the back when sewing the bias binding at the back by hand.

Jam jar cap

Techniques: machine appliqué; general

Materials
1 circle of fabric 20 cm in diameter
scraps of fabric for tree motif
matching machine thread
iron-on interlining
pattern (p. 118)

Trace the pattern onto the shiny side of the iron-on interlining. Iron it onto the wrong side of the different fabric scraps and cut out the motifs. Tack the motifs in position on the round piece of fabric and appliqué, using the machine appliqué method (p. 25). Hem the edge of the jam jar cap with a decorative machine stitch or sew a narrow piece of lace around the edge.

Key holder

Techniques: machine appliqué; pasting; general

Materials
35 cm x 25 cm brown fabric
10 cm x 17 cm yellow fabric
12 cm x 22 cm unbleached calico
14 cm x 24 cm batting
12 cm x 22 cm piece of wood about 1 cm thick
iron-on interlining
matching thread
4 or more screw-hooks
pattern (p. 119)

Trace the pattern onto the shiny side of the iron-on interlining. Iron it onto the wrong side of the yellow fabric. Cut out and machine appliqué (p. 25) onto the brown fabric.

Paste the batting on the front of the wood with 1 cm protruding at both ends. Place the fabric over the batting. Make sure the motif is in the centre of the wood. Fold the fabric over neatly to the back and glue it. Take a piece of unbleached calico and paste or staple it neatly to the back. If you wish, stitch two curtain rings to the calico beforehand so that the key holder can be hung on a wall.

Carefully pierce holes in the fabric with a sharp object and screw in the hooks.

Refrigerator magnet

Techniques: machine appliqué; general

Materials
assorted fabric remnants
iron-on interlining
matching machine thread
1 small magnet
small piece of batting
pattern (p. 118)

Trace the motif onto the shiny side of the iron-on interlining. Iron onto the wrong side of the assorted fabric scraps and cut out the motifs. Machine appliqué (p. 25) with a slightly smaller stitch than usual onto the interlining.

Take a scrap of fabric (e.g. unbleached calico) that is slightly larger than the sheep motif and lay it down, then place the batting on this fabric and the sheep motif on top of the batting. Sew all round the edges, using straight stitching. Trim any excess fabric and the batting close to the machine stitching. Set the size of the machine stitches as usual for appliqué and stitch all round the motif. Paste the magnet to the back.

Cottage biscuit container

Techniques: hand or machine appliqué; pasting; general

Materials
55 cm x 1.15 m yellow fabric
25 cm x 1.15 m brown fabric
scraps of fabric for windows and decoration
1.25 m rick-rack braid
1 m lace, width of 1 cm
25 cm x 80 cm batting
matching thread
80 cm piping cord
polyester filling
50 cm x 80 cm firm cardboard

Cut four pieces of cardboard, each 17 cm x 20 cm, for the walls, one 17 cm x 17 cm piece of cardboard for the base, one 21 cm x 21 cm piece of cardboard for the lid, and one 42 cm x 72 cm piece of yellow fabric.

Fold the fabric, right sides together, in half lengthwise to form a 21 cm x 72 cm strip. Stitch together one side and the bottom end 1 cm from the bottom. If you are using thick cardboard, leave a smaller seam allowance. Turn the work right side out. (First measure the position of the windows and doors. Appliqué these from fabric scraps before securing the walls – it will be easier to sew.)

Cut four pieces of batting the same size as the cardboard and glue them to the cardboard to form the walls. Insert one piece of cardboard into the tube of fabric. Sew exactly along the cardboard, using the zipper foot of your machine. Insert the second piece of cardboard into the fabric tube.

Again, machine stitch close to the cardboard. Repeat with the third piece of cardboard and lastly insert the fourth piece. Fold the excess fabric over to the inside and close the tube with small oversewing stitches.

Secure the first and last wall with small oversewing stitches. Cut two 19 cm x 19 cm pieces of fabric. Place the right sides together and stitch on three sides, 1 cm from the side. Turn the work right side out. Insert the piece of cardboard to form the base. Fold the seam allowance over to the inside and secure with small oversewing stitches. Press the base into position and secure to the four walls.

Cut a 23 cm x 23 cm square from the brown fabric, and four triangles with a base of 23 cm and sides measuring 18 cm. Attach three of the four rectangular bases, right sides together, to three of the sides of the square. Place right sides together and sew each side of the triangles one at a time. Turn right side out.

Insert the 21 cm x 21 cm piece of cardboard to fit snugly. Stuff the roof firmly with polyester filling. Stitch down the opening. Sew a round button on the tip of the roof to lift the lid.

Cut five 5 cm x 5 cm squares from the yellow fabric. Join the squares, right sides together with stitching 5 mm from the edge to form the chimney. Turn right side out. Stuff with polyester filling. Fold the raw edges towards the inside and sew the chimney to the roof. (Fold the edges of one side over further to make the chimney stand erect.)

If you wish, sew piping cord just inside the edge in a square of approximately 16.5 cm x 16.5 cm. This will prevent the lid from sliding or shifting.

Line the container with aluminium foil before using to protect the fabric.

Message board

Techniques: pasting; general

Materials
1 piece of wood about 60 cm x 50 cm
60 cm x 50 cm thick batting
80 cm x 70 cm fabric
7 m ribbon
small nails
glue

Glue the batting to the right side of the wood. Place the fabric over the batting and fold it over to the back. Shape the corners neatly, as you would when covering a book. Fold the raw edges over. To secure the fabric, drive small nails into the back, or staple with a staple gun. Arrange the ribbon in a criss-cross pattern across the message board, and secure with nails.

Gladys
VITA
ENGLISH

Study

Good colour and fabric choice can help to create a restful ambience in a study. The pen holder, writing pad, book ends and photograph frames are practical and make excellent gifts for Father's Day or birthdays. They are simple enough for small children to help with.

Writing pad

Techniques: pasting; general

Materials
78 cm x 35 cm fabric
52 cm x 29 cm felt
52 cm x 32 cm firm cardboard
40 cm ribbon
glue (cold glue or Bostik)

Fold the two short sides of the fabric over 3 cm to the wrong side. Stitch about 4 mm from the folding edge. Put glue on the underside of the cardboard and place, glue side down, exactly in the centre on the wrong side of the fabric.

Snip the fabric to the four corners of the cardboard (fig. 43). Fold the top and bottom edges over about 3 cm and glue to the cardboard. Place the felt on the cardboard with exactly the same amount of fabric protruding at the top and bottom. Glue.

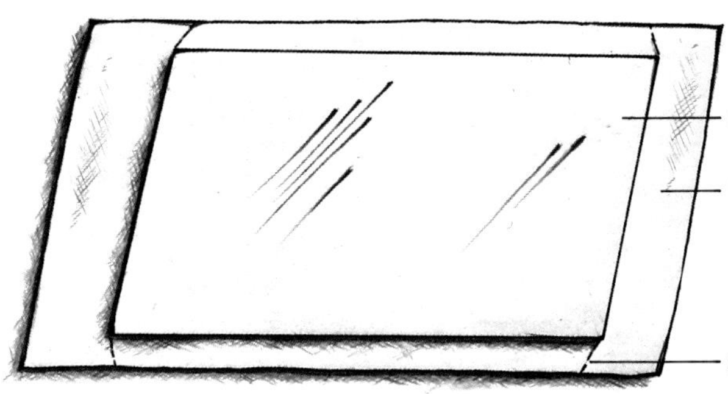

Figure 43

Fold the sides over to the front. Fold the seam over at the top and bottom. If the fabric frays easily, first fold a small seam and then the remainder. Glue the hem down firmly. Glue two pieces of ribbon diagonally across each corner on the right side, with the raw edges of the ribbon folded over about 3 cm to the back. Glue the points to the back. Use clothes pegs to hold in position until the glue has dried.

Book ends

Techniques: woodwork; pasting; general

Materials (to make one 15 cm x 15 cm book end)
two pieces of wood, respectively 15 cm x 15 cm x 1.5 cm and 15 cm x 8 cm x 1.5 cm
3 nails
30 cm x 22 cm fabric
20 cm x 13 cm felt
glue

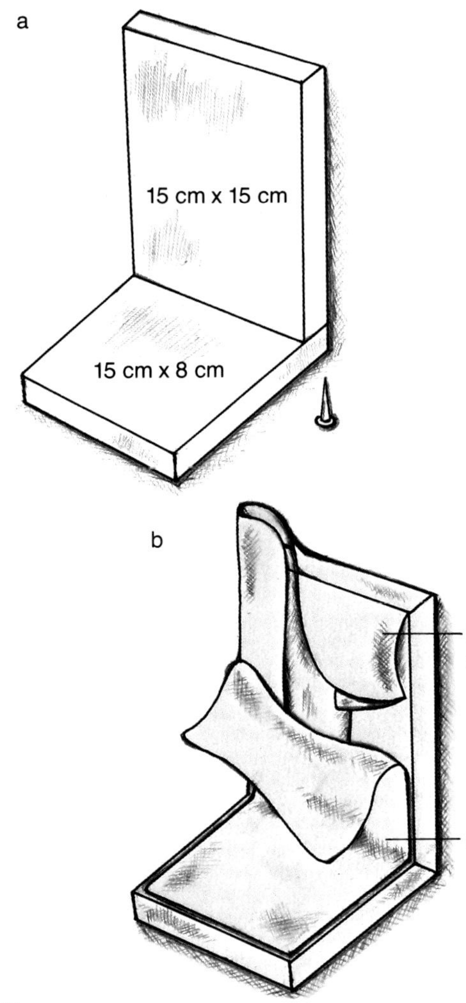

Figure 44

Place the largest piece of wood in an L-shape over the smaller block (fig. 44a) and fix it with the nails to form the book end.

Glue the fabric to the outside of each book end. Fold the raw edges over to the inside of each book end and glue (fig. 44b). Then glue a piece of felt to the inside of each book end to cover the raw edges.

Pen holder

Techniques: pasting; general

Materials
an empty tin (in this case 11 cm high and 23 cm in diameter)
15 cm x 25 cm fabric
11 cm x 23 cm batting
23 cm x 25 cm felt
glue

Glue the batting to the tin. (If you are using a smooth tin without grooves, you need not glue the batting.) Wrap the fabric around the tin, leaving 2 cm protruding at the top and bottom. Fold the raw edge over along the side and glue the fabric. Make small notches in the fabric at the base, fold over and glue. (The fabric must overlap.) Fold the excess fabric at the top over to the inside and glue.

Trace the base of the tin twice onto the felt. Cut the circles 3 mm inside the pencil lines. Cut two circles. Glue one felt circle onto the outside base of the tin, and one onto the inner base of the tin. Cut a 23 cm x 10 cm strip of felt. Glue onto the inside with the felt just meeting at the edges. You may have to trim the strip of felt slightly to make it fit snugly.

Trace the pattern onto four pieces of iron-on interlining and cut out. Iron onto the wrong side of the fabric and cut out the four fabric pieces with seam allowances. Tack the seam allowances following the inlay method (p. 19).

Place two of the fabric pieces with right sides together and sew up four sides. Turn right side out. Repeat with the other two pieces. Cut two patterns from the old X-ray film. Slide it into the opening. Sew the opening closed, but remember to secure the key ring before sewing the last few stitches.

Sew a small piece of Velcro to each side of the key ring, and another piece to each of the two sides of the holder. Place the two hexagons together and sew four of the sides. The key ring will serve a dual purpose – a key ring and a pouch for parking money.

Duck wall hanging

Techniques: hand appliqué; quilting; general

Materials
40 cm x 40 cm background fabric
fabric remnants
40 cm x 40 cm underlayer
40 cm x 40 cm thin batting
20 cm x 20 cm iron-on interlining
matching machine thread
1 small glass or plastic eye
pattern (p. 120)

Trace the pattern onto the shiny side of the iron-on interlining. Cut out the pattern pieces and iron onto the wrong sides of the fabric remnants. Remember to add seam allowances where one pattern piece is overlapped by another. Cut the pattern pieces from the fabric. Tack the panels onto the background fabric. Follow the hand appliqué method (p. 24). Embroider an eye or paste a ready-made eye onto the duck. Place the appliqué over the batting and backing fabric. Quilt the duck using the outline method, and quilt the water and grass. The wall hanging is ready for framing.

Key ring and meter-money holder

Techniques: inlay patchwork method; general

Materials
assortment of fabric scraps
remnants iron-on interlining
old X-ray film
1 key ring
Velcro strip
matching thread
pattern (p. 119)

Guinea fowl wall hanging

Techniques: hand appliqué; quilting; general

Materials
40 cm x 40 cm background fabric
20 cm x 25 cm dotted fabric
fabric remnants
backing fabric
iron-on interlining
thin batting
matching machine thread
1 small glass or plastic eye
pattern (p. 120)

Trace the pattern onto the shiny side of the iron-on interlining. Cut out the pattern pieces and iron onto the wrong side of the fabric remnants. Remember to add seam allowances where one pattern piece is overlapped by another. Cut the pattern pieces from the fabric. Tack the panels onto the background fabric. Follow the instructions for the hand appliqué method (p. 24). Embroider an eye or glue a ready-made eye in place. Place the appliqué over the batting and the backing fabric. Use the outline quilting method for the guinea fowl, and quilt the grass and ground motifs. The wall hanging is ready for framing.

Folding photograph frame

Techniques: pasting; general

Materials
20 cm x 80 cm of first fabric
20 cm x 50 cm of second fabric
20 cm x 50 cm batting
20 cm x 50 cm thin, firm cardboard
2 m piping cord
carpet adhesive tape
glue (cold glue or Bostik)
pattern (p. 119)

Cut four 15 cm x 18 cm rectangles from cardboard, two 18 cm x 21 cm rectangles from first fabric, two 18 cm x 21 cm rectangles from second fabric, two 15 cm x 18 cm rectangles from batting and one 16 cm x 28 cm rectangle from first fabric.

Cut a window following the pattern in two of the cardboard rectangles. Glue the batting onto the cardboard rectangles and neatly cut out the sections for the windows.

Place the two smaller rectangles cut from the first fabric over the batting. Fold it over to the back and paste with carpet adhesive tape. Cut notches in the fabric across the window, fold over and glue. Cover the two remaining pieces of cardboard with the second fabric by placing it on the fabric, folding back the seam allowance and fastening it with carpet adhesive tape. If desired, glue piping cord round the edge of the photograph frame on the wrong side.

Lay the two pieces of covered cardboard (without windows) neatly side by side with right sides facing down. Lay the larger piece of fabric exactly over the two pieces of cardboard. Fasten with carpet adhesive tape.

Place the two fronts neatly down on the bases and glue the two sides and bottom sections of each, leaving an opening at the top where the photograph can be inserted. Place a weight on the frame until the glue is dry.

SINGER

Sewing room

A sewing room is generally used only for making pretty things, and the room itself is neglected. Set to work and transform your workroom to provide you with a personal, inspiring place to work.

Make a notebook holder to hang on the wall. The measurements of a bed or window can be permanently recorded in your notebook in case you need it again. Or make a handy needlework basket. This looks neat for the times when you want to do sewing away from home. Mothers find such baskets ideal for holding the odds and ends needed for their babies while visiting.

Sewing basket

Techniques: general

Materials (for basket without lid)
one 43 cm x 28 cm basket, about 18 cm deep
52 cm x 1.5 m fabric
2 m bias binding
1.5 m ribbon
1.25 m elastic
matching thread

Leave a 1 cm seam allowance around each fabric panel.

Take the inside measurement of the base of the basket; here it is 33 cm x 20 cm. Cut a piece of fabric the same size plus a seam allowance. Cut two pieces of fabric measuring 1 m x 26 cm, add a 1 cm seam allowance all round.

Place the right sides of the two fabric pieces together. Sew a 16 cm seam on each short side. The seam allowance of the opening is folded over and stitched – this is for the handle of the basket.

Gather the stitched bottom end of the fabric to the same size as the circumference of the fabric at the base (about 1.06 m). Place the two sections right sides together and stitch. The inner lining of the basket's frill can be sewn now.

To make the frill, cut two lengths, 1.5 m x 13 cm. Stitch a 2.5 cm hem at the top and a smaller hem (5 mm wide) at the bottom. Sew along the 2.5 cm hem with large tacking stitches to enable you to gather the frill until it measures 1 m. Pin the frill to the inner lining and stitch. Work both fabric strips in this way. The 2.5 cm hem will form a pretty frill where the larger frill and the inner lining are stitched together.

Stitch the bias binding (or ribbon) over the stitches holding the frill and the inner lining together. Thread the elastic through the casing. Catch the elastic at both ends so that it does not slip back.

Sew ribbon on each side of the handle as bows. If desired, sew a piece of lace round the frill.

Materials (lid of basket)
90 cm x 30 cm fabric
45 cm x 30 cm batting
2.25 m lace
1 m ribbon

Lid decoration
± 1.7 m lace assortment
± 1.7 m ribbon assortment
matching thread

Cut two 43 cm x 28 cm pieces of fabric, plus 1 cm seam allowance all round. Cut one 43 cm x 28 cm piece of batting, plus 1 cm seam allowance all round.

Decorate the top of the lid by stitching pieces of lace and ribbon neatly on the right side of one piece of fabric.

Neatly gather 2.25 m lace. Tack onto the right side of the fabric decorated with ribbon and lace (p. 38).

Place the two layers of fabric right sides together. Place over the batting. Stitch together all round, leaving an opening of about 10 cm.

Trim the excess fabric and batting to 6 mm from the stitching. Make small notches in the seam allowance where necessary. Turn right side out. Close the edges of the opening with oversewing stitches. Sew two ribbons to each side of the lid to make bows around the handles.

Pin cushion

Techniques: single-seam patchwork method; general

Materials
assorted fabric remnants
polyester filling
20 cm lace
matching thread
pattern (p. 121)

Trace the pattern pieces onto the fabric remnants and cut out. Machine stitch together, using the single-seam method (p. 16).

Sew the lace by hand onto the curve of the fan.

Cut the back panel from a remnant to exactly the same size as the front. With right sides together, stitch the two panels around the edges leaving only a small opening. Turn right side out.

Fill the pin cushion with polyester filling and close the opening with small oversewing stitches.

Scissors holder

Techniques: general

Materials
two pieces of fabric, each 35 cm x 12 cm
35 cm x 12 cm batting
20 cm narrow ribbon
matching thread
pattern (p. 119)

Cut the pattern from the fabric and batting. Place the batting down, then the two layers of fabric, right sides together, on top. Stitch all round leaving a small opening.

Make notches in the seam allowance where necessary. Turn right side out.

Sew the opening edges. Fold the fabric as indicated on the pattern. Stitch neatly 4 mm from the side all round the outer edge.

Make a bow in the ribbon and sew to the top section.

Needle holder

Techniques: general

Materials
20 cm x 20 cm fabric
20 cm x 20 cm iron-on interlining
8.5 cm x 17 cm felt
17 cm lace
30 cm ribbon
matching cotton thread

Stitch a small piece of ribbon and lace across the right corner of the fabric square. Iron the interlining onto the wrong side of the fabric. Fold the fabric in half with right sides together. Stitch right around, leaving a small opening, and turn right side out. Stitch the opening.

Place the felt on the fabric and attach in the centre to form a booklet. Make a small bow with the remaining ribbon and sew it to the outside.

Note book/calendar holder

Techniques: machine appliqué; general

Materials
two 92 cm x 36 cm pieces of fabric
92 cm x 36 cm batting
assorted fabric remnants for appliqué motif
matching machine thread
iron-on interlining
± 20 cm narrow ribbon
40 cm dowel
pattern (p. 121)

Trace the appliqué design onto the shiny side of the interlining. Iron onto the wrong side of the fabric you intend using for the design and cut it out.

Tack the design about 10 cm from one short side (this forms the top) on the right side of one fabric piece. Appliqué following the machine appliqué method (p. 25).

Place the batting down, and the two fabric pieces on top with right sides together. Stitch all round through all three layers, 1 cm from the edge. Leave an opening of about 15 cm at the top end. Trim the excess seam allowance. Turn right side out. Sew the opening edges. Fold the top end of the fabric over about 4 cm, to form a casing for the dowel, and stitch.

Fold 29 cm of the bottom section to the front. Sew ribbon along the sides with small vertical stitches to hold pens or pencils. Use the photograph as a guide. Stitch the folded section: begin at the top on the stitching line of the casing for the dowel, sew right around ending at the top. Push the dowel through the casing and fasten a short length of cord to hang the holder on the wall.

Spectacle case

Techniques: cathedral window patchwork; general

Materials
25 cm x 85 cm plain fabric
8 cm x 40 cm print fabric
matching thread

Cut four 20 cm x 20 cm plain fabric squares, plus a small seam allowance. Cut five 8 cm x 8 cm printed fabric squares. Follow the instructions for the cathedral window method (p. 22) and join the four completed plain fabric squares to form a long strip. Sew a smaller square on top of each one. Fold the strip in half. Sew the two sides together with small oversewing stitches to form a spectacle case.

Main bedroom

Create a soft, romantic atmosphere with unbleached calico, ribbon and lace. Candlewicking stitches using cotton thread give unbleached calico a more textured effect. The candlewicking motifs on the quilt contribute to the romantic atmosphere.

Make matching cushions of different shapes decorated with lace and ribbon. The cushions can be enhanced with candlewicking.

The heart-shaped photograph frame and jewellery box are also embellished with candlewicking. Unbleached calico is fairly inexpensive in comparison with most fabrics, but combine it with satin ribbon and cotton lace for a beautiful, luxurious effect.

Candlewick quilt

Techniques: candlewicking; quilting; single-seam patchwork; general

Materials (size approx. 2.1 m x 2.65 m)
5 m x 1.5 m top layer fabric
2.75 m x 2.3 m backing fabric
3 m x 2 m batting
30 m cotton lace, 7.5 m wide
four 50 g balls no. 5 crochet cotton
one 50 g ball cotton knit
matching machine thread
needle with large eye (chenille no. 18-24)
patterns (pp. 122-125)

Stitches used
French knot
satin stitch
stem stitch
couching

Note: Add a seam allowance of 6 mm to all blocks and strips. Cut the strips slightly longer than directed, especially if you are not sure whether your measurements are exact.

Cut 12 blocks 35 cm x 35 cm from the top layer fabric. Remember to add a seam allowance of 6 mm on both sides. Establish the centre of the patterns and of the fabric squares. Trace the patterns neatly onto the fabric either with dressmaker's carbon paper or by using a light-box or window. In the latter case, place the fabric over the pattern and trace it with a pencil or erasable pen.

Decide which stitches (fig. 15a to m on pp. 27 and 28) you are going to use and embroider the patterns. Choose either a variety of stitches, or just two or three. Use the photograph as a guide for your choice of stitches. Depending on the effect required, use an assortment of threads, such as a light-coloured or luminous thread. Use either single or double thread.

Join all the completed blocks.

In this case the 7.5 cm wide lace is sewn onto the strips of fabric which are joined around the blocks. To save time the full length of fabric for the strips can be cut first. Make one strip and stitch continuously along the strip. Then cut the strips in the required lengths.

Cut 24 strips 35 cm long, plus 6 mm seam allowance on each side, and 24 strips 47.6 cm long, plus 6 mm seam allowance on each side. Sew the shorter strips to the sides, and the longer strips to the top and bottom ends.

Cut nine 8 cm x 47.6 cm fabric strips, plus 6 mm seam allowance on each side. Cut four 8 cm x 2.144 m fabric strips, plus 6 mm seam allowance on each side. Join the blocks with strips in between (p. 37). Cut two 8 cm x 1.748 strips, plus 6 mm seam allowance, and join at the top and bottom of the blocks. The joined blocks will be framed by fabric strips that will be quilted later. Attach the next row of strips. Cut two 16 cm x 2.10 m strips and two 16 cm x 2.65 m strips, plus 6 mm seam allowance on each side. Stitch a side lace strip all round along the joining line.

Use one of the methods on p. 29 to trace the pattern onto the fabric and quilt the motifs on the top layer. Cut the batting and underlayer about 1 cm larger than the top layer all round and tack (p. 31). Quilt around the outlines of each embroidered motif. This makes the motif stand out slightly and looks very attractive. Quilt the patterns in the strips.

Cut four 4.5 cm wide fabric strips as long as the four sides. Stitch with right sides together, right around, 6 mm from the side of the top layer. The batting and backing fabric should be only 1 cm longer on the sides.

Fold the strip of fabric over to the back, using the binding edge method (fig. 38 on p. 39) and sew with slipped-hem stitch.

Jewellery box

Techniques: candlewicking; pasting; general

Materials
40 cm x 90 cm unbleached calico
20 cm x 90 cm batting
40 cm x 90 cm cardboard
60 cm piping
1 m lace
matching thread
1 button
glue (cold glue or Bostik)
carpet adhesive tape
pattern (p. 126)

Cut the pattern pieces from the cardboard. Cut two 54 cm x 9 cm fabric pieces. Add seam allowances to each side. Stitch right sides together all round, leaving one short side open. Turn right side out.

Paste batting to one side of each cardboard rectangle. Insert the first cardboard rectangle into the fabric tube. Use the zipper foot of your sewing machine and sew a straight row of stitches close to the cardboard. Repeat with the remaining cardboard pieces, but remember that the sequence is important: three small ones, a large one, another three small ones and lastly a large cardboard rectangle. Fold the seam allowance of the last piece of cardboard over to the inside and sew the tube closed with small oversewing stitches. Join the two sides with small oversewing stitches to form the sides of the jewellery box.

Paste batting on two pieces of cardboard for the lid and base. Cut four fabric panels with a 1.5 cm seam allowance to cover them.

Stitch two of the fabric panels together, leaving three short sides of the one side open. Trim the excess seam allowance and corners at the sides that have been stitched together. Turn right side out. Insert one piece of cardboard with batting into the fabric. Fold the seam allowance over to the inside and stitch the open sides together with small stitches. Put glue on the edge of the base and push it through from underneath. The base can also be stitched together, but this will prove difficult.

Decorate one piece of fabric with candlewicking and lace for the lid. Then cover the two cardboard pieces for the lid: Place the decorated piece of fabric over the batting and the other piece over the cardboard without batting. Fold the seam allowance of both fabric pieces over the cardboard and paste it to the back with carpet adhesive. Glue the piping onto the wrong side of the top of the lid. Then glue the lace onto the piping. Glue the top and bottom lid sections together. Secure them with clothes pegs until the glue has dried.

Place the lid on the base of the jewellery box and stitch together at the back in the middle to facilitate opening and shutting. Sew a button in front at the bottom; use the ribbon to make a loop and stitch to the lid to button the box up.

Photograph frame

Techniques: candlewicking; pasting; general

Materials
25 cm x 1 m fabric
20 cm x 20 cm batting
20 cm x 80 cm thin, firm cardboard
1.2 m piping
1 m lace
matching thread
carpet adhesive tape
glue (cold glue or Bostik)
pattern (p. 126)

Stitches used
French knot
stem stitch

Cut the following pieces: two 17 cm x 17 cm cardboard squares, two 20 cm x 20 cm fabric squares, one 16 cm x 16 cm fabric square, one 17 cm x 17 cm batting square, two of each 9 cm x 11 cm fabric rectangles, and 7 cm x 9 cm cardboard rectangles for the stand.

Cut the window following the pattern from one of the cardboard squares. Glue the batting onto the cardboard and carefully cut out the window section. Trace the candlewicking pattern very lightly with an erasable pen onto one of the larger fabric squares. Embroider the pattern with candlewicking stitches. Wash the pen marks out in cold water. Cover the cardboard and glued batting with the fabric. Cut notches in the fabric across the window and fold over. Paste the fabric down at the back with carpet adhesive tape. Glue a piece of piping onto the wrong side all round the edge. Glue the lace onto the piping all round the edge.

Place the second cardboard square over the wrong side of the other large fabric square. Fold the fabric over to the back and paste with carpet adhesive tape. Glue the 16 cm x 16 cm fabric piece over the seam allowances and cardboard so that both sides of the cardboard are covered with fabric.

Glue the two sides and the bottom of the covered cardboard pieces together with wrong sides together. Insert the photograph into the opening from above.

Cover the two small cardboard pieces and paste the seam allowances to the back with carpet adhesive tape. Glue the cardboard together with wrong sides together. Score and bend the cardboard about 1.5 cm from the top and glue the top part in the centre to the back of the photograph frame to form the stand.

Granny's room

This blue and white quilt will make Granny feel she truely belongs. The blue candlewicking motifs are colourful but not too bright. The motifs on the cushions match those used on the cream-coloured candlewicking quilt (p. 72). In the mornings Granny will enjoy her coffee and croissant in bed served on a pretty lap tray. The photograph frame is ideal for photographs of the grandchildren. And if she enjoys writing letters, the pen case will make an excellent gift.

Blue candlewick quilt

Techniques: candlewicking; quilting; single-seam patchwork method; general

Materials
3 m x 1.5 m white fabric for the top layer
75 cm x 1.5 m white fabric for the frill
2 m x 1.6 m fabric for the backing fabric
14.5 m lace approximately 7 cm wide
2 m x 1.6 m batting
one 250 g ball of blue no. 5 cotton crochet yarn
matching quilting and machine thread
needle with large eye (chenille no. 18-24)
patterns (pp. 127-130)

Stitches used
chain stitch
French knots
stem stitch
satin stitch
couching
blanket stitch

Cut 12 blocks, each measuring 42 cm x 42 cm (1 cm seam allowance has been included) from the top layer fabric. Trace the patterns onto the blocks. Use dressmaker's carbon paper (first test the fabric to make sure the lines will wash out).

If you have one, use a light-box, or paste the pattern onto a window. Place the fabric over it and trace the outlines. This can be done with an ordinary pencil or an erasable pen.

Decide on the stitches you will use – the photograph will serve as a guide. Embroider all the patterns and then join the blocks. First stitch the side seams of the three blocks to form the top row. Then join the side seams of the three blocks for the second row. Repeat with the blocks for the third and fourth rows. Join the first row to the second row and the third row to the fourth row. Make sure the seams fit neatly over one another. The blocks will consist of two sections, each with six blocks. Join them neatly as well (fig. 31 on p. 37).

Cut two border strips 17 cm wide and 1.62 m long (1 cm seam allowance included) and two border strips 17 cm wide and 1.52 m long (1 cm seam allowance included). Join the border strips to the blocks and stitch the lace round them.

Trace the quilt motif onto the border. Follow the same instructions as for tracing the patterns onto the squares. The top layer can then be tacked onto the backing fabric and batting (p. 31).

Use outline quilting stitches round each pattern on the blocks. This must be done close to the pattern and will not show much, but it does help the pattern to stand out. Quilt the border pattern using blue quilting thread. Finish the edge (fig. 37 on p. 39). Stitch satin ribbon all round the border if you wish. Make a 10 cm wide fabric frill and sew it on right around.

Trapunto wall hanging

Techniques: trapunto; Italian quilting; quilting; general

Materials
25 cm x 50 cm white fabric
25 cm x 25 cm thin fabric (e.g. muslin)
25 cm x 25 cm batting
1 m white lace
polyester filling
pink wool
quilting thread
1 m bias binding
5 cm elastic
18 cm diameter embroidery hoop
pattern (p. 130)

Cut two 25 cm diameter circles from the white fabric and one each from the muslin and batting. Trace the pattern onto one white circle and place over the muslin. Tack the two layers together.

Sew running stitches along the pattern lines. Follow the trapunto method instructions (p. 32) for the leaves and the Italian quilting method (p. 32) for the flower outlines.

Place the top layer over the batting and backing fabric. Use outline quilting for the motif. Stitch the lace all round the edges (p. 38). Stitch the bias binding at the seam allowance. Fold the bias binding over to the back and stitch together with small hemming stitches to form a tube. Leave the beginning and end open to form a casing for the elastic. Stretch the design over the hoop, insert the elastic and pull it tight.

Make a loop of yarn or ribbon at the back to hang the wall hanging. Make a bow with ribbon over the cup hook if you wish to conceal it.

Pen case with mola appliqué

Techniques: mola appliqué; general

Materials
28 cm x 28 cm fabric pieces, in three different colours
fabric remnants
26 cm zipper
matching thread
pattern (p. 130)

Trace the design onto one half of a piece of fabric to fit one side of the case. Layer the three pieces of fabric and tack them together so that the design is on top.

Follow the mola appliqué instructions (p. 26) to get the pattern onto the fabric. The photograph will serve as a guide for decorating the mola appliqué case with embroidery stitches.

Fold the fabric in half with the mola appliqué design on one side. Fold the seam allowance at the upper edge of the top layer of fabric over to the inside and the seam allowance of the bottom two layers from below to the inside.

Position the zipper neatly between the top and two bottom layers of fabric; no seam allowance must show. Stitch on both sides. Turn the case wrong side out. Stitch the two side seams together and finish. Turn right side out.

Double photograph frame

Techniques: candlewicking; pasting; general

Materials
15 cm x 60 cm thin, firm cardboard
20 cm x 1 m fabric
15 cm x 23 cm batting
1.5 m piping
1.2 m lace
matching thread
carpet adhesive tape
glue (cold glue or Bostik)
pattern (p. 131)

Stitches used
French knot
stem stitch
daisy stitch

Cut the following pieces: two pieces of cardboard according to the pattern; two pieces of fabric according to the pattern with 1.5 cm seam allowance all round; one 13 cm x 21 cm rectangle of fabric; one 15 cm x 23 cm rectangle of batting; two 9 cm x 11 cm fabric rectangles for stand; and two 7 cm x 9 cm cardboard rectangles for stand.

Cut the windows following the pattern from one of the cardboard pieces. Glue batting onto the cardboard and carefully cut out the window sections. Trace the candlewicking pattern very lightly with an erasable pen onto one large piece of fabric. Embroider with candlewicking stitches. Wash the pen marks out in cold water. Cover the cardboard with the glued batting with fabric. Cut notches in the fabric opposite the windows and fold over. Paste it to the back with carpet adhesive tape. Glue a piece of lace and piping onto the wrong side all round the edge.

Place the second piece of cardboard over the wrong side of the other large piece of fabric. Fold the fabric over to the back and paste with carpet adhesive tape. Glue the 13 cm x 21 cm piece of fabric over the seam allowance and cardboard so that the piece of cardboard is completely covered.

Glue the two sides and the bottom part of the covered cardboard pieces with wrong sides together. The photographs are inserted through the opening at the top.

Cover the two small cardboard pieces with fabric and paste the seam allowance to the back with carpet adhesive tape.

Glue the two pieces of cardboard together with wrong sides together. Score and bend the cardboard about 1.5 cm from the top and glue the top part to the centre back of the frame.

Lap tray

Techniques: candlewicking; general

Materials
50 cm x 40 cm fabric for the top layer
1 m x 40 cm for the backing fabric
50 cm x 40 cm thin batting
1 m x 40 cm fabric for padding
polyester filling
46 cm x 35 cm hardboard
Velcro strip
cotton crochet yarn
matching thread
pattern (p. 131)

From the top-layer fabric, cut a 46 cm x 35 cm rectangle, plus seam allowances. Trace the candlewicking motif all round, about 3 cm from the edge. Embroider in French knots (fig. 15g on p. 28).

Cut two 46 cm x 35 cm pieces of backing fabric, plus seam allowances. Fold the seam allowance of the short side of one piece of fabric over to the back and stitch together.

Place the top layer with right side down over the other backing fabric piece, with the batting at the bottom. Stitch one short side together. Turn inside out so that the batting is in the middle.

Place the loose backing fabric piece over the candlewicked work, right sides together. Stitch the remaining three sides.

Trim the excess seam allowance and zigzag neatly. Turn right side out. Insert a 44 cm x 33 cm piece of hardboard into the case. The case can be sewn together with small oversewing stitches, but then the stitches must be removed whenever the article needs washing. Velcro strips or two bows are more practical.

Make the padding by folding the padding fabric over and stitching all round, leaving an opening of about 10 cm. Turn right sides out. Stuff with polyester filling.

Cut each half of the Velcro strip into four pieces. Stitch the soft sides to the tray section about 3 cm from the corners and the rough sides to the padding to make the tray fit snugly.

Guest room

Guests will soon feel at home in a room with this patchwork quilt. The quilt is cheerful without being too fussy and reminds one of days gone by. It is a good project to tackle if you want to master different patchwork and appliqué techniques at the same time and is ideal to make while watching television. Make a pretty cover for the pot plant holder and you will never need to look for fresh flowers.

Blue sampler

Techniques: single-seam, log cabin and inlay patchwork methods; clamshell patchwork; appliqué; quilting; general

Materials (size about 2,02 m x 2,4 m)
10 cm x 1.5 m first printed fabric
10 cm x 1.5 m second printed fabric
1 m x 1.5 m third printed fabric
1 m x 1.5 m cream fabric
2.5 m x 1.5 m blue fabric
2.05 m x 2.5 m backing fabric
2.05 m x 2.5 m batting
blue and cream quilting thread
matching cotton thread
patterns (pp. 131-135 and p. 141)

Remember to add seam allowances to every strip and block. To be on the safe side, cut the strips slightly longer in case your measurements differ slightly from the ones given.

Cut the following strips and blocks: Third printed fabric – two 13 cm x 1.3 m strips, two 13 cm x 1.9 m strips. Blue fabric – eight 30 cm x 8 cm strips, three of 1.16 m x 8 cm, two of 1.60 m x 10 cm, two of 2.46 m x 27 cm, and two of 1.52 m x 27 cm. (Strips can be joined.) Cream fabric – five 31 cm x 31 cm blocks.

This quilt consists of 12 blocks on which different techniques are used, e.g. single-seam method, appliqué, log cabin method, fold-over method, inlay method (hexagons and diamonds) and clamshell patchwork (see photograph).

Blocks 4, 6, 7, 9, 10 and 12 are made following the single-seam method (p. 16). Cut out the pattern pieces for each block and complete.

Blocks 1 and 3 are made following the hand appliqué method (p. 24). Cut out the pattern pieces and complete. Use two of the cream blocks for the background. Embroider a beak for the bird using satin stitch.

Blocks 2 and 5 are made following the inlay method (p. 19). Cut out the necessary pattern pieces and complete. Use two of the cream fabric blocks for the background.

Use the clamshell patchwork method (p. 20) for block 11. Cut out the pattern pieces and complete. Use a cream fabric block that has been cut for the background.

Use the log cabin method (p. 17) for block 8. The centre block measures 2.5 cm x 2.5 cm, plus a 6 mm seam allowance all round. The strips are 2.5 cm wide, plus a 6 mm seam allowance on each side. Complete four smaller blocks, and join to form one large block. Cut a cream fabric strip, 2.5 cm wide, plus a 6 mm seam allowance on each side. Stitch all round.

Join the blocks and border strips (fig. 32 on p. 37). Do the quilting pattern on the top layer following one of the methods shown on p. 29. The lines on the edge of the quilt must be about 4 cm apart. See p. 141 for the quilt motif pattern. Tack the backing fabric, batting and top layer together (fig. 22 on p. 31) and complete the quilting.

If desired, a binding (fig. 36 on p. 39) can be used. Fold in the 1 cm seam allowance, and fold the 2 cm blue edge back. Stitch together at the back with small blind stitches.

Pot plant holder

Techniques: general

Materials
newspaper
fabric
backing fabric
batting
matching thread

Make a pattern of the pot to be covered. Wrap newspaper around the pot and cut exactly along the edge of the pot. The top is cut about 2 cm longer. Cut curves around the top for a pretty border pattern (see photograph). Add seam allowances.

Cut out the pattern from the fabric, backing fabric and batting. Place the fabric and backing fabric right sides together over the batting. Stitch all round, leaving an opening of about 15 cm. Clip the seam allowance at the curves. Turn right side out. Sew up the opening. Sew the two sides together with small oversewing stitches. Lower the pot plant into the fabric holder from the top.

The pot plant holder can be decorated in different ways: sew piping between the top and bottom layer, or sew strips of ribbon and lace over the top layer before stitching it to the backing fabric and batting.

Hawaiian appliqué cushion

Techniques: Hawaiian appliqué; quilting; general

Materials
50 cm x 50 cm fabric for the top layer
45 cm x 45 cm fabric for the appliqué motif
30 cm x 70 cm fabric for the border strip
50 cm x 50 cm backing fabric
50 cm x 50 cm batting
70 cm x 50 cm fabric for the back
matching thread
pattern (p. 137)

Enlarge the pattern and trace onto the fabric. Follow the instructions for the Hawaiian appliqué method (p. 25). Complete the top of the cushion with outline quilting (p. 29). Follow the directions on p. 38 and complete.

Patchwork jacket

Techniques: fold-over patchwork method; general

Materials
75 cm x 1.5 m each of four different fabrics for the top layer
2.5 m x 1.5 m batting
2.5 m x 1.5 m backing fabric
matching thread
assortment of lace and buttons (optional)
pattern (p. 144)

Enlarge the pattern on paper or use any other simple jacket pattern without darts. Cut out the pattern from the backing fabric and batting. Place the batting pieces over the different backing fabric pieces. The right side of the backing fabric must face down, with the wrong side facing the batting. Tack together.

Cut the different fabrics in strips of different widths varying from 2 cm to about 5 cm. All the strips can also be the same width, if preferred.

The whole jacket is made according to the fold-over method. Begin at one side of each panel and stitch towards the next side (fig. 45a and b).

Place the first strip with right side facing up over the batting. Place the next strip over the previous strip, right sides together, and stitch. Fold the strip over with the right side facing up. Pin and place the next strip over this one, right sides together. Continue until all the panels are covered. (Pieces of lace may be added for variety.)

Place the front panels over the back panel with the backing fabric pieces on the outside; stitch the shoulder seams together and finish the seam. Stitch bias binding on the right side of the top, bottom and sides of pockets. Fold the bias binding over to the back and stitch, using small hemming stitches. Stitch the sides and bottom of the pockets against the bias binding on the front panels.

Stitch the side seams together. Stitch the side seams of the sleeves. Insert sleeves. Stitch the bias binding of the one side of the sleeve and side seams along the seam stitches. Trim the seam allowances to a width of about 5 mm. Fold the bias binding over and sew to form a strip covering the seams. Take one long piece of bias binding and sew all round the edge of the jacket, as well as at the sleeves on the right side. Trim the excess seam allowance. Fold the bias binding over to the back and hem stitch.

The jacket is reversible. If you do not intend wearing both sides of the jacket, it will not be necessary to sew the bias binding. Just machine zigzag the side and sleeve seams. Decorate the jacket with buttons or beads as desired.

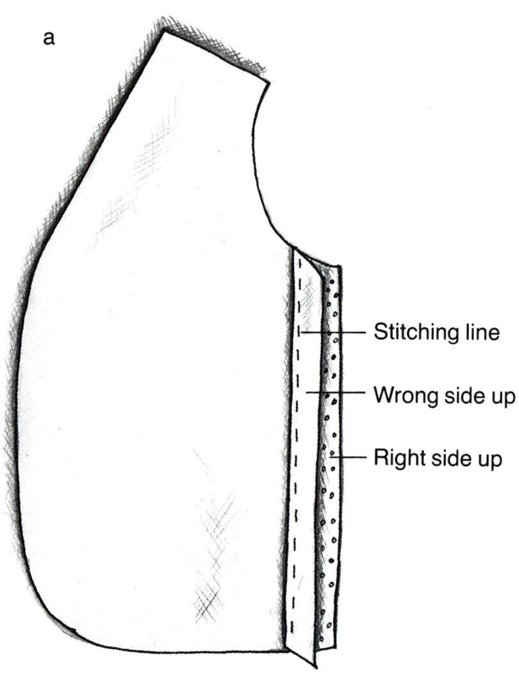

Figure 45

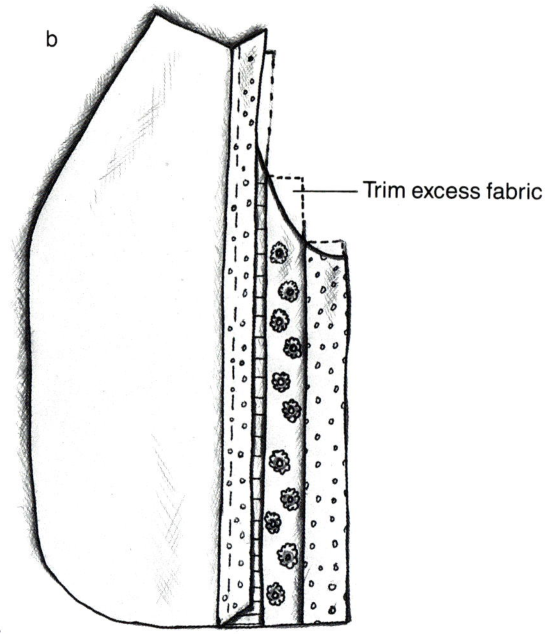

Figure 45

Handbag with strips

Techniques: fold-over patchwork method; general

Materials
37.2 cm x 62 cm and 44 cm x 26 cm unbleached calico
two 4.2 cm x 1.7 m pieces of fabric in different colours
two 4.2 cm x 2.35 m pieces of fabric in different colours
4.2 cm x 2.95 m main colour fabric
four strips of fabric each 4.2 cm x 70 cm in main colour
28 cm zipper
four strips iron-on interlining, each 4.2 cm x 70 cm
37.2 cm x 62 cm and 44 cm x 26 cm batting
matching thread
pattern (p. 136)

The maximum length of each strip of fabric for the sides of the bag is 62 cm, therefore the quantities shown above need not consist of one long strip – they can be 62 cm or shorter. A seam allowance of 6 mm is added to the end of each strip.

Place the large piece of unbleached calico down with the corresponding piece of batting on top. Tack together.

Place the first strip of fabric with right side up, over the batting against the long side. Stitch together inside the seam allowance.

Place the next strip of fabric over the first strip with right sides together. Stitch down one long side. Fold the strip over so that the right side is facing up.

Place the third strip over the second strip with right sides together. Stitch together and fold over again. Repeat the process until the whole layer of batting and unbleached calico is covered.

Follow the same method as above with the smaller piece of unbleached calico and batting. Cut out the two side panels as indicated in the pattern. If you wish, first cut out the side panels from the unbleached calico and batting and then stitch the strips onto it.

Sew a row of large tacking stitches 1 cm from each short side of the large rectangle. Gather until it measures 28 cm plus 6 mm seam allowance on each side.

Use the additional strips of the main colour and cut two 29.2 cm lengths. Place on either side of the tacking stitches with right sides together and edges aligned. Stitch the strips. Fold the seam allowance of the strips over 6 mm and fold the strip over to about 1.5 cm wide. Slip-hemstitch it to the back.

Fold the large rectangle in half lengthwise to find the centre and mark it. Place one side panel with right sides together and centre points on top of each other over the large rectangle. Pin to fit neatly, especially on top at the diagonal strips where the zipper should go. Tack. Repeat with the other side panel. Stitch and zigzag all round. Open the zipper, place it on the inside of the handbag at the two diagonal strips and stitch.

Make the handles as follows: Iron the four strips of iron-on interlining onto the wrong side of the four strips of fabric. Place two strips with right sides together, and stitch 6 mm from the side all round, leaving one end open. Repeat with the other handle. Turn the work right side out and iron. Fold the edge of the open end over to the inside and stitch a row of stitches 6 mm from the side all round. Place the handles in position on the bag (10 cm from the top and 6 cm from the side) and stitch down.

If desired, a lining can be made for the bag. Cut out an additional 37.2 cm x 62 cm piece of fabric and two additional sides. Tack the lining to the top and bottom as for the outside of the bag, join the diagonal strips and stitch the sides. Place the lining, wrong sides together, inside the bag before sewing in the zipper. Tack the zipper between the diagonal strips and stitch.

POETRY
詩
COPPER CANYON PRESS

Teenager's room

Many teenagers also use their rooms as entertainment areas for their friends – drinking coffee and chatting. It is also a place where they can express their individuality. Teenage girls, in particular, like to decorate their bedrooms. Some like frills and lace, while others prefer a dramatic look. The motif quilt patterns and the floral fabric used here soften the harder patchwork lines. The room is feminine but not childish. Note the use of colour – light (cream or beige), medium light (patterned or floral), medium (peach), and dark (rust) fabrics – to create a subtle effect with the quilt.

Seminole quilt

Techniques: Seminole patchwork; single-seam patchwork method; quilting; general

Materials
2 m x 1.5 m unbleached calico
1.8 m x 1.15 m floral fabric (1.8 m x 1.5 m)
1 m x 1.15 m rust-coloured fabric (1 m x 1.5 m)
1 m x 1.15 m peach-coloured fabric (1 m x 1.5 m)
2.2 m x 1.7 m batting
2.2 m x 1.7 m backing fabric
matching machine thread
quilting thread
rotary cutter, cutting board and long ruler
patterns (pp. 138 and 139)

Cut the following strips: a) Unbleached calico – one 31.2 cm x 1.452 m strip. b) Floral fabric – two 8.2 cm x 1.632 m strips, one 8.2 cm x 81.2 cm strip. c) Rust fabric – two 3.2 cm x 1.702 m strips, one 3.2 cm x 85.2 cm strip. d) Unbleached calico – two 5.2 cm x 1.722 m strips, one 5.2 cm x 93.2 cm strip. e) Peach fabric – two 3.2 cm x 1.762 m strips, one 3.2 cm x 97.2 cm strip. f) Floral fabric – two 8.2 cm x 1.782 m strips, one 8.2 cm x 1.112 m strip. g) Unbleached calico – two 5.2 cm x 2.032 m strips, two 5.2 cm x 1.612 m strips.

Cut the following squares (then cut through diagonally to form triangles): Unbleached calico – 27 blocks measuring 11 cm x 11 cm (= 54 triangles). Floral fabric – 25 blocks measuring 11 cm x 11 cm (= 50 triangles). Unbleached calico – 25 blocks measuring 10 cm x 10 cm (= 50 triangles). Floral fabric – 26 blocks measuring 10 cm x 10 cm (= 52 triangles). Floral fabric – one block measuring 18 cm x 18 cm (= 2 triangles). Unbleached calico – one block measuring 18 cm x 18 cm (= 2 triangles).

A 6 mm seam allowance has been included in the measurements.

For the seminole strips, cut the following: Rust fabric – 1.62 m x 5.2 cm. Unbleached calico – 1.62 m x 3.2 cm. Peach fabric – 1.62 m x 5.2 cm. Floral fabric – 1.62 m x 5.2 cm. (Shorter strips of each colour can be joined to obtain the total length, or the total length can be subdivided to form shorter seminole strips.) Join the strips lengthwise in the same order as above. Divide this strip into 50 small strips, each 3.2 cm wide (A, fig. 46a).

Then cut the following: Unbleached calico – 1.68 m x 3.2 cm. Rust fabric – 1.68 m x 3.2 cm. Unbleached calico – 1.68 m x 3.2 cm. Peach fabric – 1.68 m x 5.2 cm. Join the strips in the same order as above. Divide this strip into 52 small strips, each 3.2 cm wide (B, fig. 46a).

Now cut the following: Unbleached calico – 1.15 m x 3.2 cm (10 strips). Rust fabric – 1.15 m x 5.2 cm (10 strips). Unbleached calico – 1.15 m x 3.2 cm (10 strips). Peach fabric – 1.15 m x 5.2 cm (10 strips). Floral fabric – 1.15 m x 3.2 cm (10 strips). Join the strips in the same order as above. There should be 10 seminole strips. Divide into 332 smaller strips, each 3.2 cm wide (C, fig. 46a).

Then join 300 strips from C (fig. 46a) together in groups of three (each strip should protrude 2 cm beyond the end of the previous one). At 49 of these groups the blocks should run to the top right when the strips are turned vertically (D, fig. 46b) and at 51 groups to the bottom right (E, fig. 46b). Then stitch a strip from A onto the right of the 28 D-group; a strip from B onto the right of the 29 E-groups; a strip from B onto the left of the 21 D-groups and a strip from A onto the left of the 20 E-groups. Two groups from E remain unchanged.

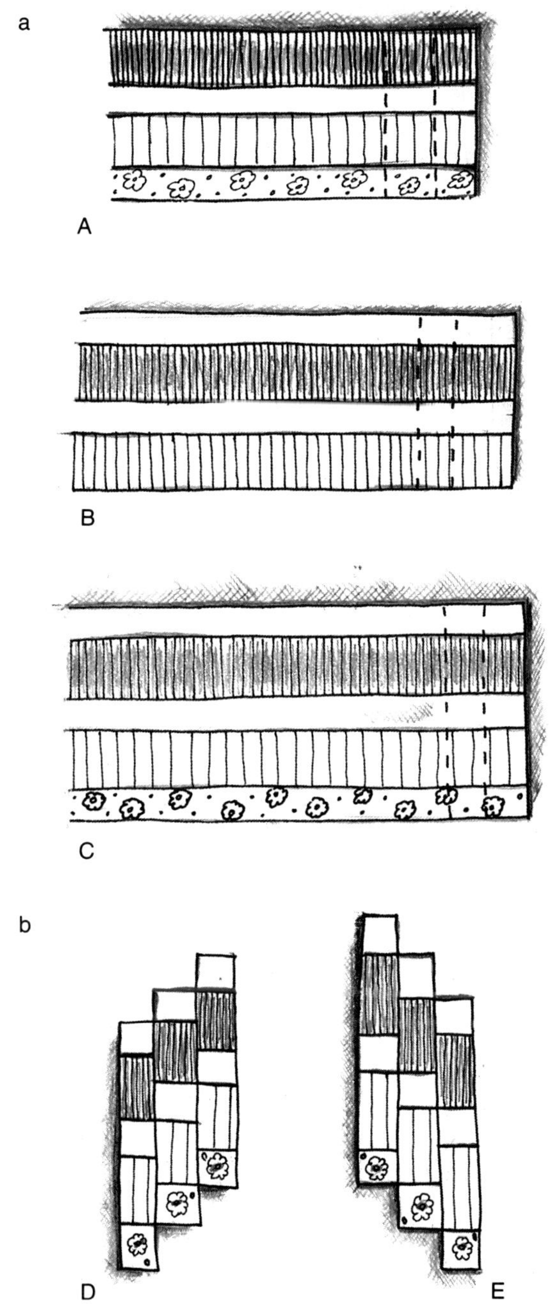

Figure 46

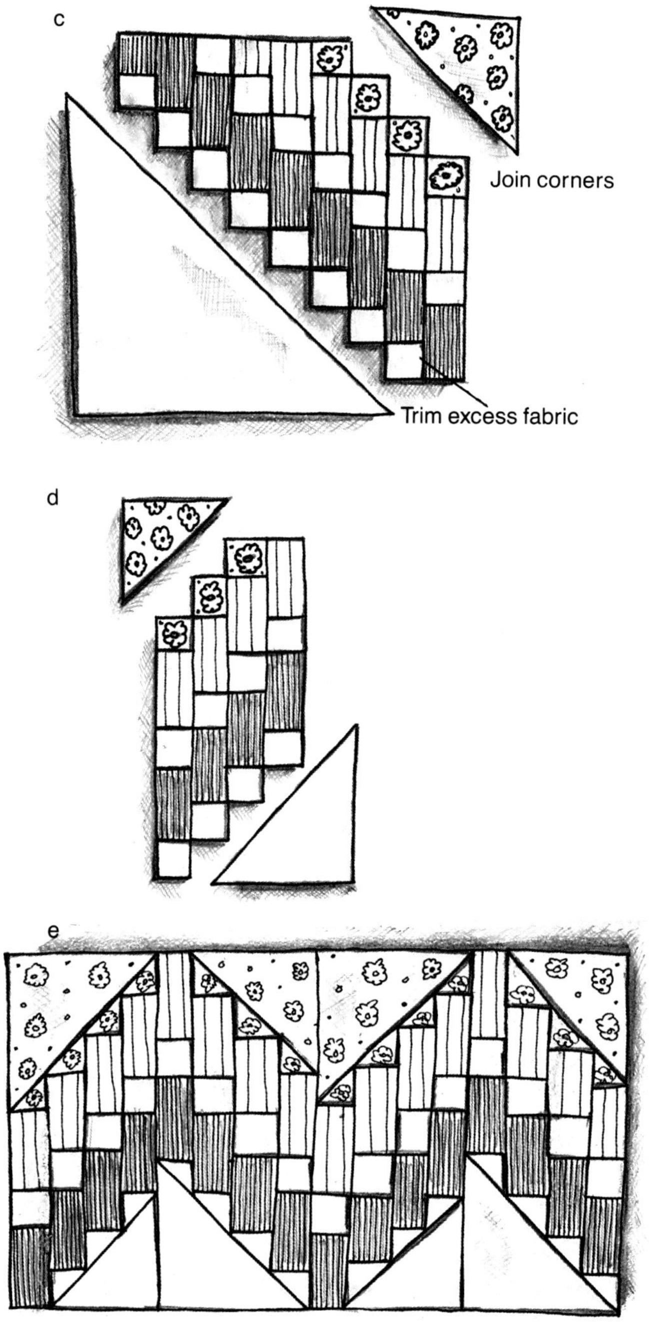

Figure 46

For the four corners, join every eight strips from C, two in the same direction as D (fig. 46b) and two in the same direction as E (fig. 46b). Stitch a strip from A onto one D-type corner to the left side and a strip from B onto the other D-type corner on the left side. Stitch a strip from B onto one E-type corner on the right side and a strip from A onto the other E-type corner on the right side. All the seminole pieces are ready to be joined to the three triangles.

The seminole pieces of the corners are first joined to their triangles (fig. 46c). Two corners are predominantly peach and two predominantly rust. Join the large calico triangle to one side and the smaller floral triangle to the other side of the rust seminole corners. Join the large floral triangle to the one side and the smaller unbleached calico triangle to the other side of the peach seminole corner. Trim all the excess fabric with the rotary cutter.

The zigzag seminole strip is joined together as follows: First stitch the triangles onto both sides of the seminole piece. Stitch the smaller triangles to each side of the piece consisting of only three blocks and the larger triangles to the piece consisting of four blocks (fig. 46d).

The two sections with three seminole strips instead of four fit into the corners. Follow the diagram and complete the seminole sections that fit between the corners, and then the seminole sections that fit along the sides (fig. 46d).

Join the top layer. Begin at the strip of unbleached calico (a). Follow with a seminole strip, then add the strips b, c, d, e and f. Add another seminole strip. Join the strip of unbleached calico (g). Complete the quilting pattern on the top layer.

Tack the backing fabric, batting and top layer together and complete the quilting. Fold a 6 mm hem in the unbleached calico and fold a 2 cm edge over to the back. Stitch, using small hemming stitches.

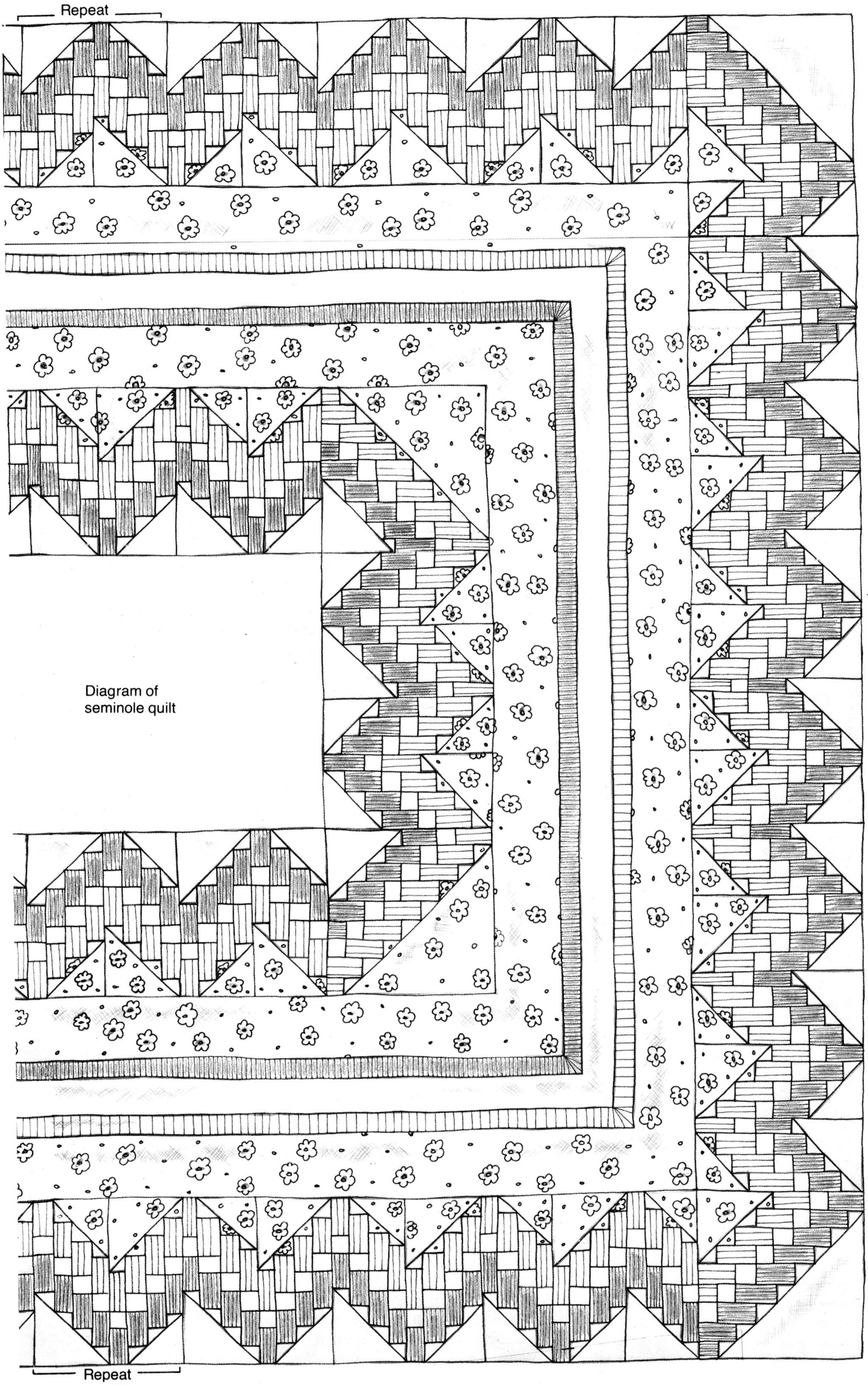
Repeat
Diagram of
seminole quilt
Repeat

Tissue box container

Techniques: machine quilting; general

Materials
25 cm x 75 cm printed fabric
25 cm x 75 cm backing fabric
25 cm x 75 cm batting
2.7 m bias binding
matching thread
2 press studs
pattern (p. 136)

Enlarge the pattern pieces. The 6 mm seam allowance has been included in the pattern. Cut out the pattern pieces from the floral fabric, batting and backing fabric. Trace the quilting lines 2.5 cm apart on the print fabric using an erasable pen. Place the printed fabric over the batting and backing fabric and machine quilt. If preferred, quilt the fabric before cutting out the pattern pieces.

Cut two pieces of bias binding, each 26 cm, and sew each one, right sides together to the top of the sides. Fold the bias binding over to the back and stitch, using small hemming stitches.

Place the edges on each side exactly in the centre over the other fabric strip with wrong sides together and the edges matching. Stitch to the three raw edges on the right sides. Stitch a strip of bias binding along the seam allowance around the right side. Fold the bias binding over to the back and stitch using small hemming stitches. Sew the press studs in place.

Mirror frame

Techniques: machine quilting; pasting; general

Materials
1 mirror
1 piece of hardboard, large enough to cut out the frame
printed fabric
batting
backing fabric
matching thread
piping
colourless glue
cold glue
carpet adhesive tape
mirror adhesive

The mirror is secured to the wall with screws, so the weight is not on the frame.

The quantity of fabric will depend on the size of the mirror.

From the hardboard, cut a frame of about 10 cm wide, with the inside measurement about 2 cm smaller than the mirror. Glue two layers of batting to the mirror frame. Use the wooden frame as a pattern and cut a piece of fabric, batting and backing fabric about 4 cm larger than the frame right around. Draw the quilting lines 2.5 cm apart on the printed fabric using an erasable pen. Lay the three layers on top of one another. Machine quilt. Place the fabric over the batting on the frame and neatly fold over to the back.

Make small nicks in the fabric on the inside of the frame so that they will fold back neatly. Paste to the back with carpet adhesive tape or use a staple gun. Glue the piping to the back of the frame, so that it looks neat at the front. Paste the mirror to the frame with mirror adhesive tape. For the back, cut a piece of fabric to fit, fold in the seam allowance and staple or glue it neatly. A piece of hardboard can also be stapled or pasted to the back with mirror adhesive. Make small holes in the back for the screws attaching the mirror to the wall.

Tote bag

Techniques: machine quilting; general

Materials
50 cm x 1.5 m plain fabric
50 cm x 1.5 m backing fabric
50 cm x 1.5 m batting
2.2 m x 2.5 cm cotton or nylon tape for the handles
45 cm zipper
matching thread

Cut two circles, each with a 25 cm diameter (add 1 cm seam allowance), from the plain fabric, backing fabric and batting. Cut one 75 cm x 45 cm rectangle each from the plain fabric, backing fabric and batting.

Place the plain fabric and backing fabric rectangles, right sides together, on top of the batting. Stitch the two short sides. Turn right side out. Place the circles of plain fabric on top of the backing fabric and the batting. Machine quilt the circles and the rectangle in lines 2 cm apart.

Place the right side of the length of the rectangle on the right side of a circle. Stitch all round and repeat with the other circle. Zigzag each seam and turn right side out. Tack the zipper at the opening on the inside of the bag.

Divide the strip of tape for the handles in two and stitch the ends of each together to form two circles. Begin 10 cm from the zipper and 6 cm from the side and stitch the tape to the bottom of the bag, ending 10 cm from the zipper again. Back-stitch at the end to strengthen.

Stitch the other circle in exactly the same way to the other side of the bag to form handles on both sides of the bag.

Cosmetics bag

Techniques: machine quilting; general

Materials
30 cm x 90 cm printed fabric
30 cm x 90 cm backing fabric
30 cm x 90 cm batting
1.50 m bias binding
matching thread
2 press studs
pattern (p. 137)

Add a 6 mm seam allowance to all pattern pieces. Cut the pattern pieces from the printed fabric, batting and backing fabric. Trace the quilting lines 2.5 cm apart on the printed fabric using an erasable pen. Place the printed fabric over the batting and backing fabric and machine quilt. If preferred, the whole piece of fabric can be quilted beforehand.

Sew bias binding to either end of the side strip and to the top end of the front panel. Turn the bias binding over to the back and stitch, using small hemming stitches.

Pin the front with wrong sides together to one long end of the side strip, and the back with wrong sides together on the other long side of the side panel. Machine stitch. Stitch a strip of bias binding along the seam allowances all round on the right side. Fold over to the back and stitch, using small hemming stitches. Sew the press studs in place.

Coaster

Techniques: machine quilting (optional); general

Materials (for one)
20 cm x 40 cm fabric
20 cm x 40 cm iron-on interlining
matching thread
pattern (p. 136)

Trace the pattern twice onto the shiny side of the iron-on interlining and cut out. Iron both onto the wrong side of the fabric. Add a seam allowance of 7 mm all round and cut out. Tack the seam allowance towards the wrong side of the fabric.

Lay the two sections right sides together and sew all round with oversewing stitches. Leave one side open. Turn the right sides out and stitch the last seam. Pull out the tacking threads. If preferred, use the machine quilting method.

2
4
1
3

Nursery

For small children, the nursery is their kingdom. They sleep, play and keep their toys here – and a teddy bear has pride of place on almost every windowsill.

In winter especially, small children spend much of their time indoors. An interesting, brightly coloured room will stimulate a small child, which is why the three primary colours – blue, red and yellow – with a touch of green, is a popular colour scheme. There is a good balance between the warm (yellow and red) and the cold (blue and green) colours for the room not to appear too warm or too cold.

Make the toy blocks yourself, and to improve his co-ordination, a book from which the child can learn to tie shoelaces and buttons. The book is fully washable, provided all the fabric is pre-shrunk.

Wall hanging

Techniques: machine appliqué; general

Materials
40 cm x 60 cm background fabric
40 cm x 25 cm green print fabric for the grass
assorted remnants
iron-on interlining
matching machine thread
pattern (p. 115)

Enlarge the pattern. Trace the pattern pieces onto the shiny side of the iron-on interlining, cut out and iron onto the wrong side of the different fabric pieces. Cut out. Place the green printed fabric for the grass onto the background fabric.

Appliqué the motifs following the machine appliqué method (p. 25). Embroider the leaf and tree trunk detail by hand or machine, or leave as is. The wall hanging can now be framed. A fabric frame (p. 36) can look striking, but remember you then need enough fabric for the backing fabric and the border.

Building blocks

Techniques: machine appliqué; general

Materials
12 cm x 72 cm fabric for each block
assorted remnants for appliqué
matching thread
polyester filling
pattern (p. 143)

Cut six 10 cm x 10 cm squares for each block, adding a 1 cm seam allowance all round. Trace the appliqué pattern pieces onto the shiny side of the iron-on interlining and cut out. Iron onto the wrong side of the fabric and cut out. Place over the squares and follow the machine appliqué method (p. 25) instructions.

Join the blocks as follows: Sew two squares with right sides together on one side. Then begin again at the stitching just completed. Pin two adjoining sides of a third square to the tops of the first two squares. Stitch together. Repeat with the other three squares.

Pin the two completed parts together to form a block. Stitch all the sides, except one. Trim the seam allowances. Turn right side out. Stuff the block with polyester filling and close the seam with small oversewing stitches.

A small bell inside one of the blocks will make it more interesting.

Nursery quilt

Techniques: log cabin patchwork method; quilting; general

Materials (for small bed: 1.275 m x 1.8 m; single bed: in brackets)
light yellow fabric – 28 cm x 1.1 m (36 cm x 1.1 m)
medium yellow fabric – 50 cm x 1.1 m (75 cm x 1.1 m)
dark yellow fabric – 90 cm x 1.1 m (1.2 m x 1.1 m)
light blue fabric – 40 cm x 1.1 m (52 cm x 1.1 m)
medium blue fabric – 75 cm x 1.1 m (90 cm x 1.1 m)
dark blue fabric – 1 m x 1.1 m (1.2 m x 1.1 m)
centre block (white) – 12 cm x 1.1 m (16 cm x 1.1 m)
binding strip (blue) – 40 cm x 1.1 m (50 cm x 1.1 m)
batting – 1.3 m x 1.8 m (1.5 m x 2 m)
backing fabric – 1.3 m x 1.8 m (1.5 m x 2 m)
for log cabin motif – 3 m x 1.1 m (4 m x 1.1 m)
matching machine thread
rotary cutter, cutting board and long ruler

The whole quilt is joined by machine. Each completed block measures 17.5 cm x 17.5 cm.

Cut out all the yellow and blue fabric blocks except those for the binding strips, to measure 2.5 cm wide plus a 6 mm seam allowance on each side (= 3.7 cm wide). Cut 70 (88) 3.7 cm x 3.7 cm centre blocks from the white fabric. Cut 70 (88) squares, each 20 cm x 20 cm, from the base fabric if you intend stitching the log cabin motif on a background. The background may be left out and the motif stitched onto paper which is removed afterwards.

Follow the instructions for the log cabin method (p. 17). Use a colour twice before beginning with the next strip – use the photograph on p. 97 as a guide. As soon as the squares are complete, join them all. The blocks can be arranged in many different ways (fig. 5a and b on p. 19). Begin with the top row and stitch the blocks together at the side seams to form a long strip. Repeat with the next rows until there are 10 (11) strips.

Then join the long strips. Make sure the seam lines correspond exactly. If paper was used, remove it. Tack the top layer onto the batting and backing fabric (p. 31). Make sure the batting and backing fabric are exactly 2 cm larger than the top layer all round. Quilt as desired, e.g. on the seam line of each centre block.

Cut binding edges 6.2 cm wide. Place these, right sides together, on top of the backing fabric. Stitch 6 mm from the edge. Fold the fabric over to the back. Fold a small hem over and use small slip-hemming stitches to form a 2.5 cm binding.

Charl

Activity book

Techniques: hand or machine appliqué; embroidery; general

Materials
50 cm x 1.5 m denim fabric
assorted felt scraps
matching thread
3 buttons
Velcro strips
2 shoelaces
24 shoelace eyelets
8-10 cm zipper
cotton tape or leather buckle
2 press studs
patterns (p. 143)

Pre-shrink the felt and fabric to make the book washable. Fabric rather than felt can be used, but appliqué the patterns with satin stitch. For felt an ordinary straight stitch will do.

Divide the denim into seven sections, each about 21.5 cm x 50 cm. Appliqué the pictures onto the right half of each piece of fabric. Embroider the child's name on the front cover.

Page 1: Nurse
Appliqué the nurse's face, hair and cap onto the denim. Embroider a nose. Sew one half of a press stud in position for each eye, and the other half behind the loose eyes. Sew one piece of Velcro in position for the cross on the hat and the mouth, and the other one behind the two loose pattern pieces.

Page 2: Apple tree and basket
Appliqué the apple tree and basket onto the denim. Sew a piece of Velcro on the basket and six pieces on the tree. Sew another piece of Velcro onto the back of the apples.

Page 3: Raincoat and cloud
Iron interlining onto the back of the felt for the coat to reinforce the buttonholes. Make three buttonholes on one side and sew three buttons onto the other side. Sew the arms and side seams of the coat and the cloud in position.

Page 4: Boot
Cut out the whole boot and separate flaps from the felt following the pattern. Appliqué the boot onto the denim. Stitch the detail with zigzag stitching. Press three shoelace eyelets into each boot flap and sew the side seams of the boot. Thread the shoelace.

Page 5: Caravan and tent
Stitch the zipper onto the tent. (Cut a long zipper shorter if necessary, but stitch down securely where it is cut off.) Mark the position where the man's sleeping bag is to be and appliqué it along the sides and at the bottom. Appliqué the tent, caravan and plants into position. Put the man in the sleeping bag so that the child can take him out. Sew one section of the Velcro to the loose caravan door, window and wheel, and the other section to the corresponding sections on the caravan itself.

Page 6: Little man
Appliqué the little man in position. Make a belt and buckle from fabric or leather (felt is not very strong and may tear), by cutting two strips and sewing a buckle to one end. Sew one section onto each side to form the belt.

Complete each page of the book and fold over with right sides together. Stitch 5 mm from the edge all round, leaving a 10 cm opening, and turn right side out. Stitch the opening and sew a row of fancy stitches around each page. Press two eyelets on the left side of each page so that a shoelace can be threaded through. Place the front page with the child's name right on top. Thread the shoelace through all the pages and tie it.

Baby's room

Every expectant mother enjoys preparing her new baby's room. Here we used cheerful printed fabric and motifs that are suitable for both boys and girls. These practical items will help to make a mother's life more easy, and are excellent gift ideas for a friend's stork party. The utility bag on the wall will help to keep the room neat and tidy and later to keep dangerous items; such as pins, out of baby's reach.

Quilt for a baby's room

Techniques: machine appliqué; embroidery; general

Materials
66 cm x 44 cm fabric for the top layer
two 90 cm x 13 cm strips and two 70 cm x 13 cm strips for the border
70 cm x 90 cm backing fabric
8 cm x 6 m (or 32 cm x 1.5 m) dark fabric for the frill
6.5 cm x 6 m (or 26 cm x 1.5 m) pink fabric for the frill
additional fabric for cat motif
70 cm x 90 cm batting
2.5 m ribbon
matching machine thread
30 cm x 45 cm iron-on interlining
pattern (p. 140)

Cut the strips for the border and sew them around the top layer rectangle. Follow the instructions for the mitred corner method (fig. 29 or 30 on pp. 36 and 37) to fit the border strips. Enlarge the cat motif and trace onto the shiny side of the iron-on interlining. Cut out the pattern pieces and iron onto the wrong side of the appliqué fabric. Follow the instructions for the machine appliqué method (p. 25). Embroider the cat's face and other detail using stem stitch.

Embroider the eyes using satin stitch or sew ready-made eyes in place. Sew 15 cm of ribbon to each side of the neck and stitch.

Stitch ribbon over the seam line where the inside and border strip are joined.

Hem the fabric for the frills at the top end. Machine stitch two rows of tacking stitches to the bottom. Gather until the frill measures 3.16 m. Follow the instructions on p. 38 and first stitch the narrow pink frill and then the broad pattern fabric frill. Place the batting down, then the backing fabric and the top layer, right sides together, and the frills folded to the inside. Make sure that the layers are not puckered.

Stitch all round, leaving a large enough opening, and turn right side out. Stitch the opening using small oversewing stitches.

Tack all three layers together neatly. Work from the inside outwards, and quilt the cat.

Baby's bib

Techniques: shadow appliqué; general

Materials
25 cm x 60 cm fabric
25 cm x 30 cm thin, transparent fabric, e.g. organdie
assorted fabric remnants for appliqué motif
75 cm ribbon
1.5 m lace
matching thread
glue stick
pattern (p. 140)

Trace the appliqué motif onto the right side of the fabric remnants and cut out. Cut two bib patterns from the fabric and one from the transparent fabric. Glue the appliqué motif in position on one layer of fabric and place the transparent fabric over it. Tack the layers together. Follow the instructions for the shadow appliqué method (p. 26).

Gather the lace to fit around the bib. Place it on the edge of the bib, right sides together, with the raw edges of the fabric and straight edge of the frill matching. Tack. Place the second layer of fabric over the shadow appliqué motif, right sides together. Stitch all round, leaving an opening of about 10 cm. Trim the excess seam allowance and clip the curves. Turn the work right side out. Stitch the opening.

Sew two pieces of ribbon to the neck for fastening the bib. Make a bow and stitch onto the cat's neck.

Utility bag

Techniques: machine appliqué; general

Materials
48 cm x 62 cm fabric for the top layer
48 cm x 62 cm backing fabric
16 cm x 20 cm and 18 cm x 13 cm pink fabric for pockets 1 and 4
15 cm x 11 cm and 22 cm x 19 cm dark printed fabric for pockets 3 and 6
24 cm x 17 cm and 38 cm x 17 cm striped fabric for pockets 2 and 5
12 cm x 18 cm dark printed fabric for the loops
scraps of plain blue fabric and iron-on interlining for the appliqué motif
ribbon
2.25 m lace frill
matching machine thread
pattern (p. 140)

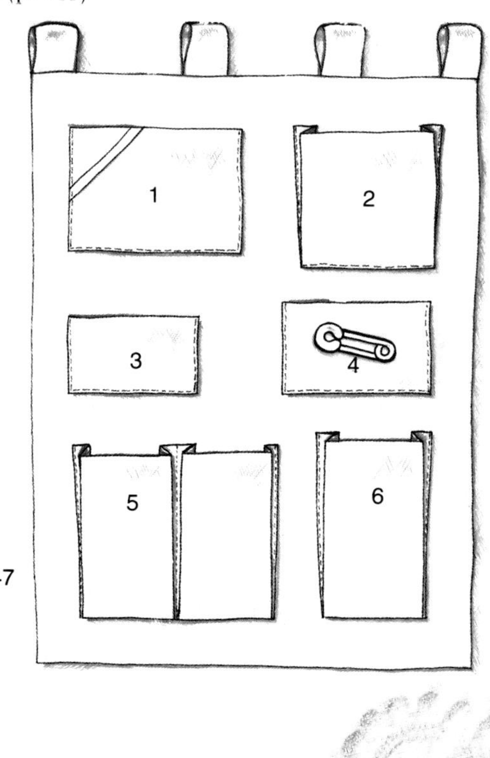

Figure 47

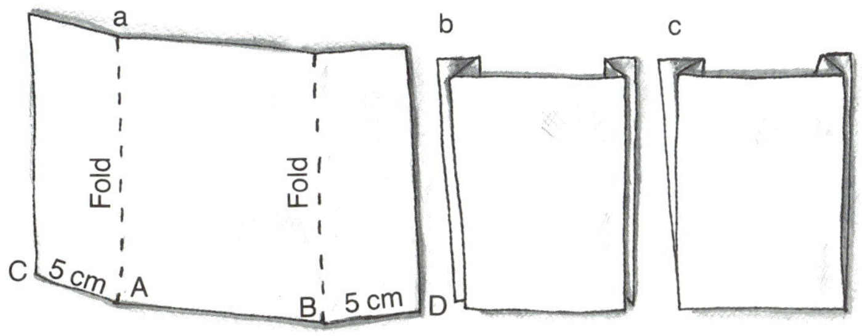

Figure 48

Trace the appliqué motif onto the shiny side of the iron-on interlining and appliqué it onto pocket no. 4 (fig. 47), using the machine appliqué method (p. 25). Stitch the ribbon onto pocket no. 1. Hem the top edges of the six pockets (a seam allowance of 1 cm has been included in the measurements). Fold back the remaining seam allowances of pockets 1, 3 and 4 and tack into position on the top layer. Make pockets 2, 5 (double pocket) and 6 by folding a flat seam on each side (a double flat seam at no. 5 also in the centre) (fig. 48). Stitch the pockets in the positions indicated. Pocket no. 5 must also be stitched from top to bottom where the two folds meet (fig. 47).

Fold the fabric for the loops lengthwise with right sides together. Stitch the two sides together 6 mm from the edge. Divide into four equal parts and turn right side out. Iron flat and pin into position with raw edges together. Stitch.

Place the completed top and backing fabric with right sides together. Stitch all round, leaving a large enough opening to turn the work right side out. Stitch the opening, using small stitches. Stitch the lace frill all round.

Buffer strip

Techniques: machine appliqué; embroidery; quilting; general

Materials
30 cm x 1.8 m light-coloured fabric (it may be joined)
30 cm x 1.8 m backing fabric
8 cm x 4.5 m (24 cm x 1.5 m) dark printed fabric for the frill
15 cm x 70 cm additional dark printed fabric for cat motifs
15 cm x 60 cm pink fabric for cat motif
two 30 cm x 1.8 m strips of batting
2.5 m; 4.5 m and 1 m satin ribbon
20 cm x 75 cm iron-on interlining
matching machine thread for appliqué
patterns (p. 140)

Trace the cat motifs onto the shiny side of the iron-on interlining. Cut out the pattern pieces and iron them onto the wrong side of the fabric. Space the cats on the light-coloured printed fabric, with one cat in the centre and the other two about 15 cm from the sides. Follow the instructions for the machine appliqué method (p. 25).

Embroider the cat faces and other details with stem and satin stitches. Use the photo as a guide. Make a 5 mm hem on one edge of the frill. Stitch the satin ribbon about 1 cm from the hem onto it. Gather until it measures 2.36 m long, forming small gathers.

Follow the instructions for the method on p. 38 and stitch, but remember that only the two sides and the top have a frill, not the bottom. Place the two layers of batting down, then the backing fabric and top layer with right sides together and the frill folded in between them. Stitch all round, leaving a large enough opening to turn the work right side out. Use small stitches to sew the opening.

Outline quilt all around the cat motifs. Take the inner measurement of the cot, e.g. 60 cm across. Establish the centre of the buffer strip. Sew a row of machine stitches away from the centre point towards each side from top to bottom, so that the buffer strip fits snugly in the cot. Cut 2.5 m ribbon in four equal sections. Mark the centre point of each of the four ribbons, but do not cut through. Sew to the back just alongside the frill so that the buffer strip can be tied to the cot. Sew one to each end of the buffer strip and the other two at the stitching in the corners of the cot. Cut the 1 m ribbon in half and sew each section down into a corner so that the buffer strip can also be tied at the bottom.

Bathroom

Patchwork accessories can brighten up your bathroom. The towelling fabric used here is an excellent choice. By using different coloured fabrics and mixing and matching, you can create an interchangeable colour scheme. With two or three sets of towels the bathroom can look different every week. The cute duck can serve as a doorstop or ornament. Should it accidentally land in the water, it won't matter, since it is fully washable.

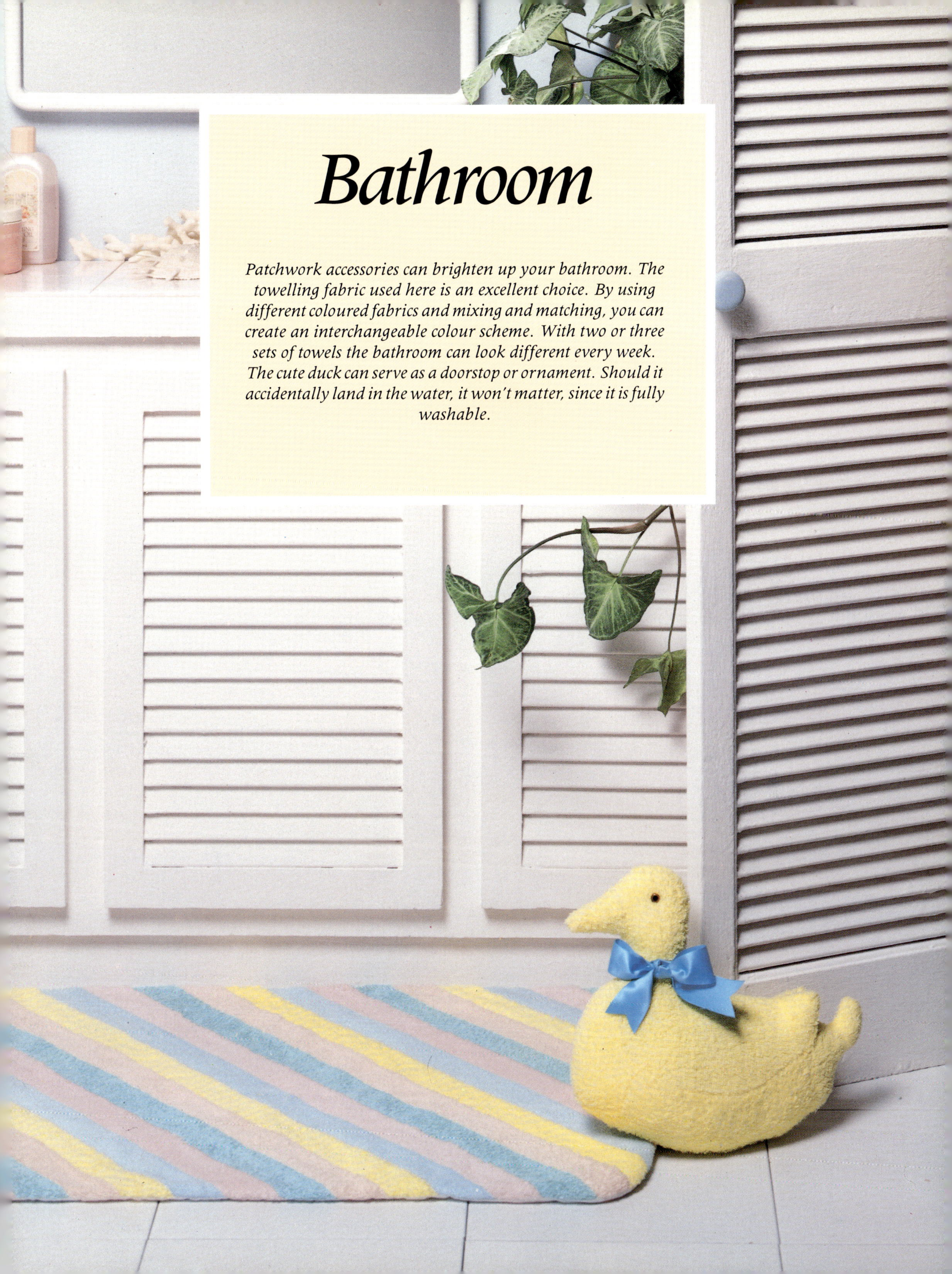

Bathroom set

Techniques: fold-over patchwork method; general

Materials (for the whole bathroom set)
1 m x 1.5 m backing fabric
four 50 cm x 1.5 m strips of towelling fabric in different colours
1 m x 1.5 m background fabric
1 m x 1.5 m batting
70 cm elastic
matching thread

Cut the towelling fabric in 5.2 cm wide strips. Stitch the strips onto the background fabric, using the fold-over method (fig. 49). Place the first strip in position and stitch. Place the next strip over the first, right sides together. Stitch and fold the strip back. Repeat with all strips. It is easier to stitch the central strip first and work towards the corners. There will be less chance of making errors. Cover the whole piece of background fabric with strips.

Enlarge the patterns on paper and cut out. Make a pattern for the toilet lid cover by tracing its shape onto paper. Cut a rectangle of 65 cm x 13 cm for the side panel of the toilet roll holder. Arrange neatly on the fabric. Cut out. Cut a 90 cm x 50 cm rectangle for the bath mat. Trim the corners to form curves.

Floor mat (toilet)

(Pattern on p. 142)

Cut the backing fabric and batting exactly the same size as the top layer. Place the top layer and backing fabric with right sides together over the batting. Stitch all round, leaving an opening of about 20 cm. Trim the seam allowances and clip at the curves. Turn right side out. Stitch the opening, using small stitches. Sew a row of stitches 1 cm from the edge all round.

Bath mat

(Size: 90 cm x 50 cm)

Cut the backing fabric and batting exactly the same size as the top layer. Place the top layer and backing fabric with right sides together over the batting. Stitch all round, leaving an opening of about 20 cm. Trim the seam allowances and clip at the curves. Turn right side out. Stitch the opening using small stitches. Stitch about 1 cm from the edge all round.

Toilet lid cover

Trace the outer edge of the toilet lid onto a piece of paper. Mark one side of the hinge point A and the other side point B. Add a seam allowance of 5 cm along the curve from point A to B. Cut the backing fabric and top layer according to the pattern. (It is not necessary to add batting.) Place the top layer and backing fabric with right sides together. Stitch all round from point A to point B. Leave an opening at the lower end. Turn right side out. Sew a row of stitches around the cover from point A to point B, about 1 cm from the side. Thread the elastic through. Stitch the elastic at the beginning and end. Stitch the opening.

Toilet roll holder (for 2 rolls)

(Pattern on p. 141)

Cut backing fabric and batting for each panel of the top layer. Place the long rectangle of batting down first, then the backing fabric and top layer with right sides together. Stitch

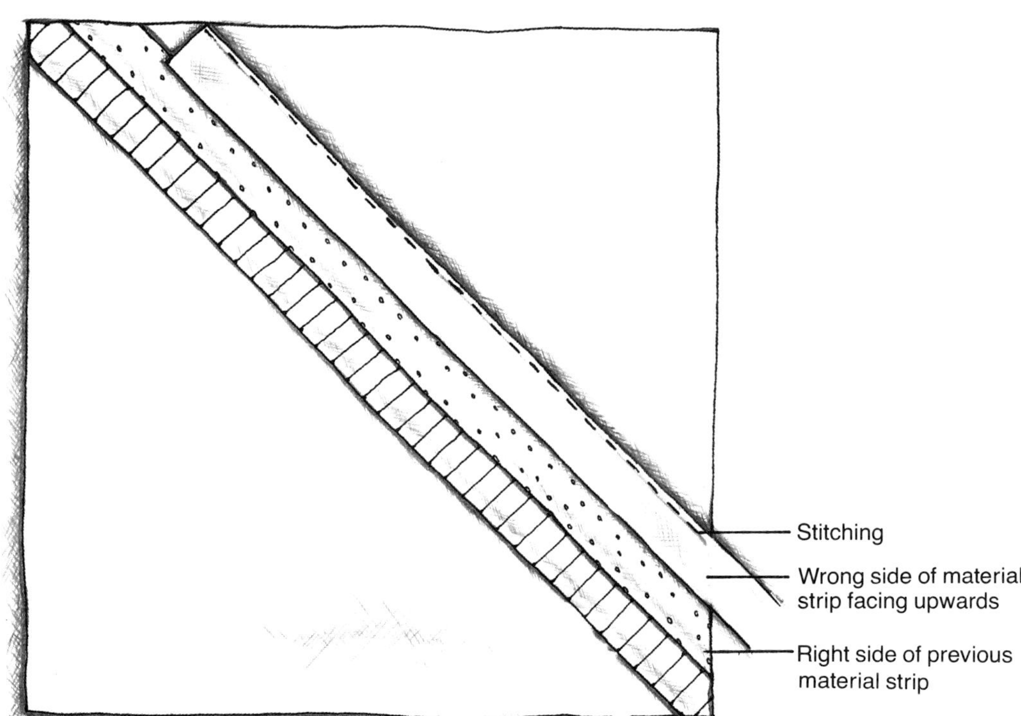

Figure 49

along the two short sides and one long side. Turn right side out.

Place the batting between the backing fabric and top layer of the base. Stitch all round. Pin the raw edges of the long strip onto the raw edge of the base, right sides together, and stitch all round. Trim the excess seam allowance and machine zigzag neatly. Sew the sides where they meet at the back with small oversewing stitches.

To make the lid, stitch the top layer and backing fabric, right sides together, over the batting. Leave a small opening and turn right sides out. Stitch the opening, using small stitches. Sew a row of stitches about 1 cm from the edge right round.

Attach the lid at the back of the holder with about 8 cm of small stitches. Make a small loop of ribbon and sew to the front of the lid in the centre. Sew a button on the holder. The holder can also be made without the loop and button.

Duck

Techniques: general

Materials
25 cm x 1 m fabric
2 eyes
polyester filling
matching thread
pattern (p. 142)

Since the duck is stuffed firmly and the seams are under tension it is a good idea to make a few back stitches at the beginning and end of each seam to reinforce them. Use good quality fabric that will not fray.

Enlarge the pattern and all the parts from the fabric.

Stitch darts at the tail and side panels. Stitch one panel of the breast to the side panel. Stitch the side to the tail at seam B and stop on dot 1.

Attach wing to the breast, side and tail. Pin the sections with right sides together and match with dot 2. Stretch or take in the fabric slightly to fit exactly round the wing. When neatly pinned, the seams can be stitched. Attach the bottom section to the side.

Attach the head section at the neck to the breast and wing. Repeat with the other half of the duck.

Place the right sides of the two halves of the duck together. Stitch from the beak opening, leaving an opening of about 12 cm at the bottom, and then stitch the breast section.

Stitch the two beak sections closed with right sides together, leaving an opening for the beak. Clip the seam allowance at the curves. Stitch the beak as you would when attaching a sleeve: Place the beak in the opening at the head, with right sides of the beak and head together on the inside. Pin neatly. Tack the beak in position, then stitch carefully, a few stitches at a time, ensuring the fabric does not pucker.

Turn the work right side out. Stuff the duck firmly with small pieces of polyester filling, making sure the beak and tail are stuffed firmly.

Put half a brick in the duck if it is going to serve as a doorstop, and stitch the opening. Sew an eye to both sides of the head. First sew on one eye, push the needle through to where the other eye should be, and pull the thread tight. Sew on the second eye. Push the needle back to the first eye. Wrap the thread round the eye three times and make a knot in it by pushing the needle through the last loop and pulling tight. Cut the thread.

OOKING CLASS 3

Barbecue area

One of the easiest ways to entertain friends and family is with a barbecue. These items will help to create a cheerful barbecue area. And any barbecue enthusiast would be delighted to receive the apron or utility bag as a gift.

Pot holder

Techniques: machine appliqué; general

Materials
1.2 m x 20 cm fabric
40 cm x 20 cm thick batting
assorted remnants
2.25 m bias binding
iron-on interlining
matching machine thread
12 cm ribbon
pattern (p. 141)

Cut two long strips of fabric 80 cm x 20 cm, two 20 cm x 20 cm pieces of fabric, and two 20 cm x 20 cm pieces of batting.

Place the two long fabric strips over each other with right sides out. Place a piece of batting at each end of the strip between the two layers of fabric. Tack or machine stitch the batting all round the edge.

Take the two fabric squares and sew a narrow hem along one side. Trace the pattern onto the shiny side of the iron-on interlining. Follow the instructions for the machine appliqué method (p. 25) on one of the squares. Place over the long strip with right sides out. The hemmed edges should face each other. (The ends of the strip can also be cut to form a curve.)

Make a small loop of ribbon and pin in the centre of the strip at the edge. Stitch the bias binding round the long strip through all layers of fabric. Trim the excess seam allowance where necessary. Fold the bias binding over to the back and stitch, using small hemming stitches.

Apron

Techniques: machine appliqué; general

Materials
1 m x 1.15 m fabric
assorted remnants for appliqué motif
iron-on interlining
matching thread
patterns (p. 141)

Enlarge the pattern of the apron and cut from the fabric. Trace the appliqué motif for the pocket onto the shiny side of the iron-on interlining. Cut out and iron onto the wrong side of the remnants. Machine appliqué the motif onto the pocket piece (p. 25).

Fold a 6 mm seam allowance at the neck band and along the length of the bow and stitch. Fold a seam allowance of 1.5 cm over to the wrong side all round the apron. Place the two bands for the bow and the neck band in place and tuck the ends under the seam allowance. Stitch the seam allowance all round the apron. Fold the bands over to the front and stitch all round again, about 6 mm from the edge.

Fold a seam allowance of 1.5 cm round the pocket to the wrong side of the fabric. Stitch the top hem. Tack the pocket in position on the apron. Machine stitch the two sides and the bottom.

Place mat

Techniques. general

Materials (for 1 place mat measuring 44 cm x 33 cm)
46 cm x 35 cm top layer
46 cm x 35 cm backing fabric
46 cm x 35 cm batting
35 cm x 15 cm fabric for the pocket and strip
14 cm bias binding
40 cm ribbon
matching thread

Cut an 18 cm x 12 cm rectangle plus seam allowances from the fabric for the pocket. Fold in half with right sides together and stitch all round, leaving a large enough opening to turn right side out. Stitch a row of fancy stitches along the short side. Place the pocket in the bottom left corner of the top layer rectangle and stitch to the long sides and the bottom, using fancy stitches.

Cut the 7 cm x 14 cm strip. Fold the long sides over so that it is 3 cm wide. Stitch the bias binding lengthwise in the centre. Stitch the fabric strip to the right side by first folding the seam allowances of the short sides over to the inside and stitching with vertical stitches. Divide the strip with two more rows of vertical stitches to make spaces for a knife, fork and spoon. The top layer is complete.

Place the right sides of the top layer and backing fabric together and place over the batting. Stitch all round, leaving an opening, and turn right side out. Stitch the opening, using small stitches. Sew a row of stitches all round, about 1 cm from the edge. Sew a small piece of ribbon to the back along the one side. The cutlery can be placed in the place mat, rolled up and fastened so that each guest's cutlery is neatly in place.

Variation: "Pillowcase" place mat

Use the same materials as for the place mat, plus an additional 46 cm x 35 cm piece of fabric. Follow the instructions for the top layer. Place the right sides of the top layer and backing fabric together and place over the batting. Stitch one short side. Turn right side out, with the batting in the centre.

Cut an additional piece of backing fabric measuring 47 cm x 35 cm. Fold the seam allowance of one short side over to the back and stitch. Place the additional layer of fabric with right sides together over the place mat, with the two short finished sides together. Stitch the remaining three sides. Trim the excess batting and seam allowances and zigzag. Turn right side out. The place mat will be like a pillowcase in which you can insert a piece of hardboard measuring about 43 cm x 32 cm. It can be used as a lap tray.

Barbecue utility bag

Techniques: machine appliqué; general

Materials
1 m x 1.5 m fabric
assorted remnants
1 double wooden coat hanger
iron-on interlining
matching thread
4 cup hooks
pattern (p. 141)

Cut two 50 cm x 70 cm pieces of fabric. Place right sides together. Place the coat hanger on the 50 cm long side of the fabric, and trace the curve of the hanger with a pencil onto the fabric. This forms the stitching line for the utility bag.

Fold the fabric in half lengthwise to establish the centre at the top of the curve. When the bag is stitched, an opening of 1 cm must be left for the hanger's wire to be pushed through.

Cut the following pockets (a seam allowance of 1 cm all round has been included): 8 cm x 10 cm for matches, 25 cm x 30 cm for fire-starters, 32 cm x 25 cm for recipes, etc.

Fold the seam allowances for all the pockets to the wrong side and tack. Stitch the top hem. Fold a flat seam in each side of the pocket for the fire-starters. Trace the appliqué motif to the shiny side of the iron-on interlining. Iron onto the wrong side of the appliqué fabric and cut out. Appliqué it onto the recipe pocket, using the machine appliqué method (p. 25). Using the photo as a guide, lay all the pockets in place and stitch.

Place the two layers of fabric with right sides together. Stitch all round the bag, leaving an opening of about 20 cm. Trim the excess seam allowance if necessary and clip the seam allowances at the curves. Turn right side out. Place the hanger in position. Screw the cup hooks into the hanger. Stitch the opening.

French bread basket

Techniques: general

Materials
1 oblong basket
about 50 cm of fabric
elastic
lace
matching thread

Measure the base of the basket. Cut one piece of fabric the same size as the base plus 1 cm seam allowance all round. Measure the depth of the basket and add about 6 cm more, depending on the depth of the basket. Measure the circumference of the edge of the basket. Cut one piece of fabric as wide as the depth of the basket plus another 6 cm, and one and a half times as long as the circumference of the edge. Tack it at the bottom and stitch to the base panel, with right sides together. Fold a small hem at the top over to the wrong side and stitch. Stitch a lace frill over the hem. Stitch a piece of elastic around the back so that the fabric will fit snugly over the edge of the basket.

Patterns

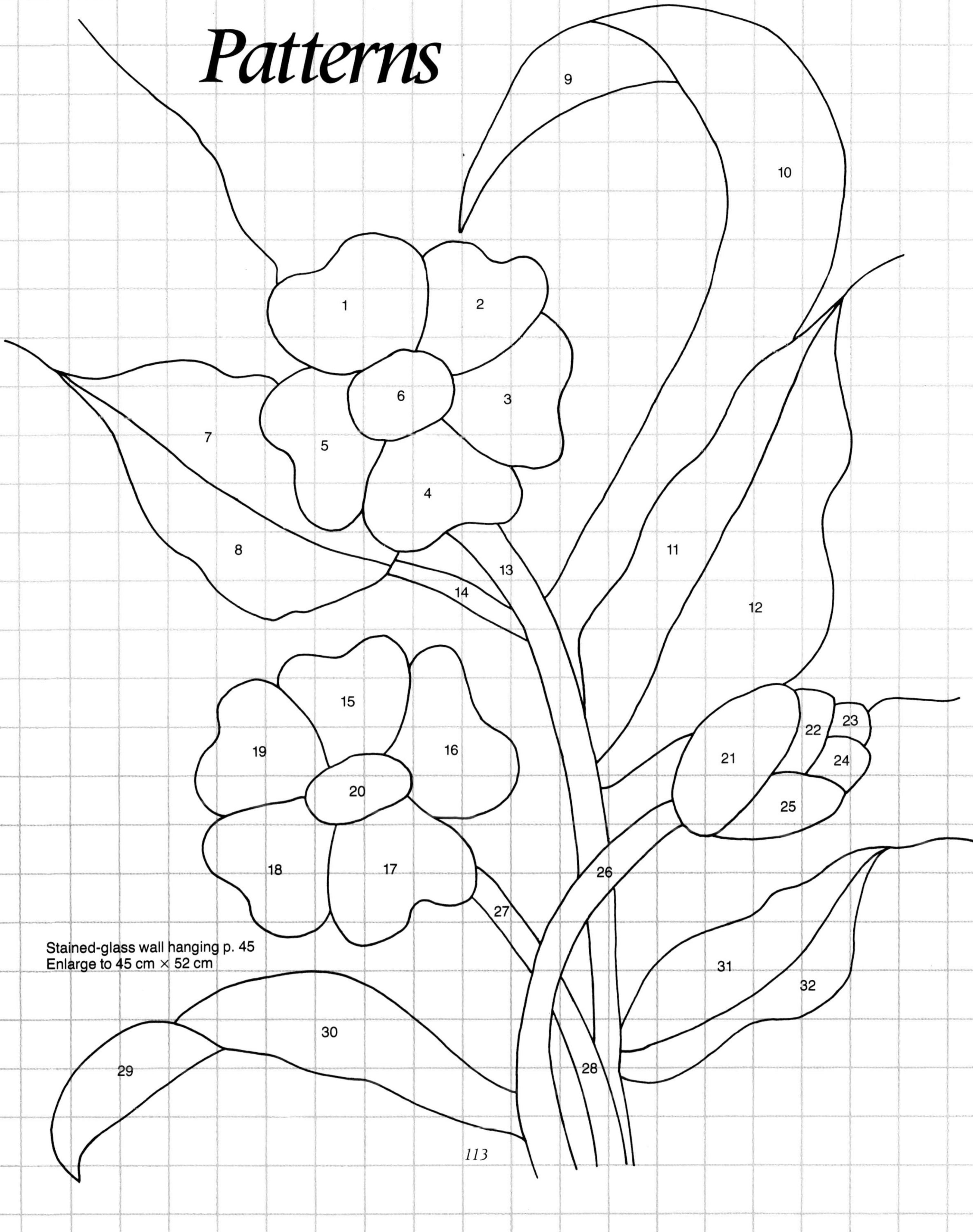

Stained-glass wall hanging p. 45
Enlarge to 45 cm × 52 cm

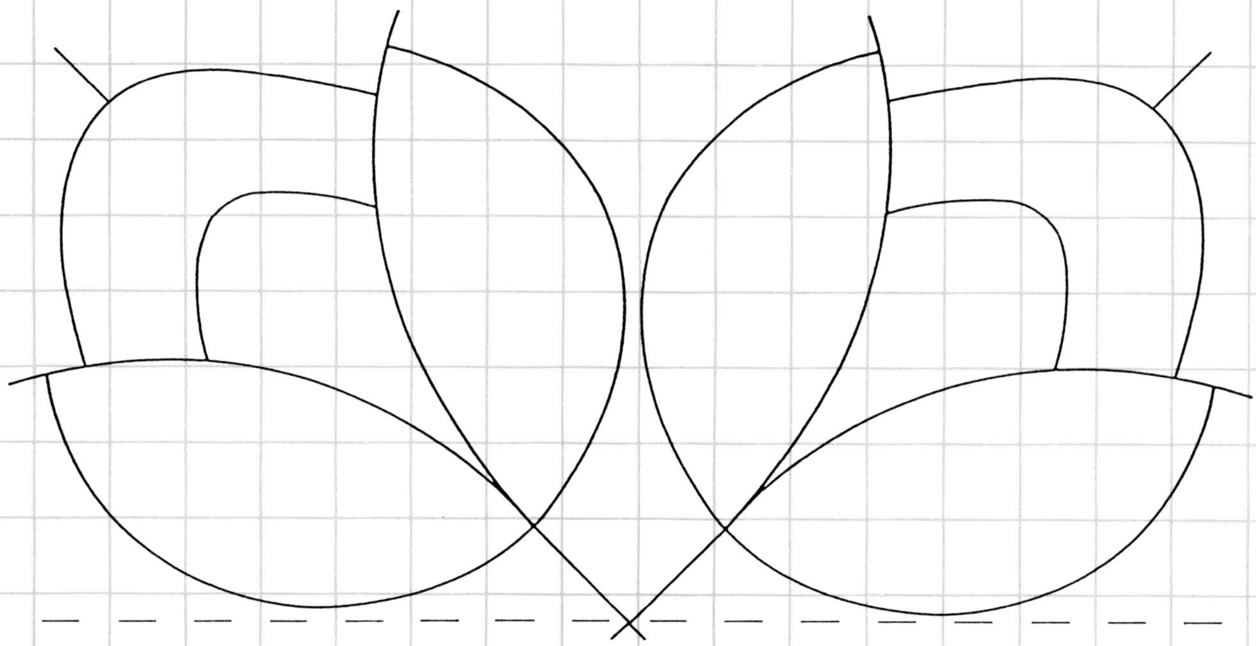

Stained-glass cushion cover p. 45
Complete and enlarge to 35 cm × 35 cm

Repeat (mirror image)

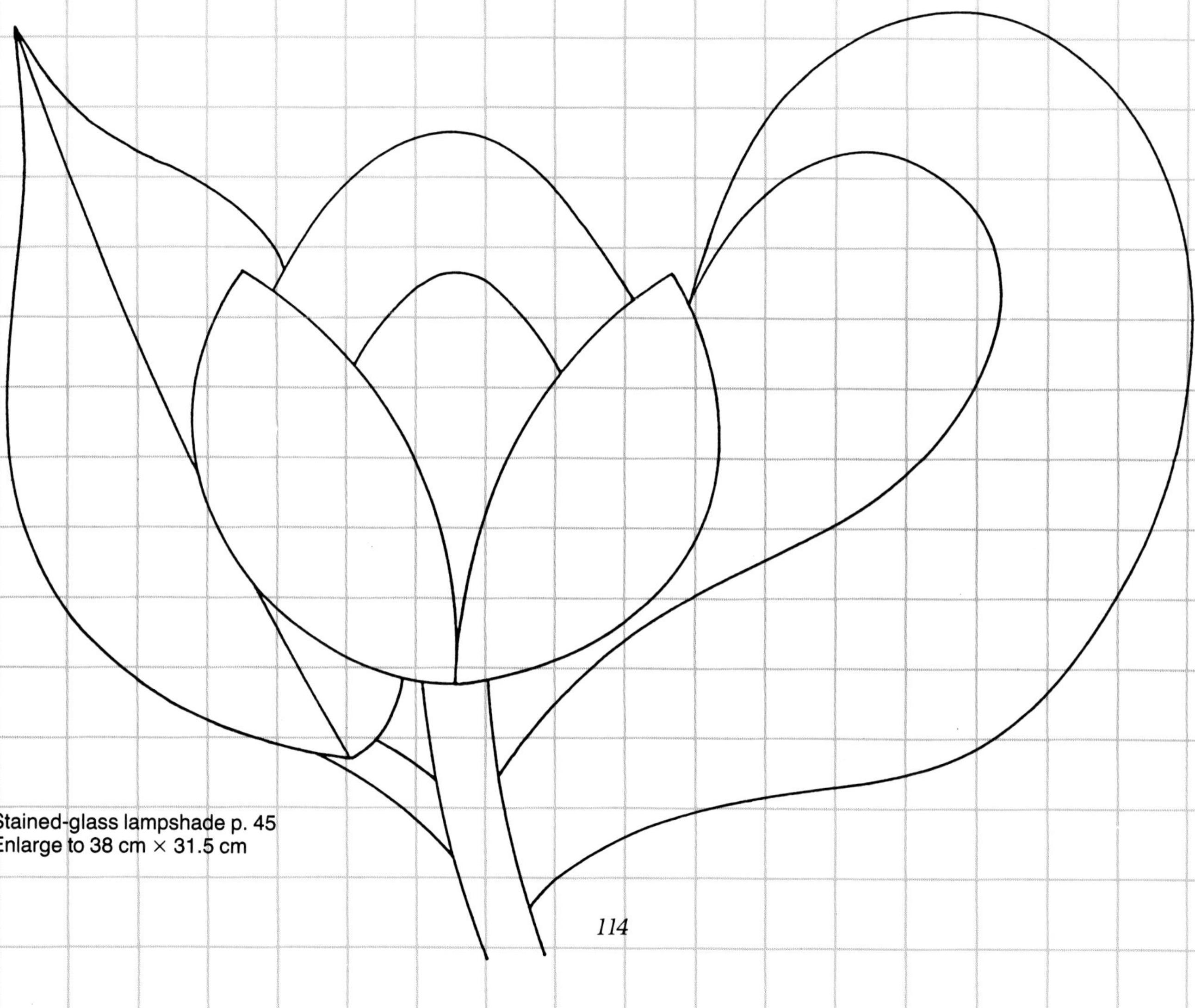

Stained-glass lampshade p. 45
Enlarge to 38 cm × 31.5 cm

Wall hanging p. 96
Enlarge to 40 cm × 60 cm

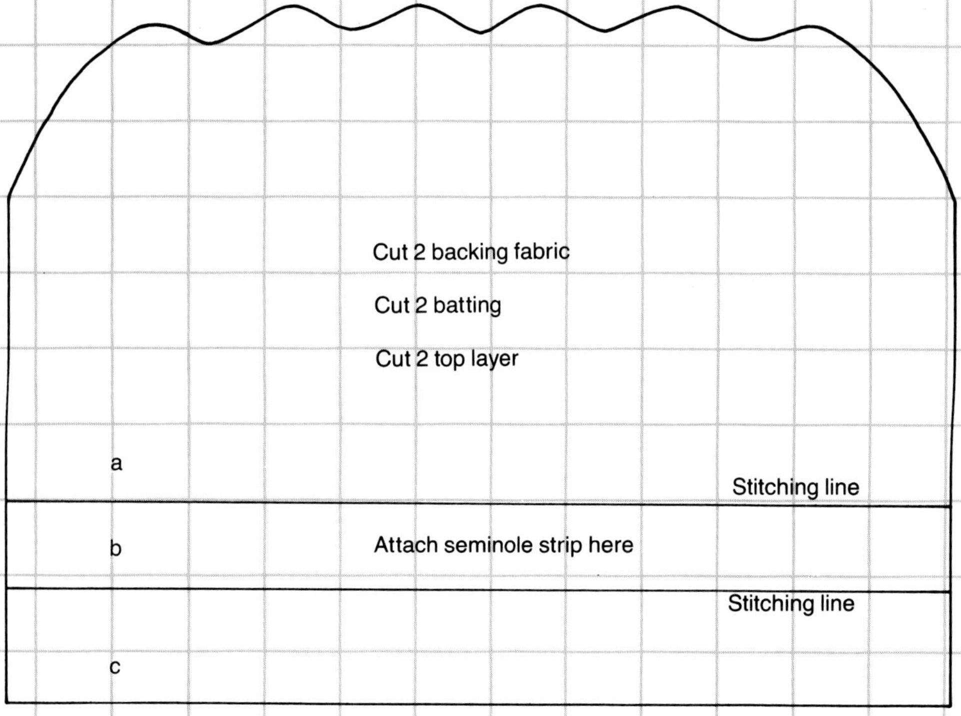

Tea cosy (side panel) p. 52
Enlarge to 30.5 cm × 22.5 cm

Tea cosy (bottom) p. 52
Enlarge to 27 cm × 27 cm

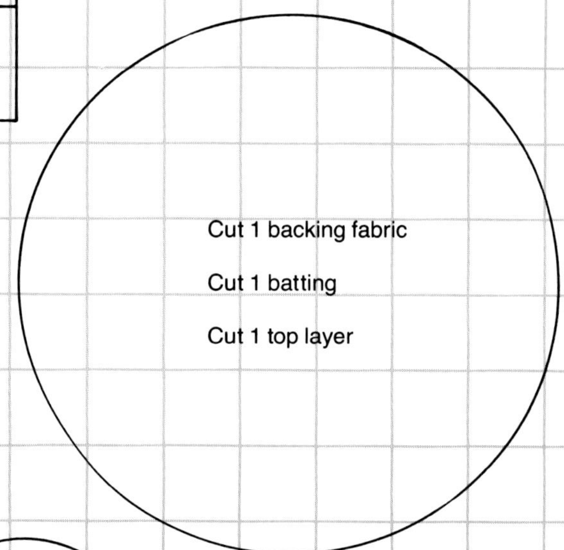

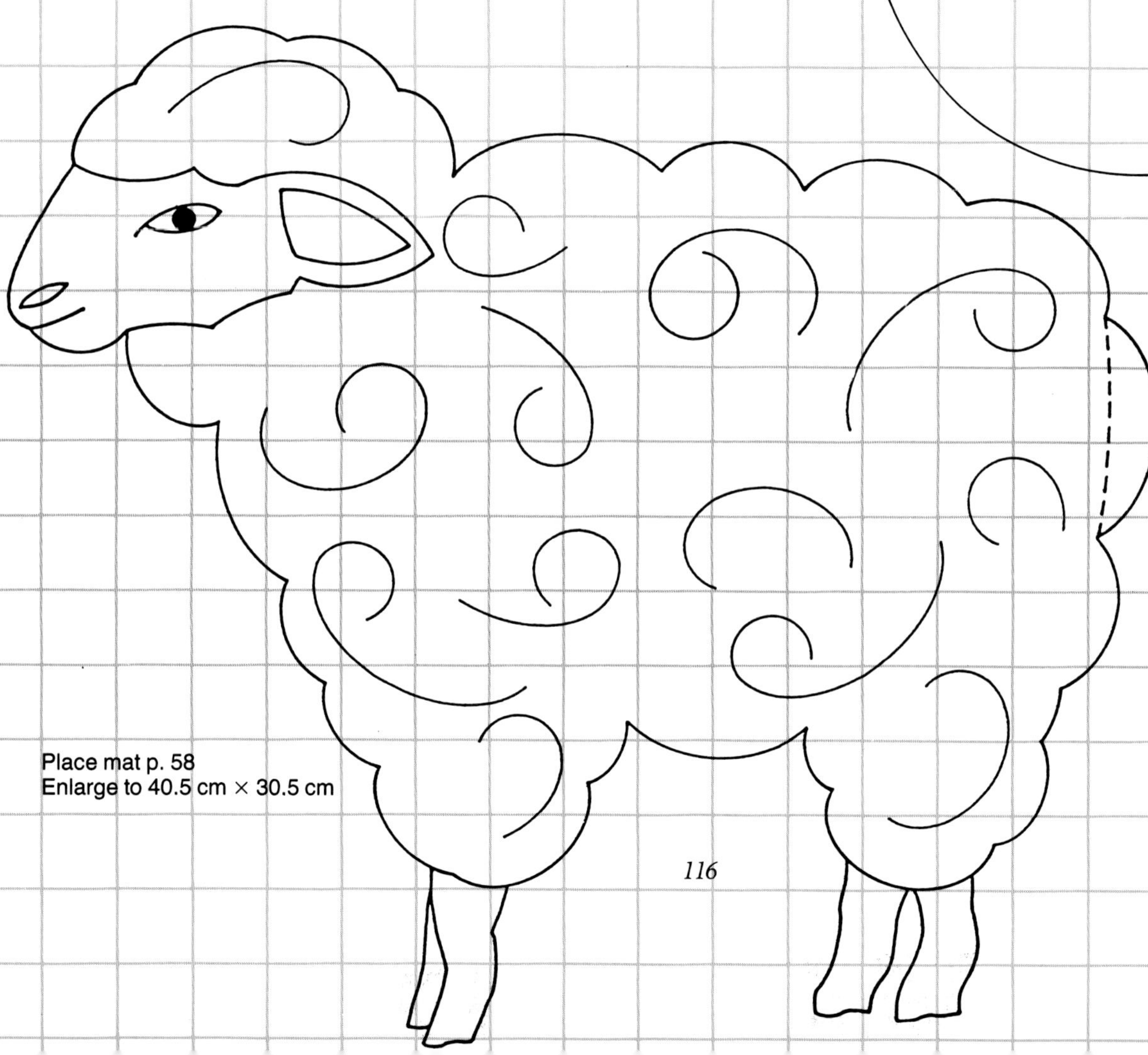

Place mat p. 58
Enlarge to 40.5 cm × 30.5 cm

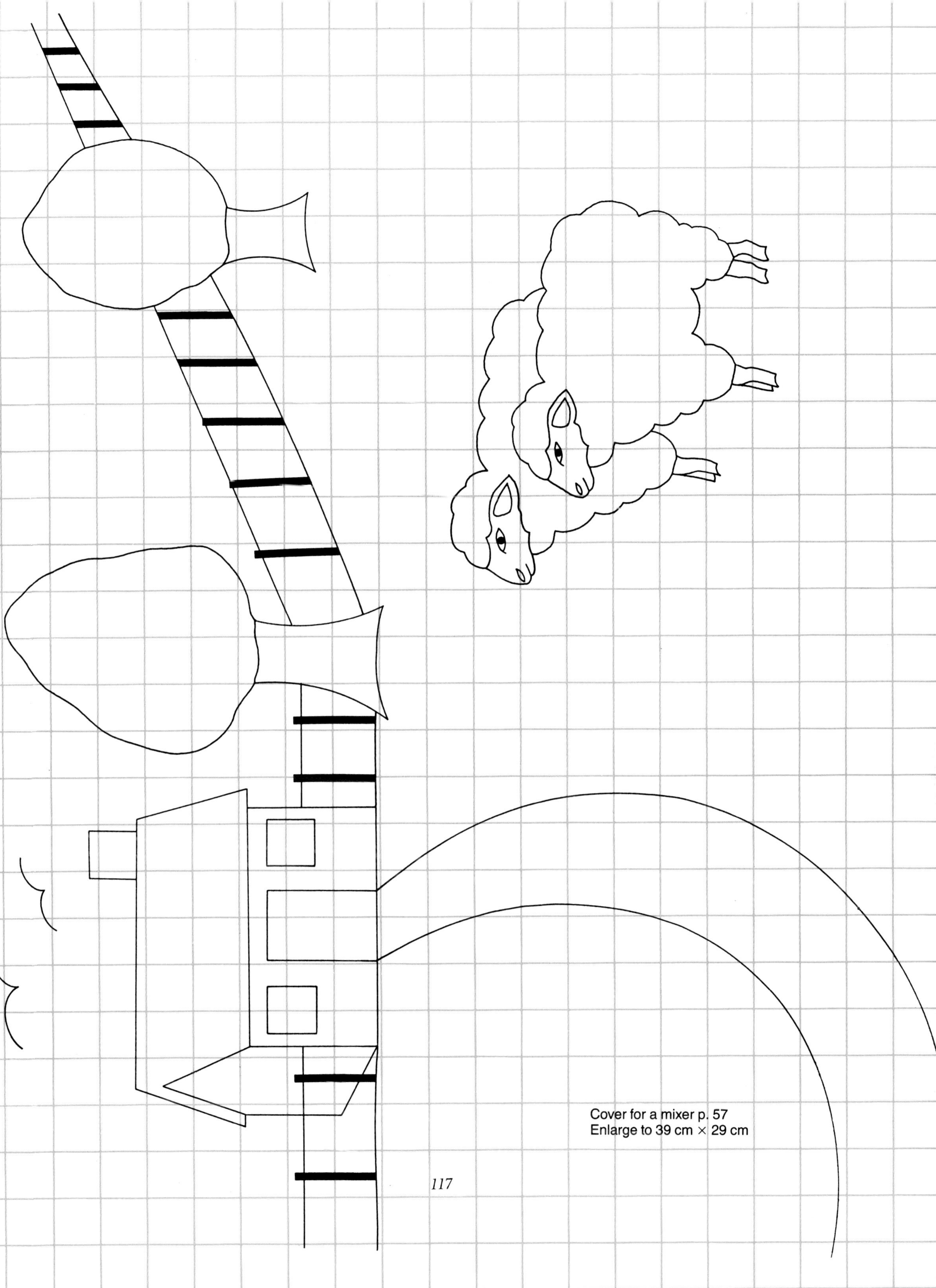

Cover for a mixer p. 57
Enlarge to 39 cm × 29 cm

Clock p. 53
Enlarge to 33.5 cm × 33.5 cm

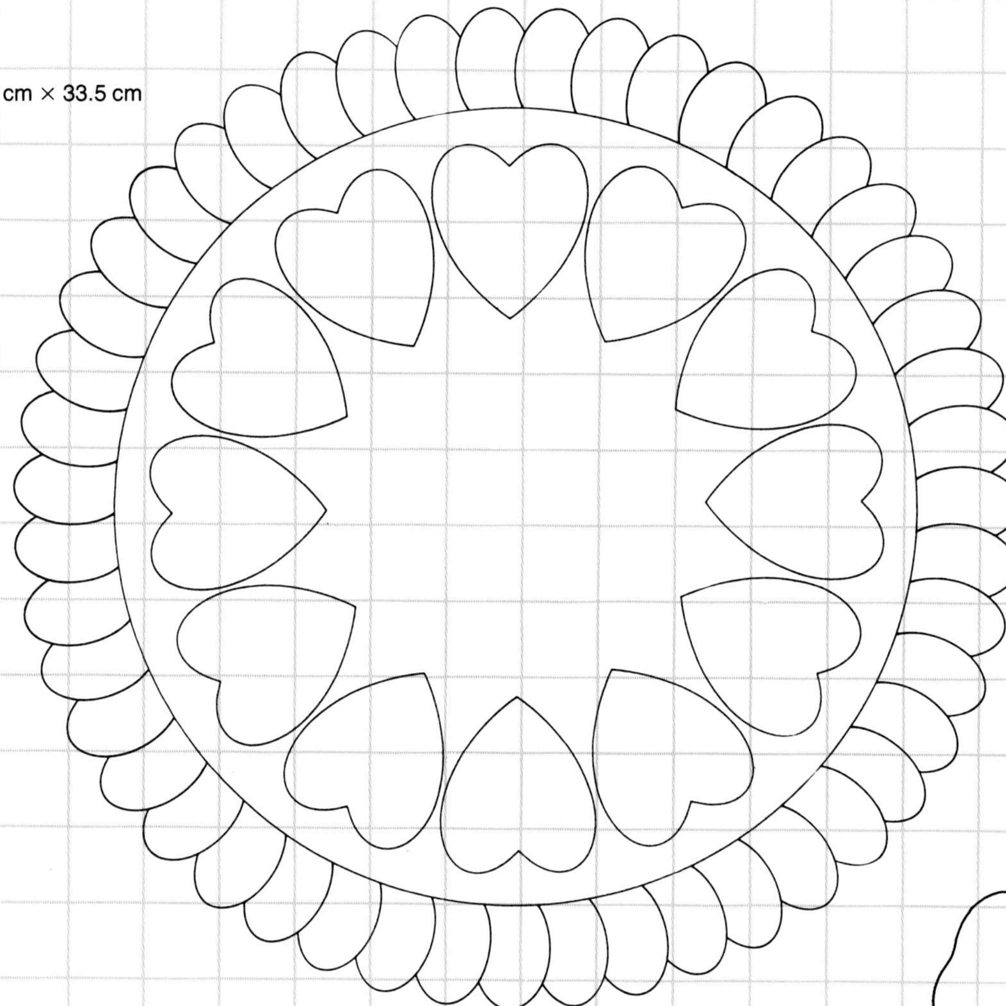

Pot holder p. 58
Enlarge to 14 cm × 11.5 cm

Jam jar cap p. 58
Enlarge to 5.5 cm × 6.5 cm

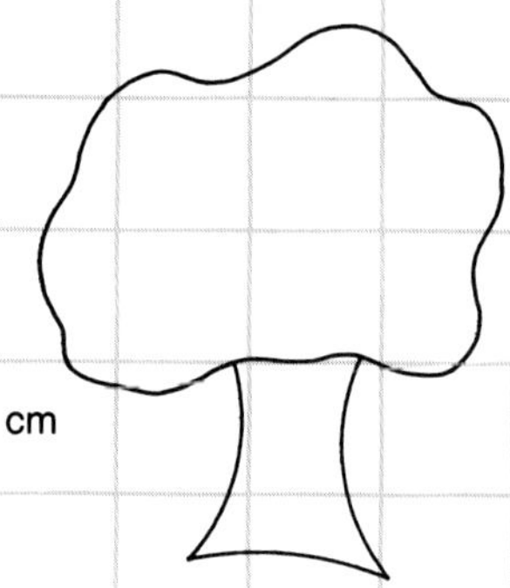

Refrigerator magnet p. 59
Enlarge to 12.5 cm × 8.5 cm

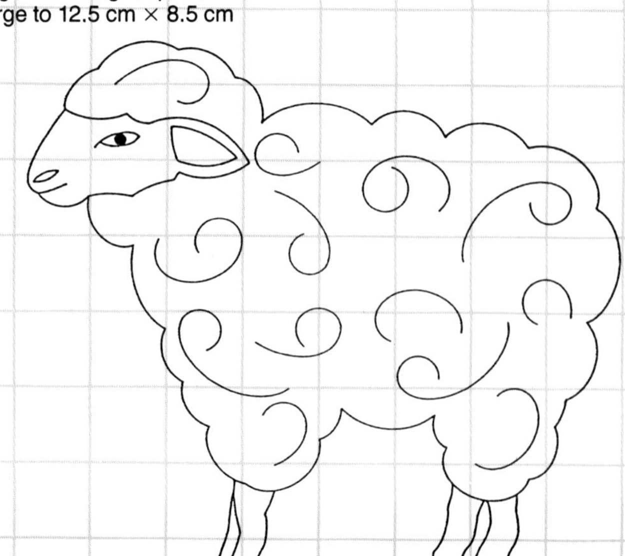

Key holder p. 58
Enlarge to 17.5 cm × 8.5 cm

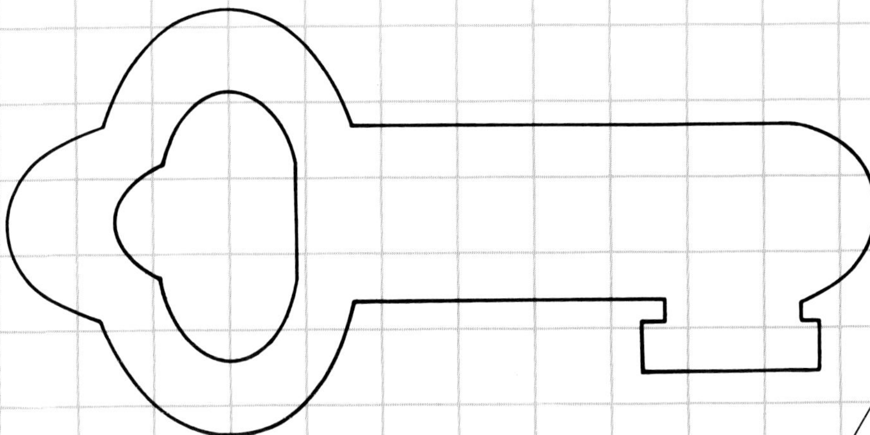

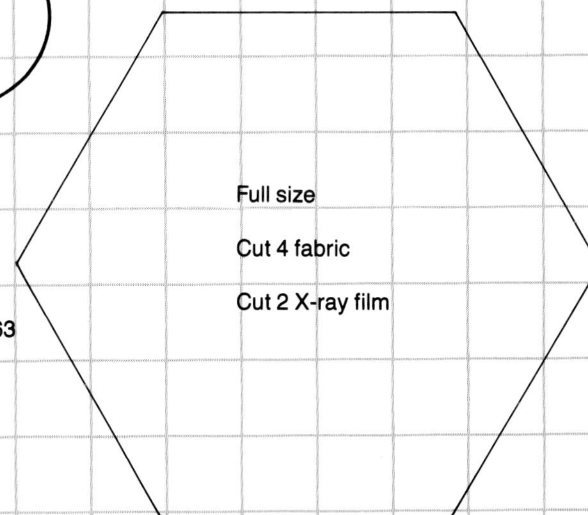

Key ring and meter-money holder p. 63

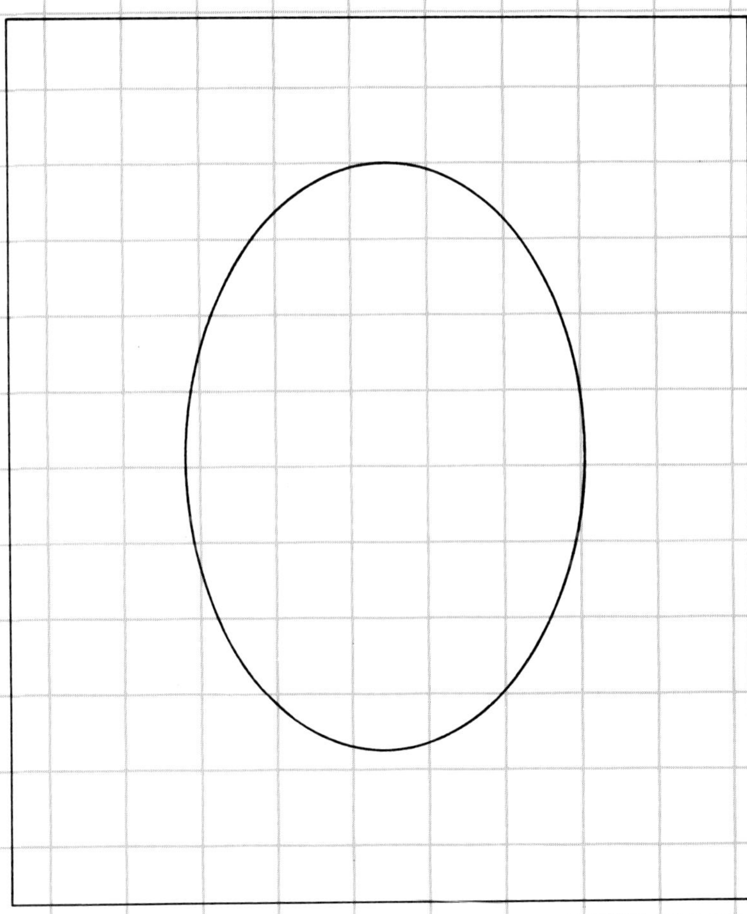

Folding photograph frame p. 65
Enlarge to 15 cm × 18 cm

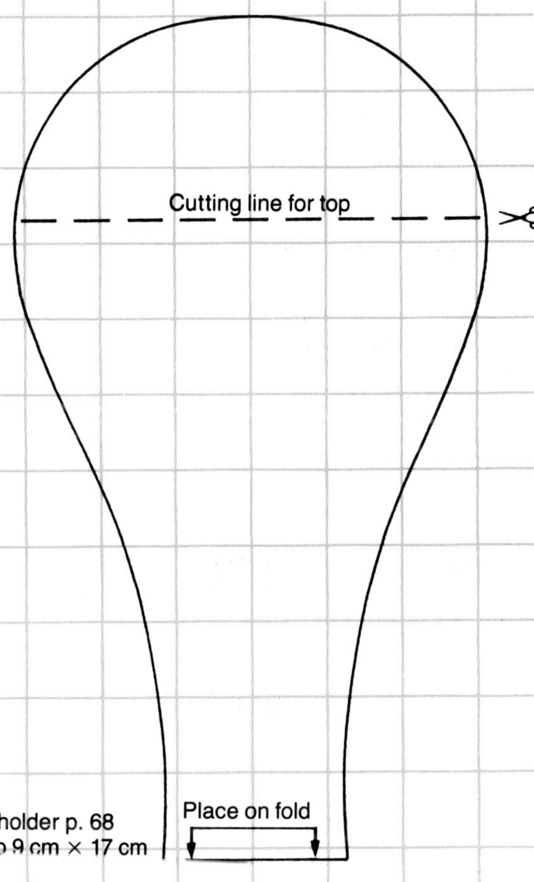

Scissors holder p. 68
Enlarge to 9 cm × 17 cm

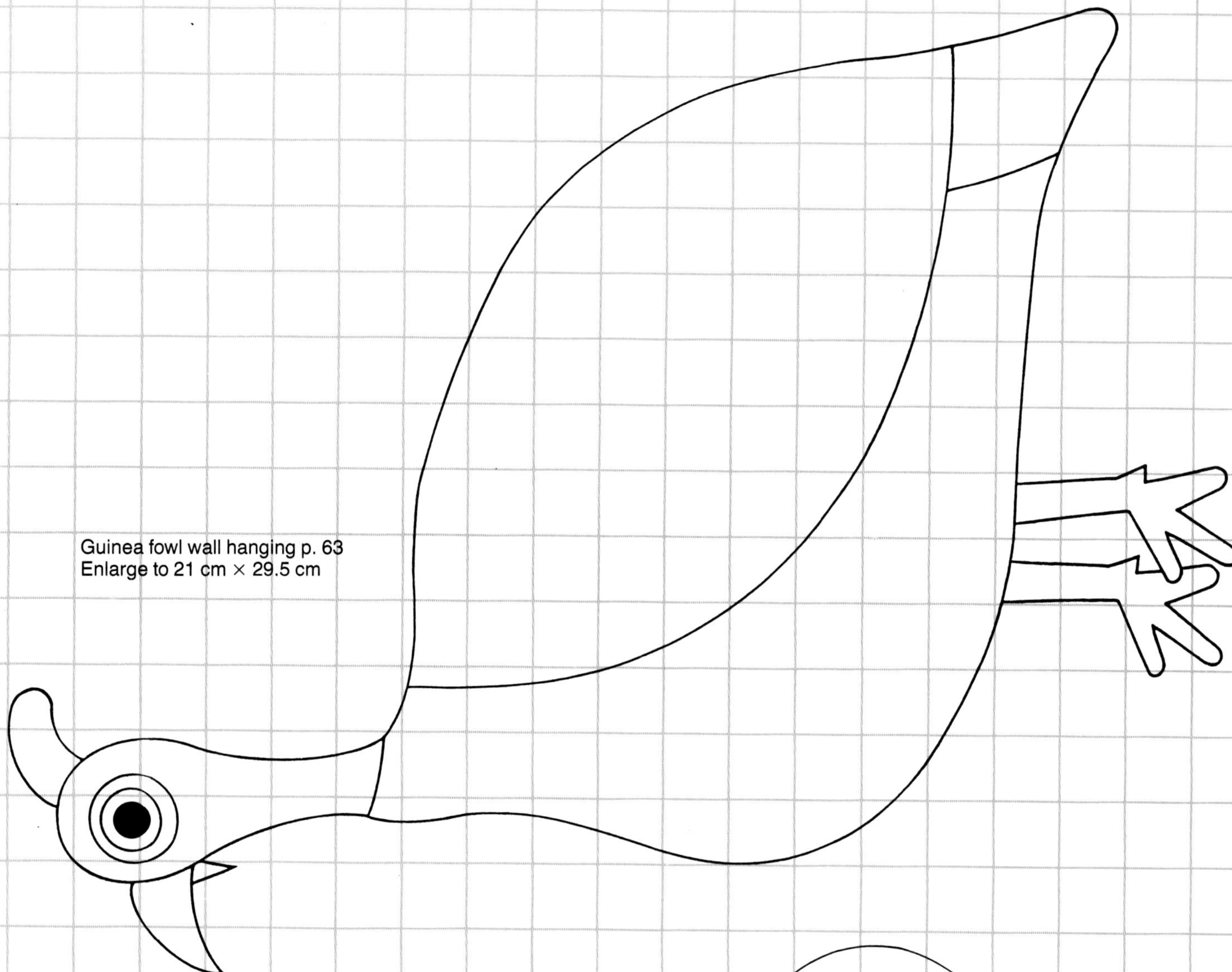

Guinea fowl wall hanging p. 63
Enlarge to 21 cm × 29.5 cm

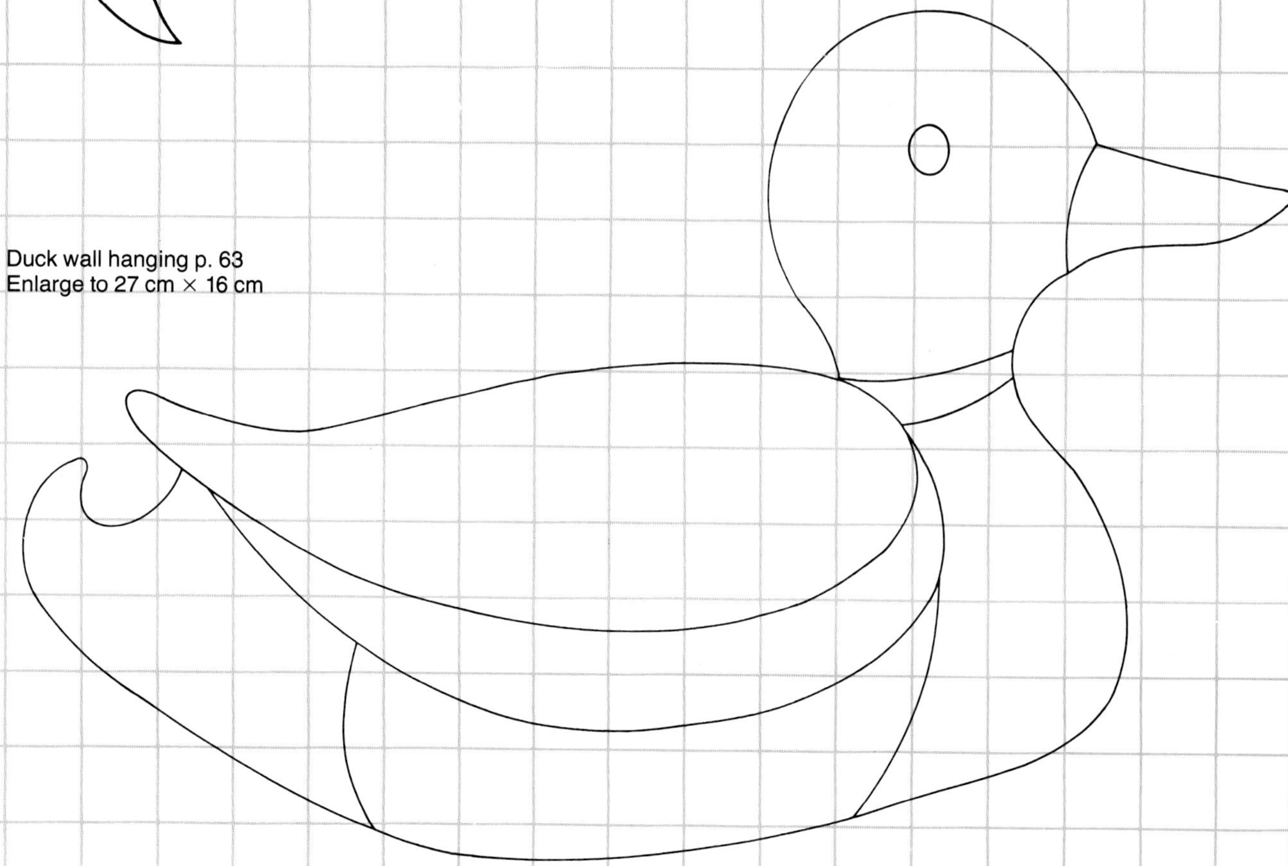

Duck wall hanging p. 63
Enlarge to 27 cm × 16 cm

Note book holder p. 69
Enlarge to 20 cm × 17.5 cm

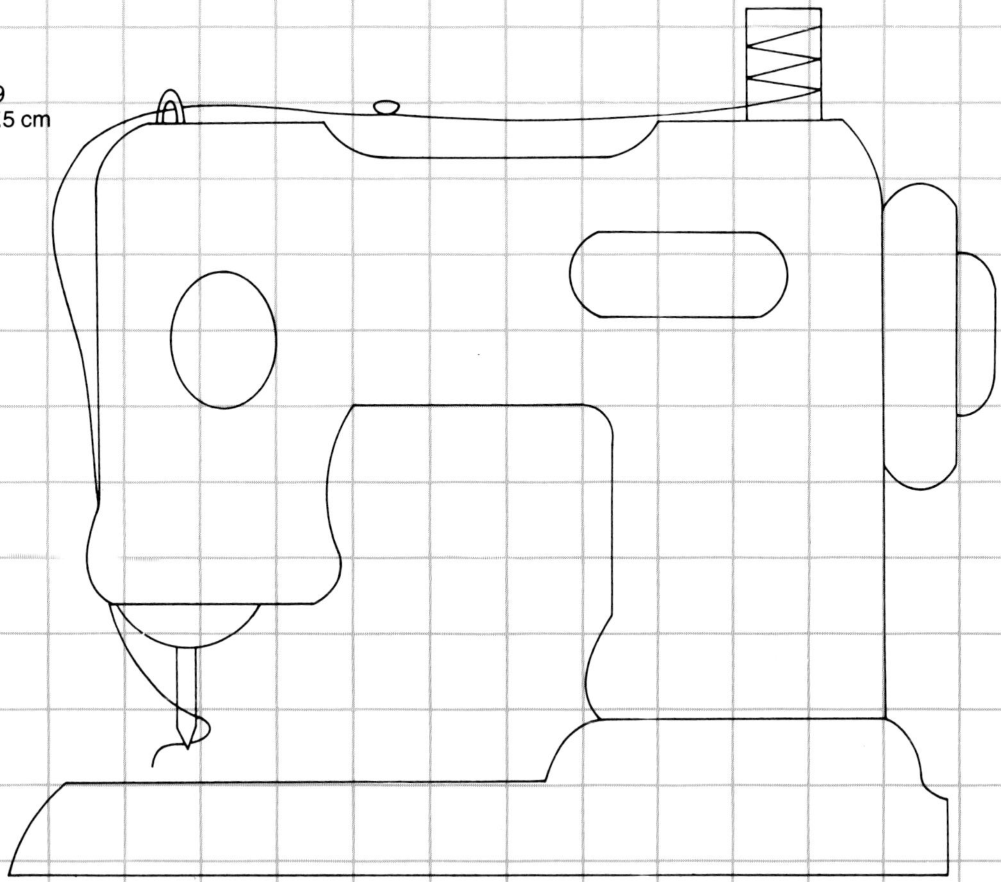

Pin cushion p. 68

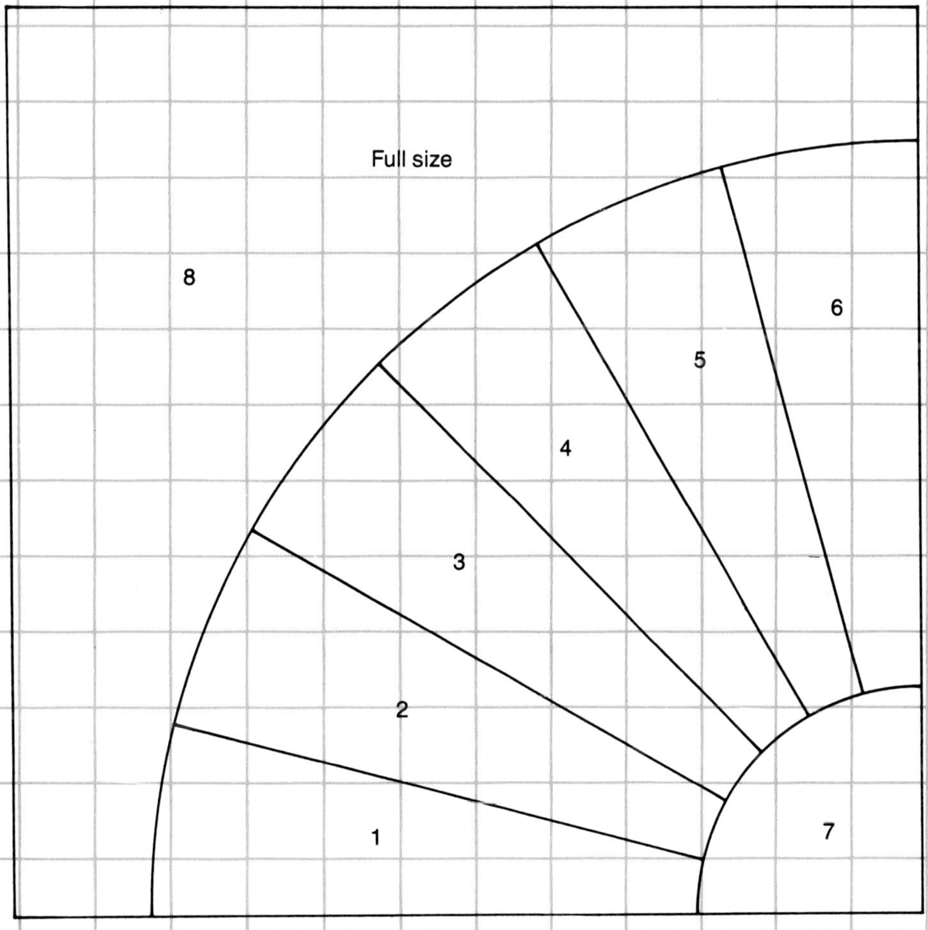

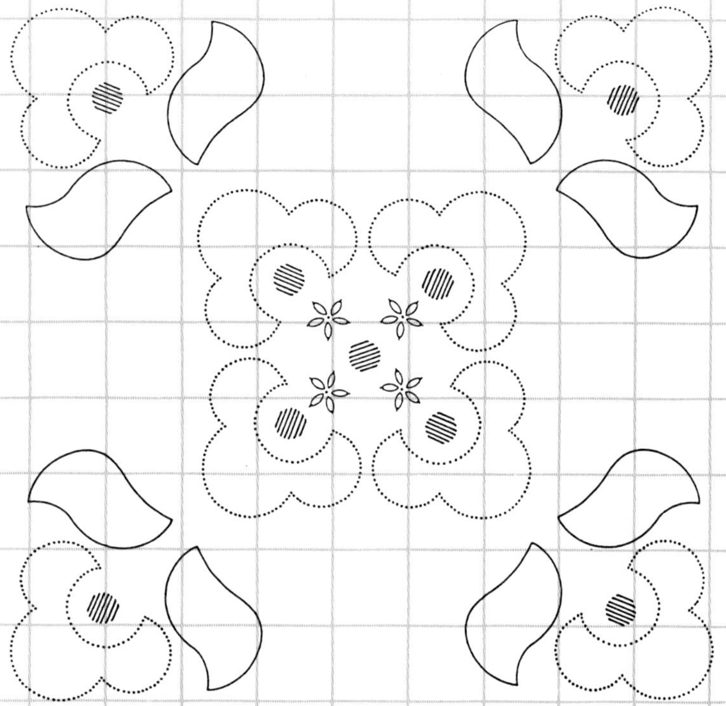

Candlewick quilt p. 72
Enlarge to 22.5 cm × 22.5 cm

Candlewick quilt p. 72
Enlarge to 22 cm × 22 cm

Candlewick quilt p. 72
Enlarge to 28.5 cm × 28.5 cm

Candlewick quilt p. 72
Enlarge to 25 cm × 25 cm

Candlewick quilt p. 72
Enlarge to 24 cm × 24 cm

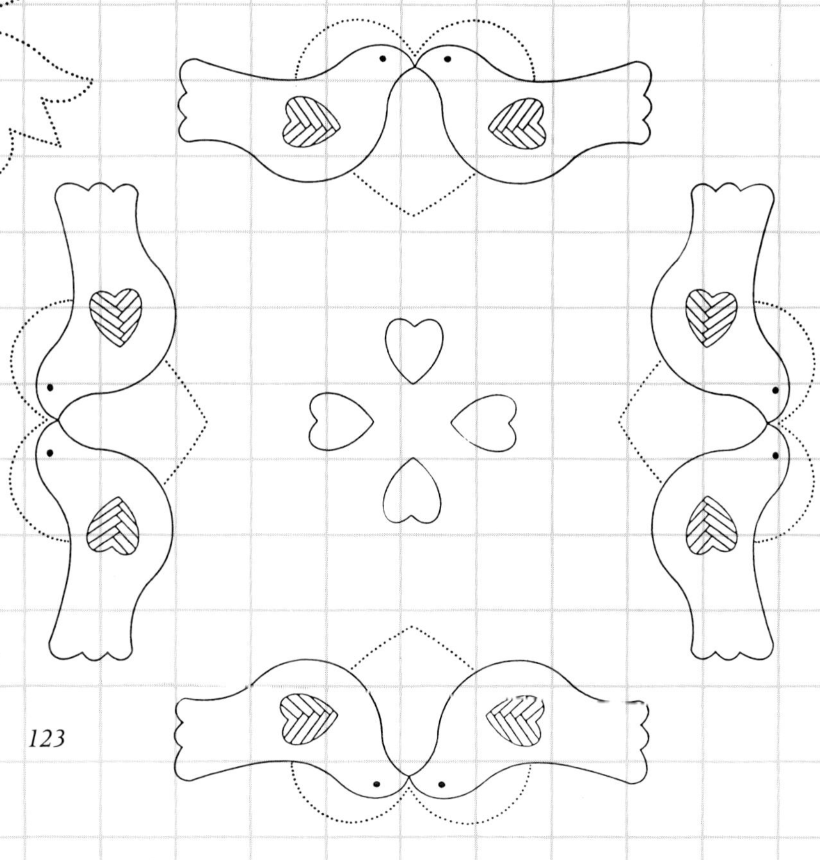

Candlewick quilt p. 72
Enlarge to 27 cm × 27 cm

Candlewick quilt p. 72
Enlarge to 22 cm × 22 cm

Candlewick quilt p. 72
Enlarge to 27.5 cm × 27.5 cm

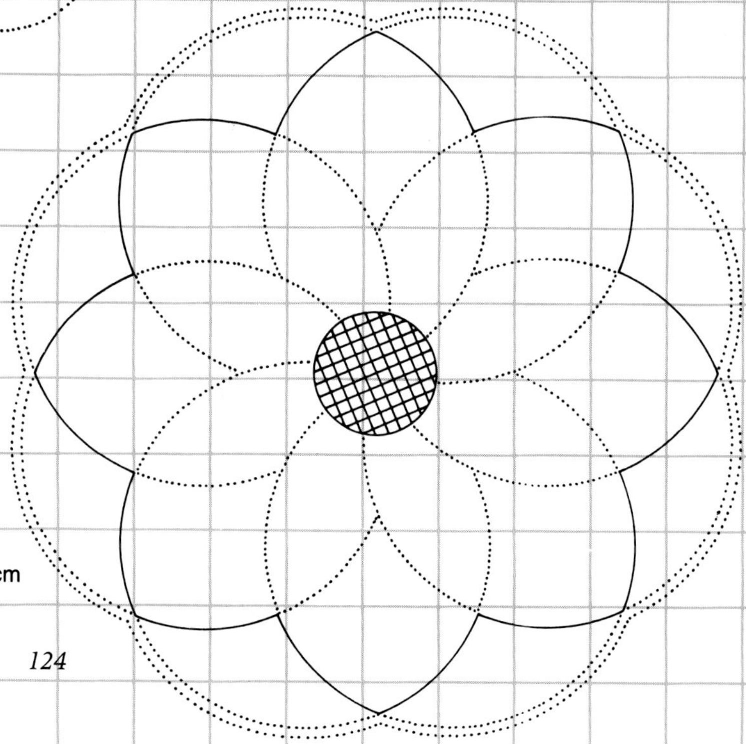

Candlewick quilt p. 72
Enlarge to 24 cm × 24 cm

Candlewick quilt p. 72
Enlarge to 26 cm × 20 cm

Candlewick quilt p. 72
Enlarge to 27 cm × 27 cm

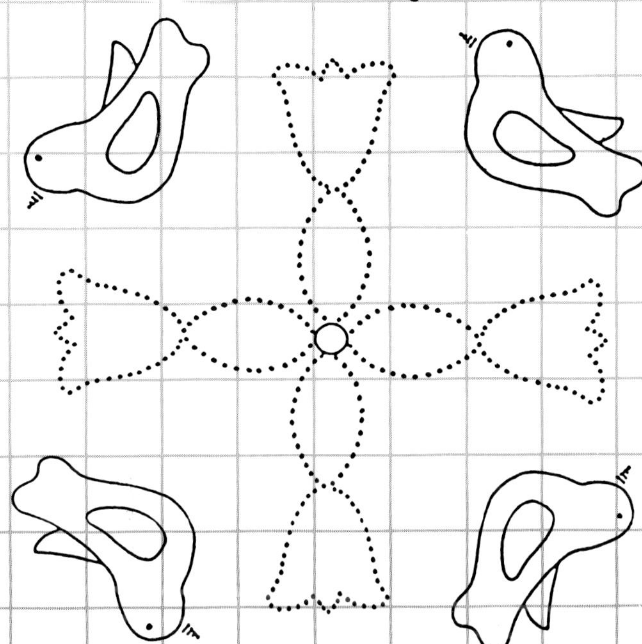

Candlewick quilt p. 72
Enlarge to 25 cm × 25 cm

Candlewick quilt p. 72
(Quilting pattern)
Enlarge to 29.5 cm × 7 cm

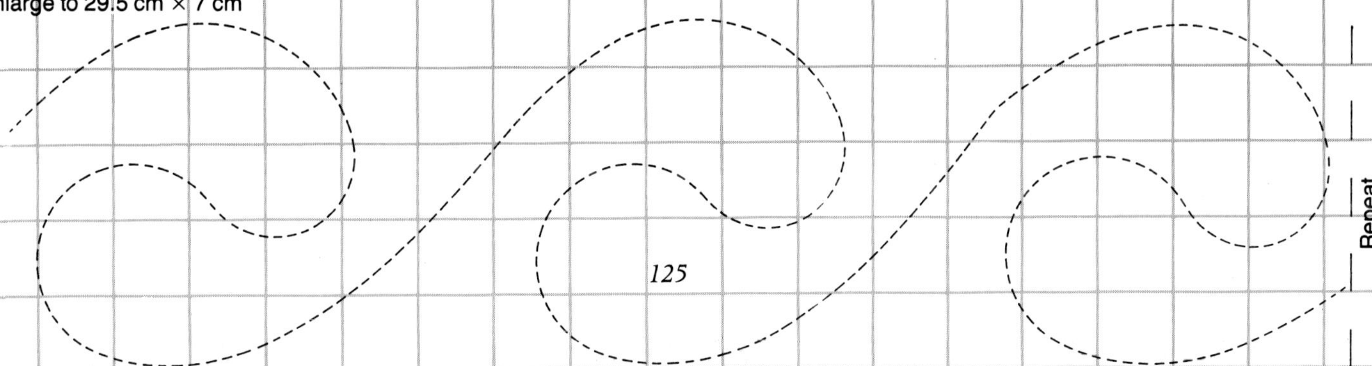

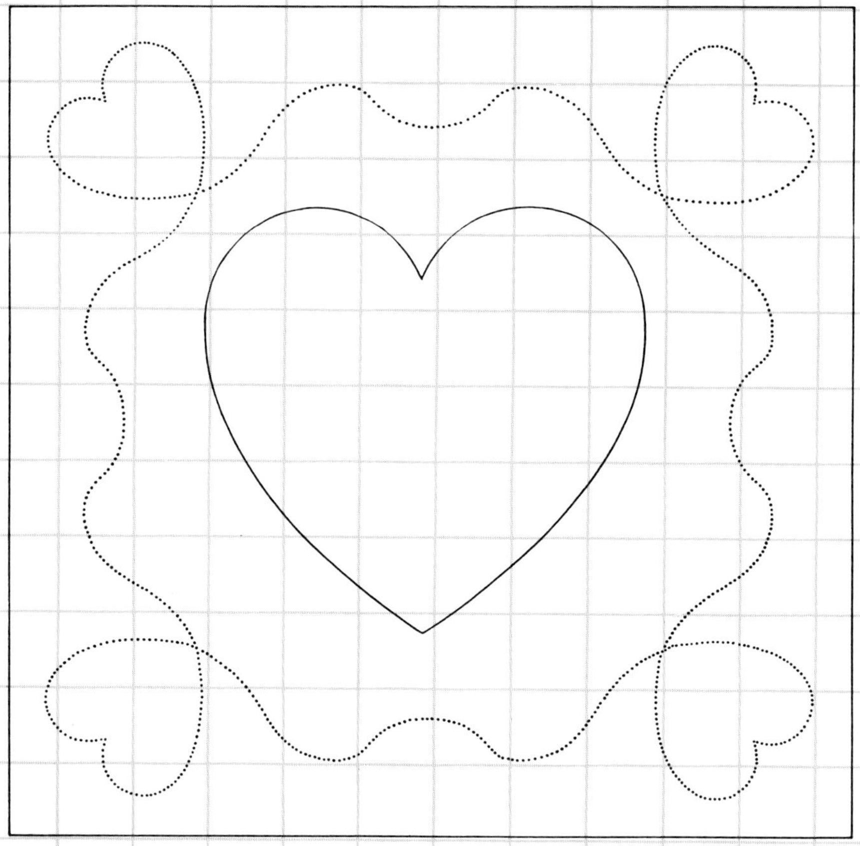

Photograph frame p. 73
Enlarge to 17 cm × 17 cm

Jewellery box (side panel 1) p. 72
Enlarge to 5.3 cm × 9 cm

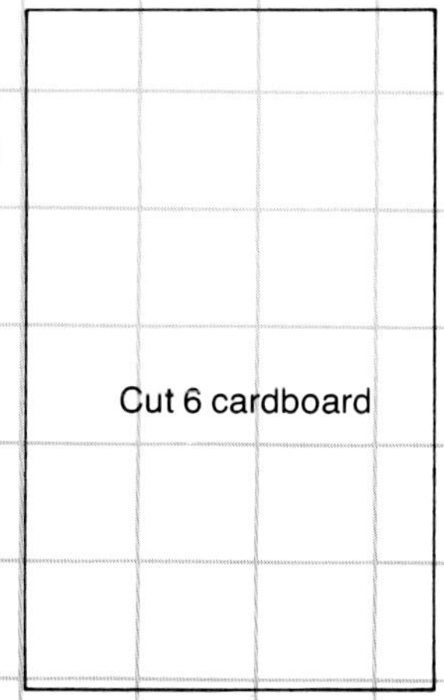

Jewellery box (lid and base) p. 72
Enlarge to 17 cm × 13 cm

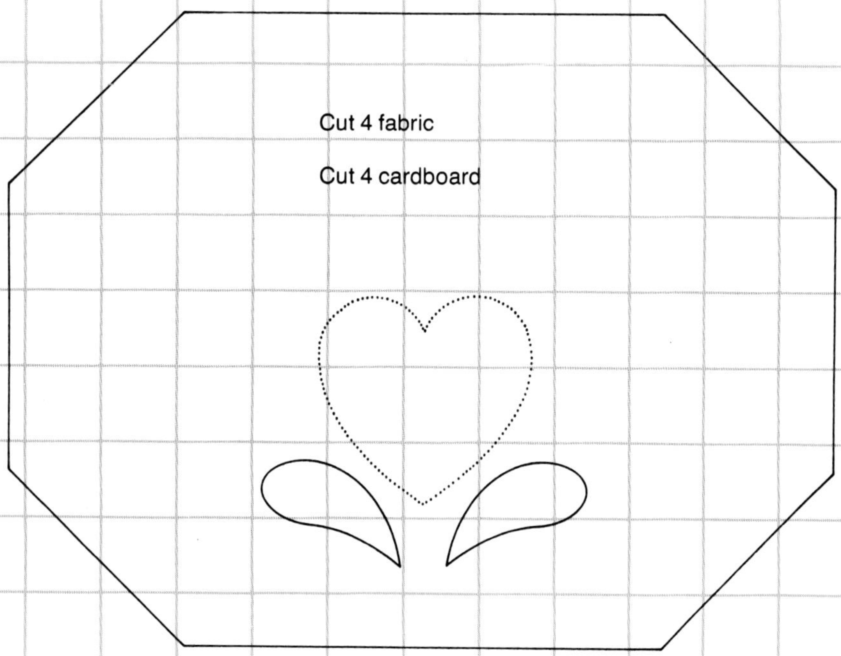

Jewellery box (side panel 2) p. 72
Enlarge to 9.7 cm × 9 cm

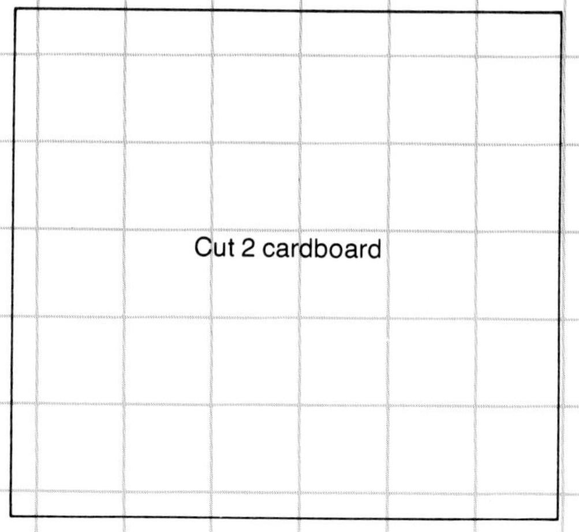

Blue candlewick quilt p. 76
Enlarge to 27.5 cm × 27.5 cm

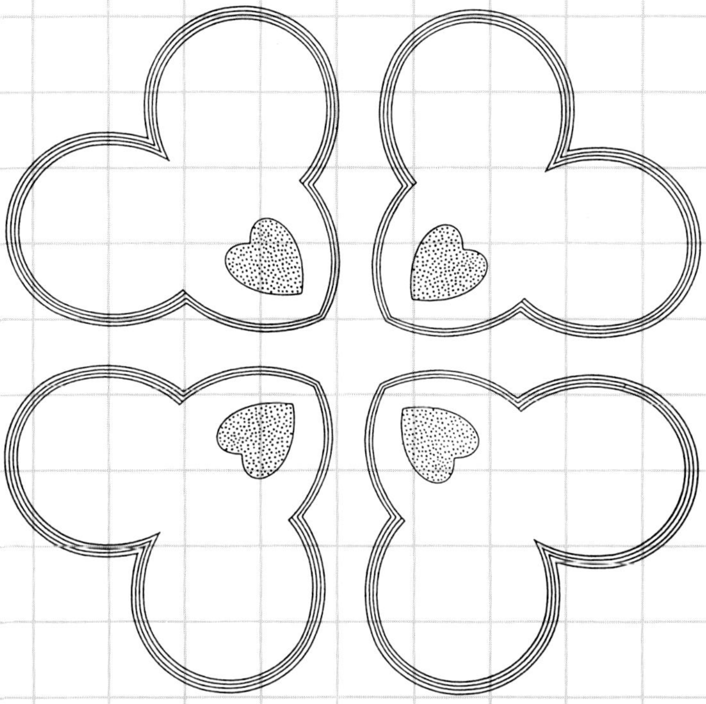

Blue candlewick quilt p. 76
Enlarge to 21 cm × 21 cm

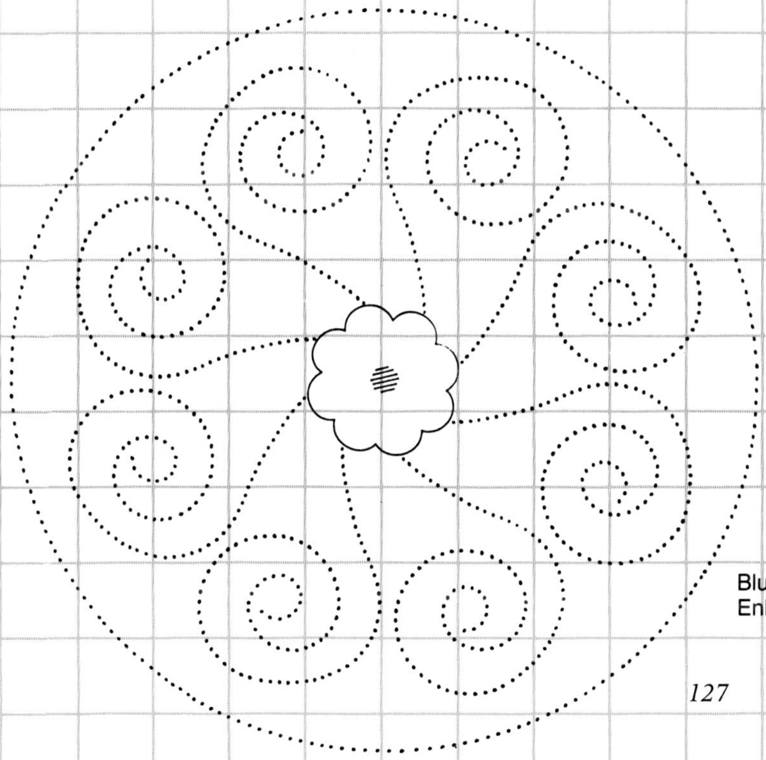

Blue candlewick quilt p. 76
Enlarge to 25 cm × 25 cm

Blue candlewick quilt p. 76
Enlarge to 22 cm × 22 cm

Blue candlewick quilt p. 76
Enlarge to 26 cm × 26 cm

Blue candlewick quilt p. 76
Enlarge to 23 cm × 23 cm

Blue candlewick quilt p. 76
Enlarge to 27 cm × 27 cm

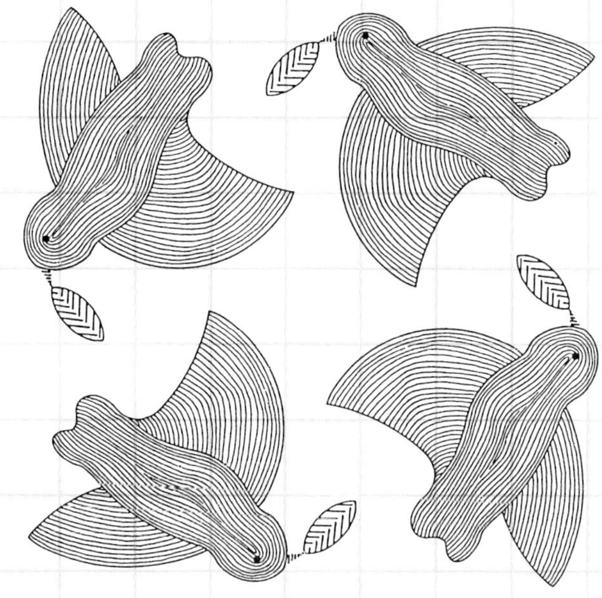

Blue candlewick quilt p. 76
Enlarge to 27 cm × 27 cm

Blue candlewick quilt p. 76
Enlarge to 24 cm × 24 cm

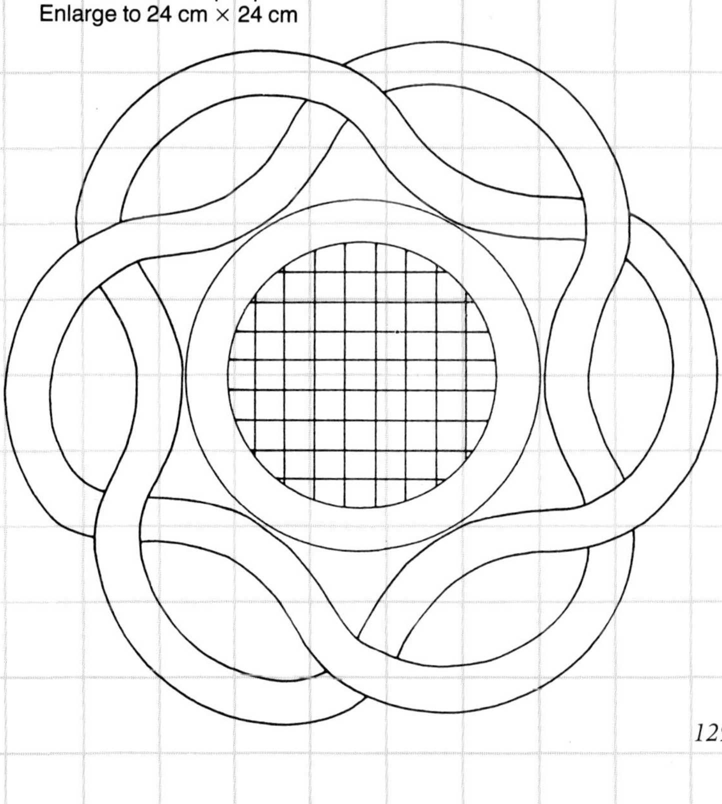

Blue candlewick quilt p. 76
Enlarge to 24 cm × 24 cm

Blue candlewick quilt p. 76
Enlarge to 25 cm × 25 cm

Blue candlewick quilt p. 76
Enlarge to 25 cm × 25 cm

Pen case with mola appliqué p. 78
Enlarge to 25 cm × 9.5 cm

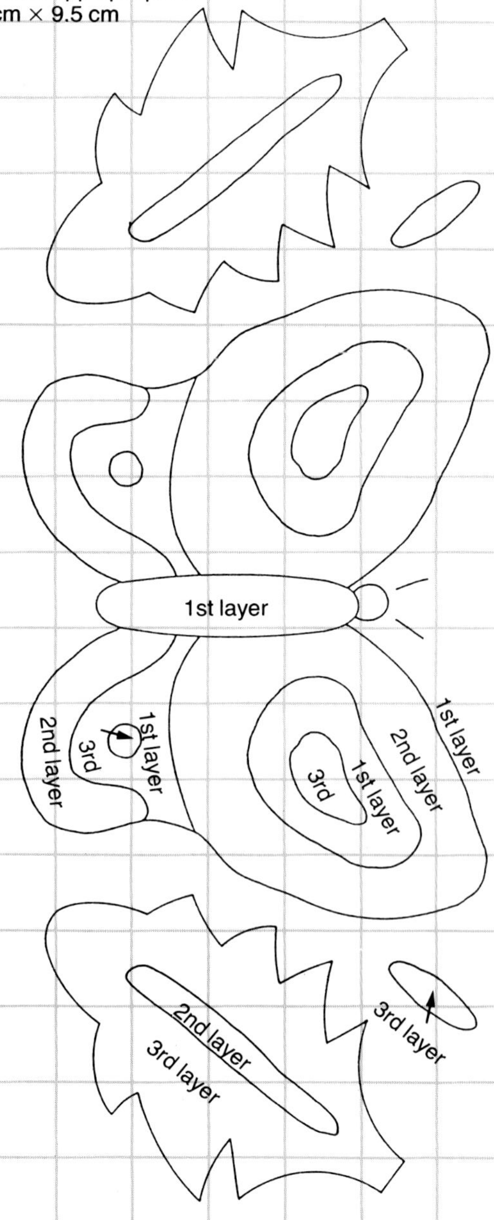

Trapunto wall hanging p. 78
Enlarge to 18 cm × 18 cm

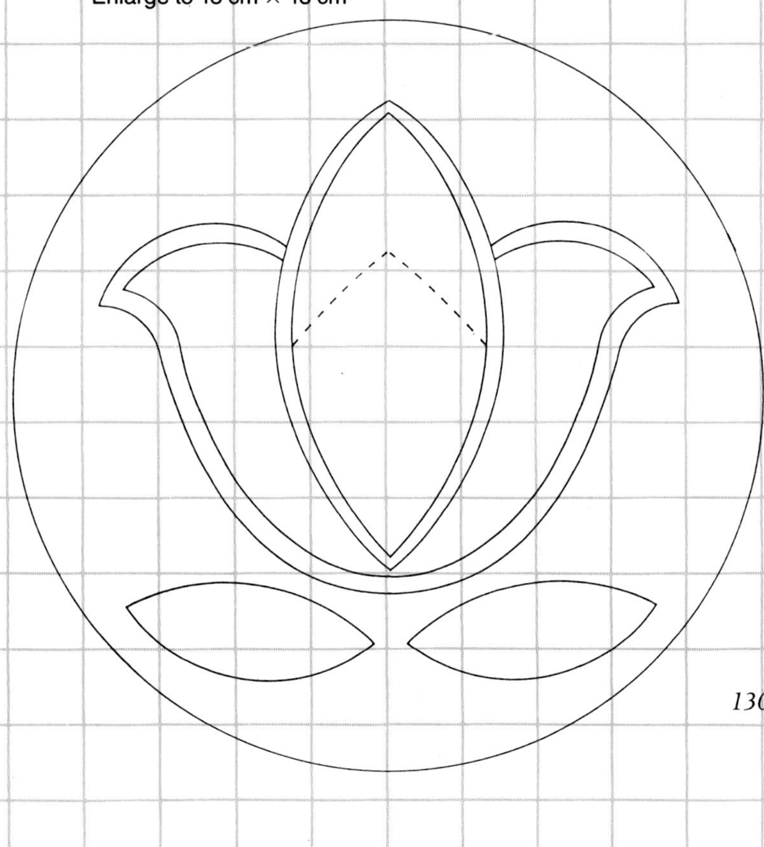

Double photograph frame p. 78
Enlarge to 22.5 cm × 15 cm

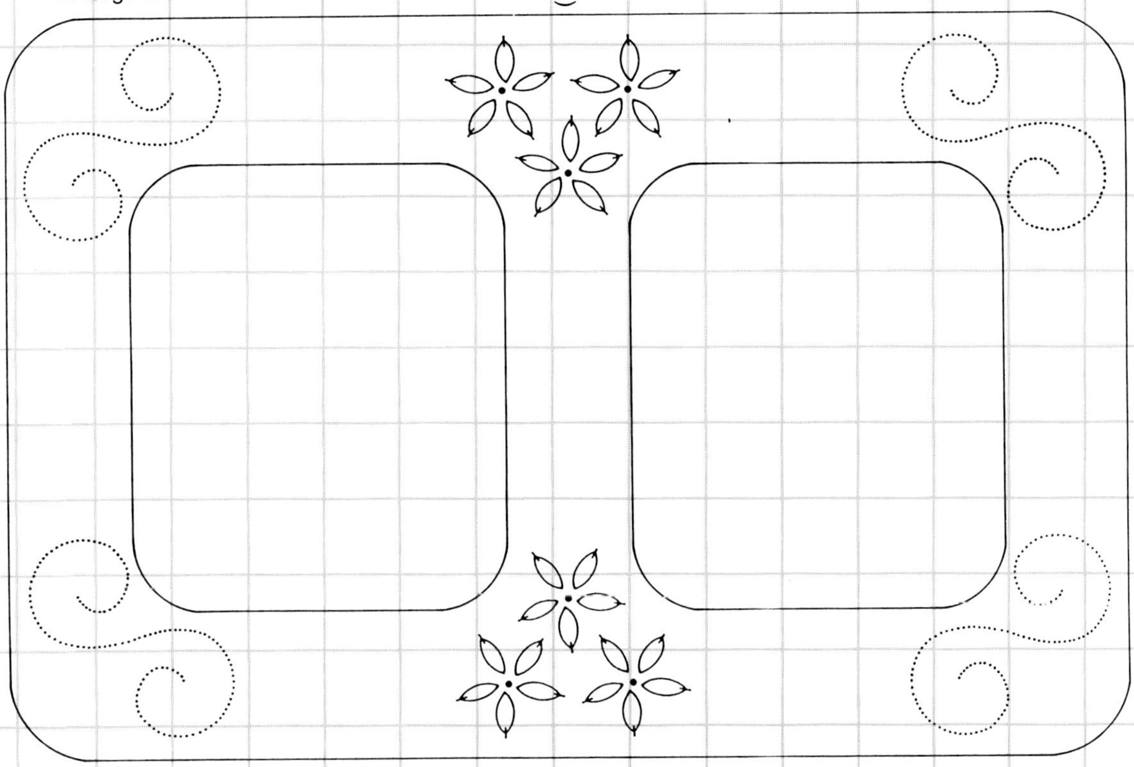

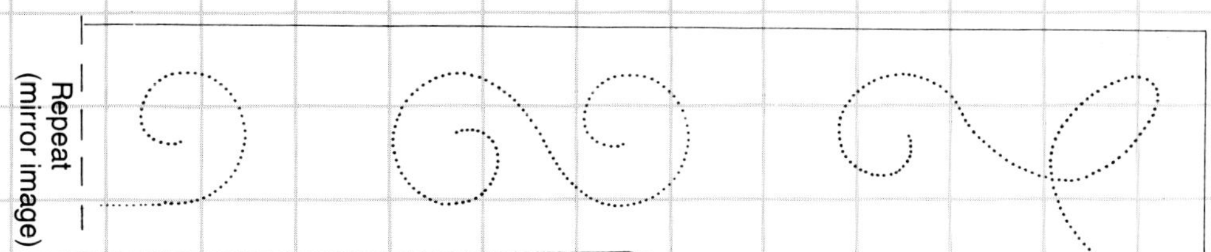

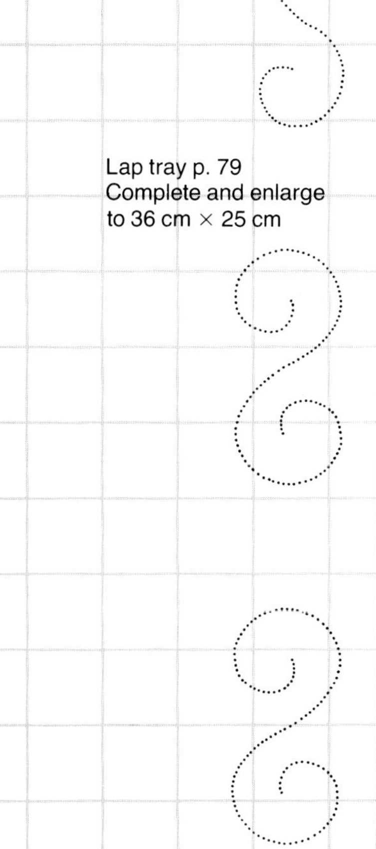

Lap tray p. 79
Complete and enlarge to 36 cm × 25 cm

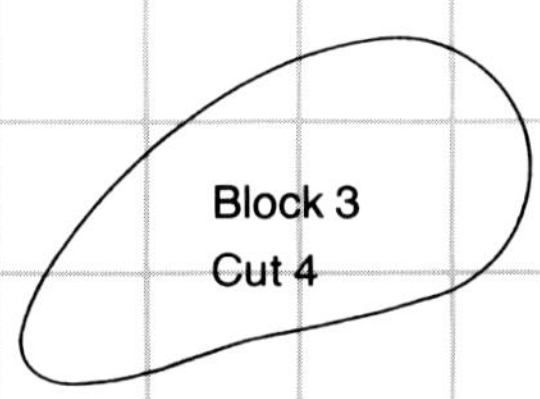

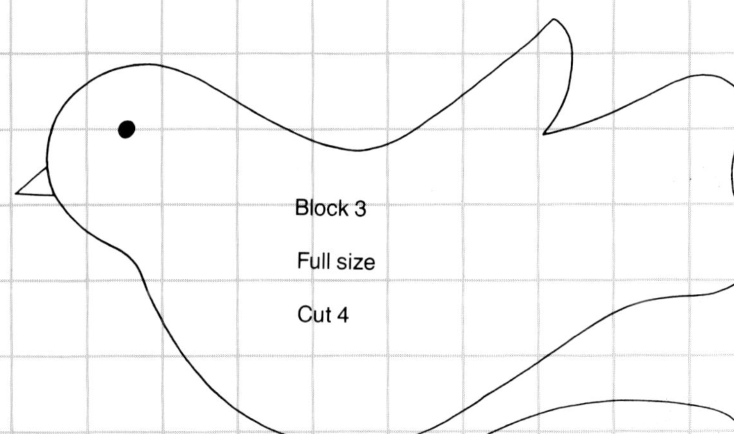

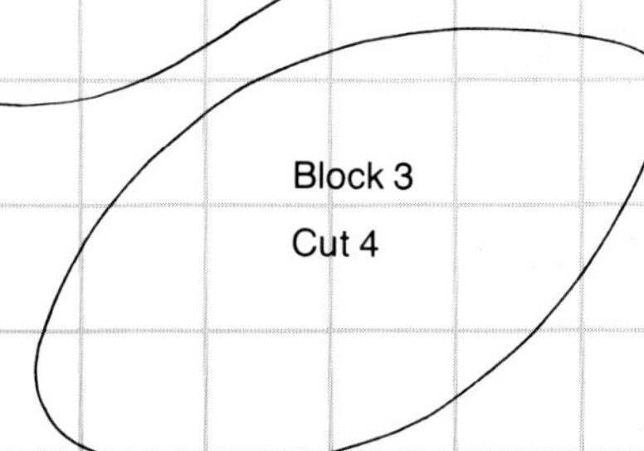

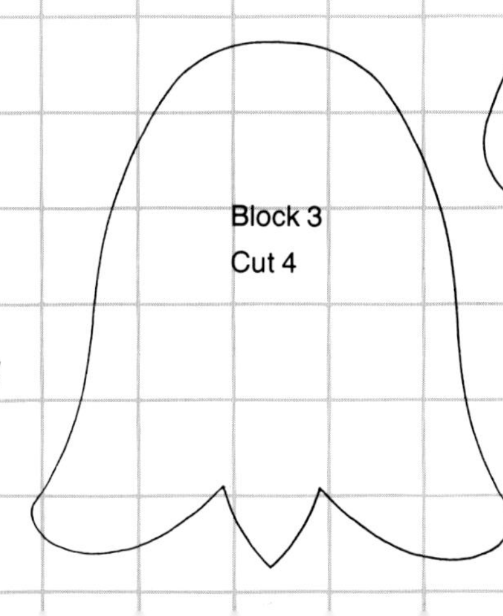

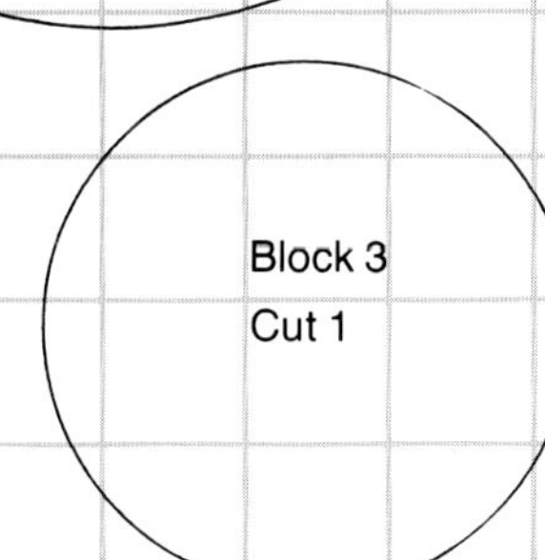

Blue sampler p. 82

Block 3

Blue sampler p. 82

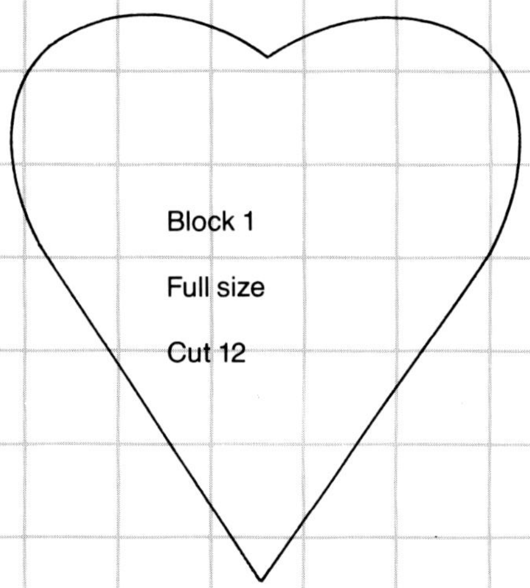

Block 4 (Bleeding hearts)

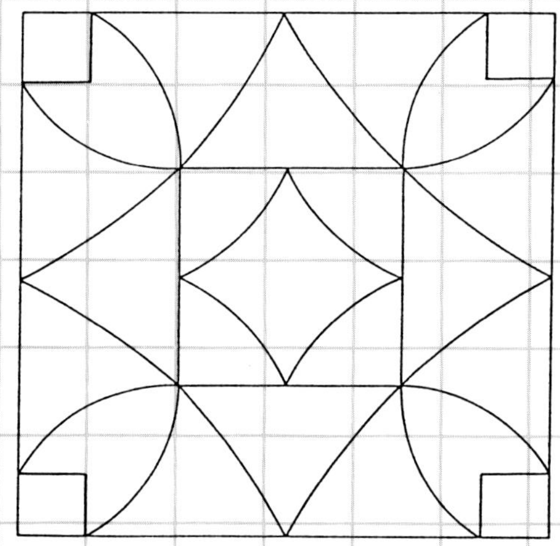

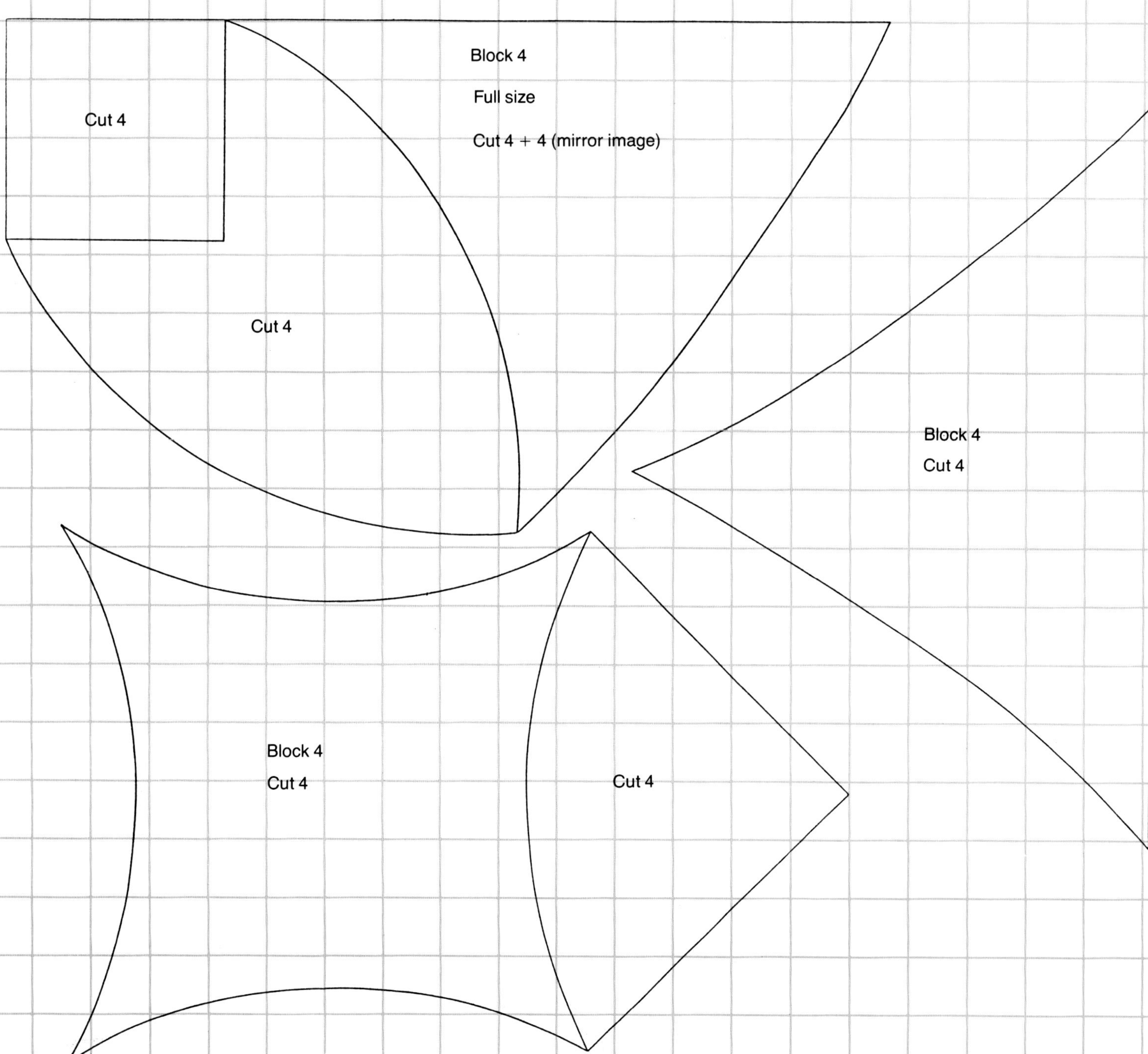

Blue sampler p. 82

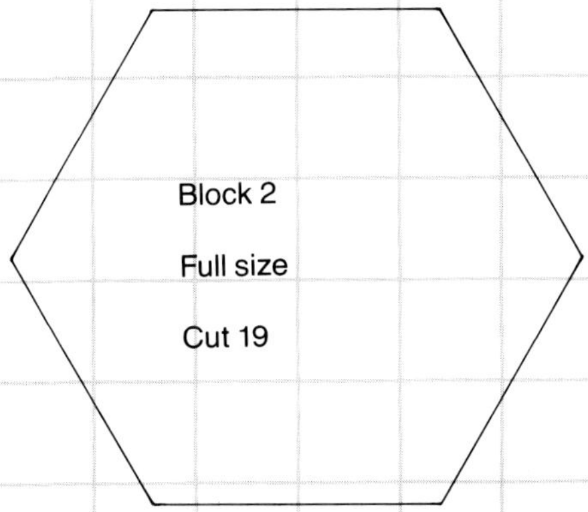

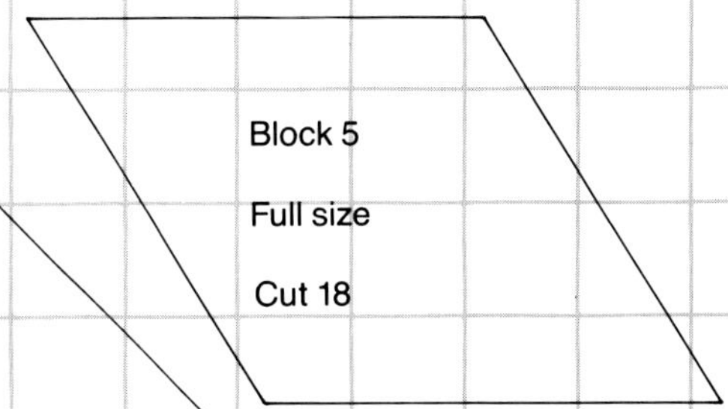

Block 6 (Hearts and gizzards)

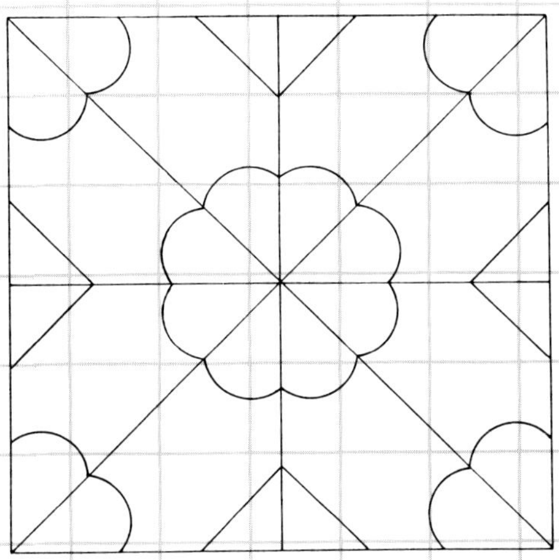

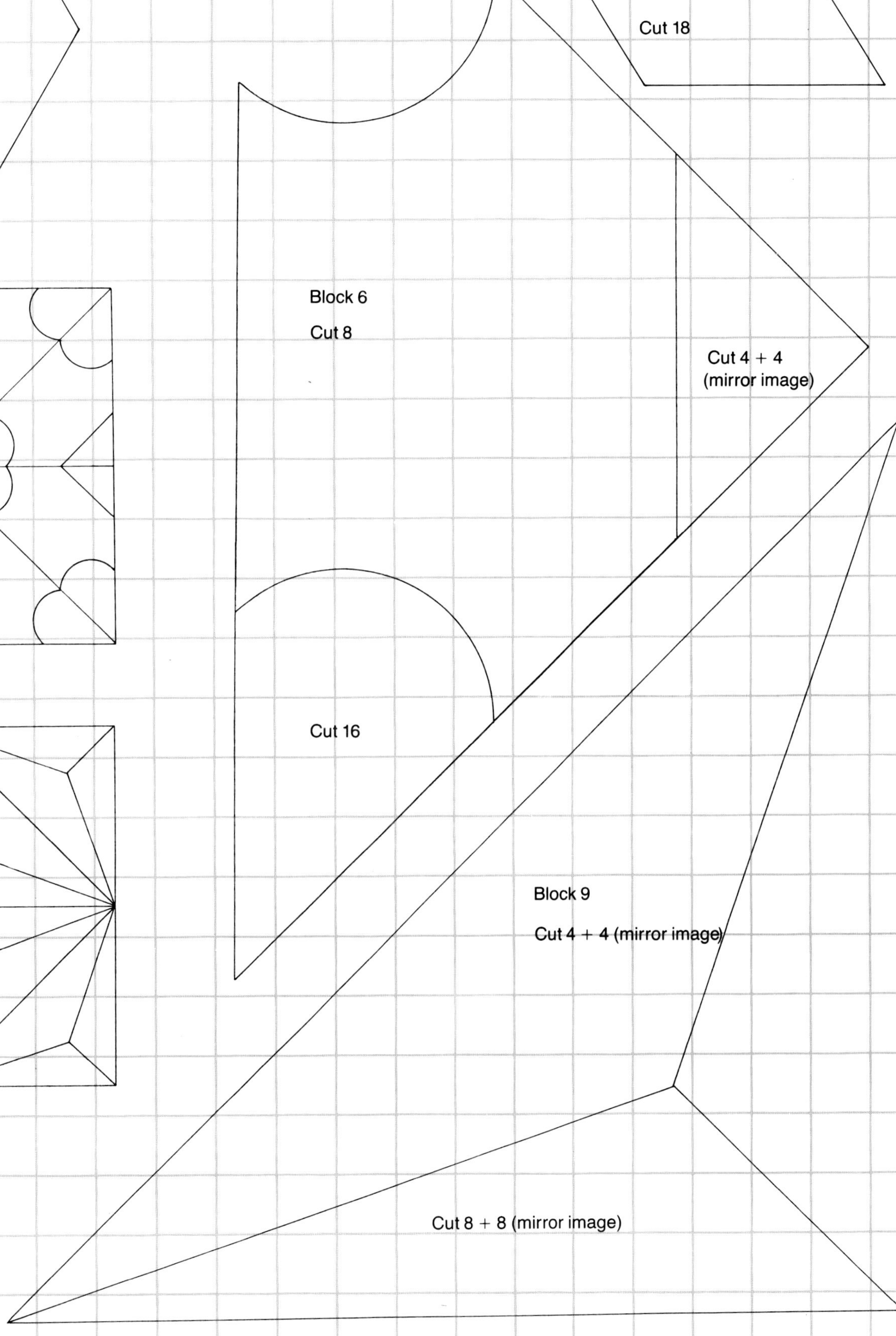

Block 9 (Diamondring)

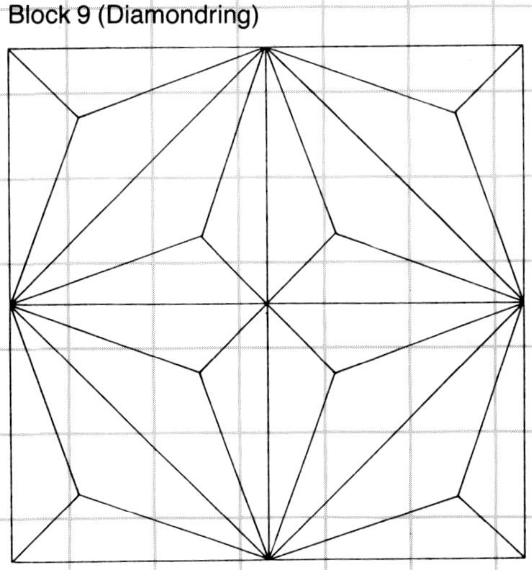

Blue sampler p. 82

Block 7 (Louisiana)

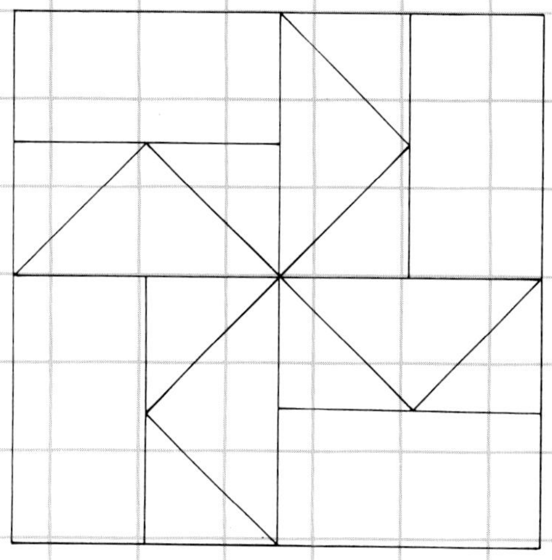

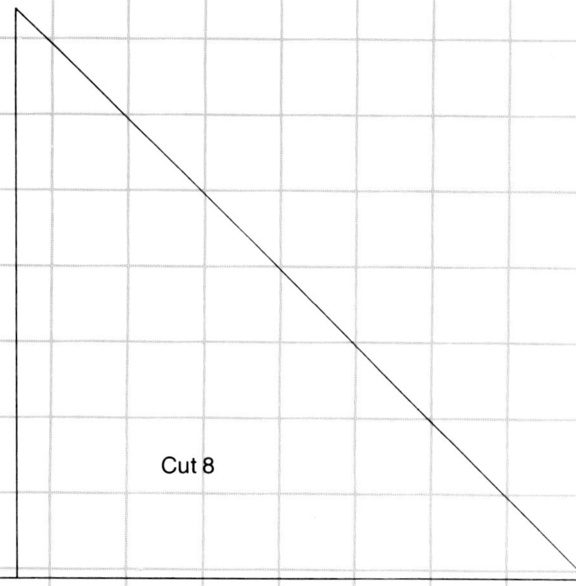

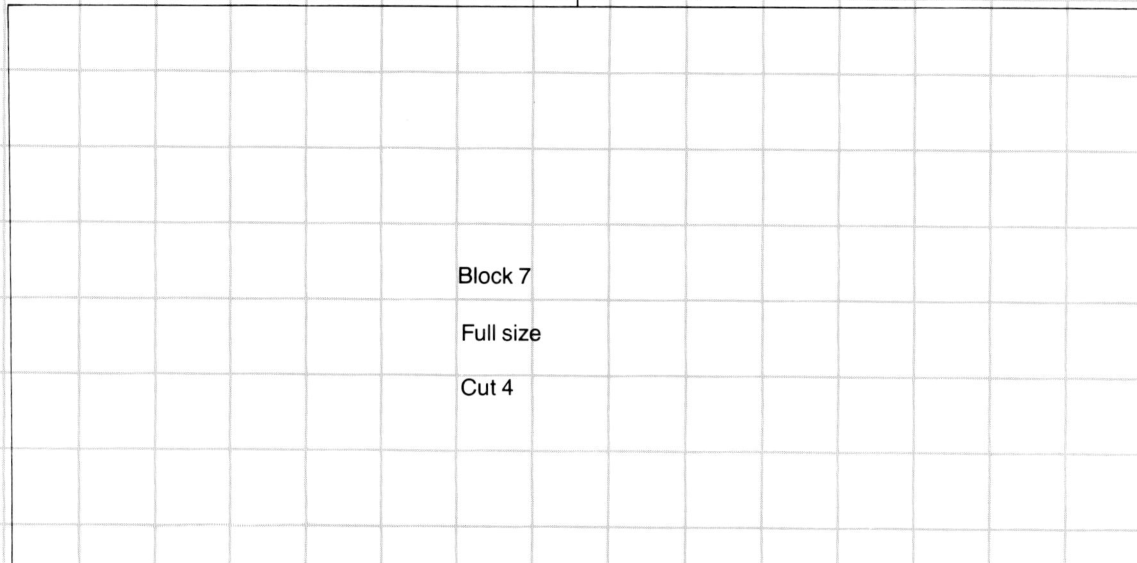

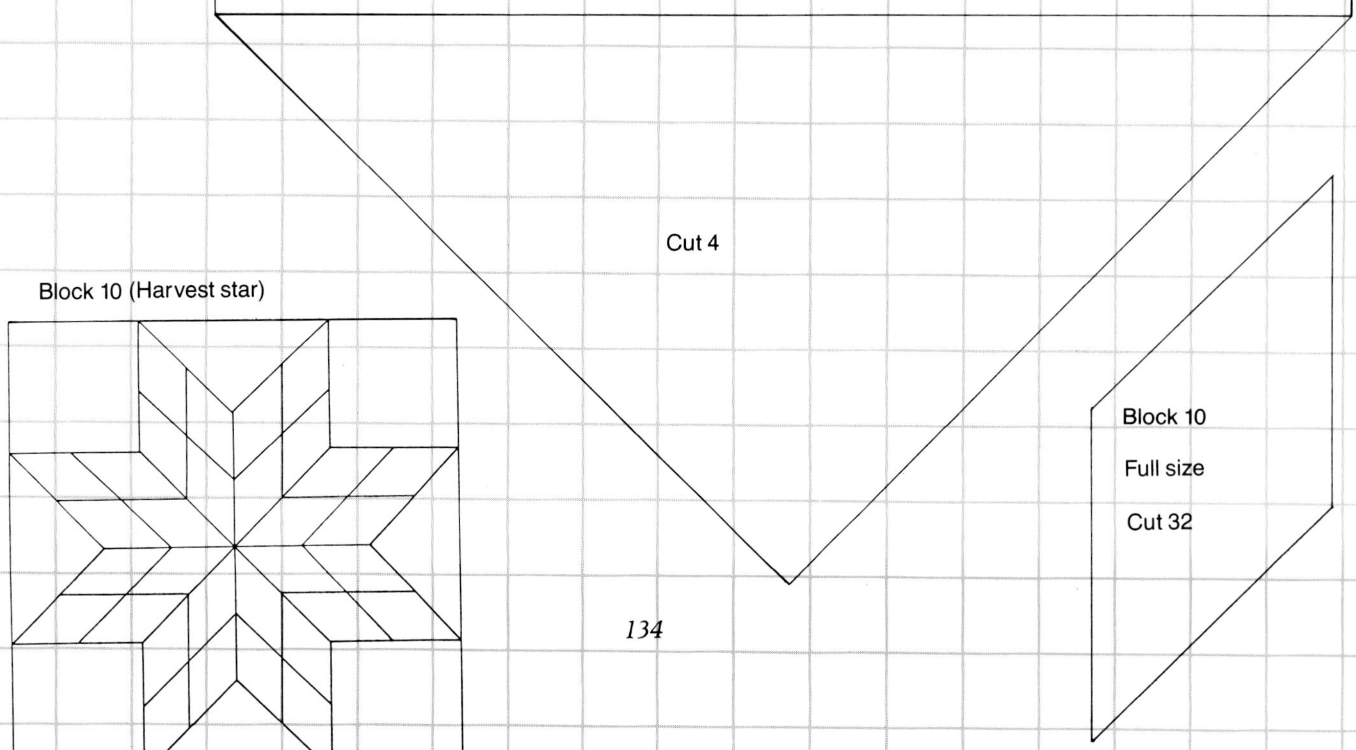

Block 10 (Harvest star)

Blue sampler p. 82

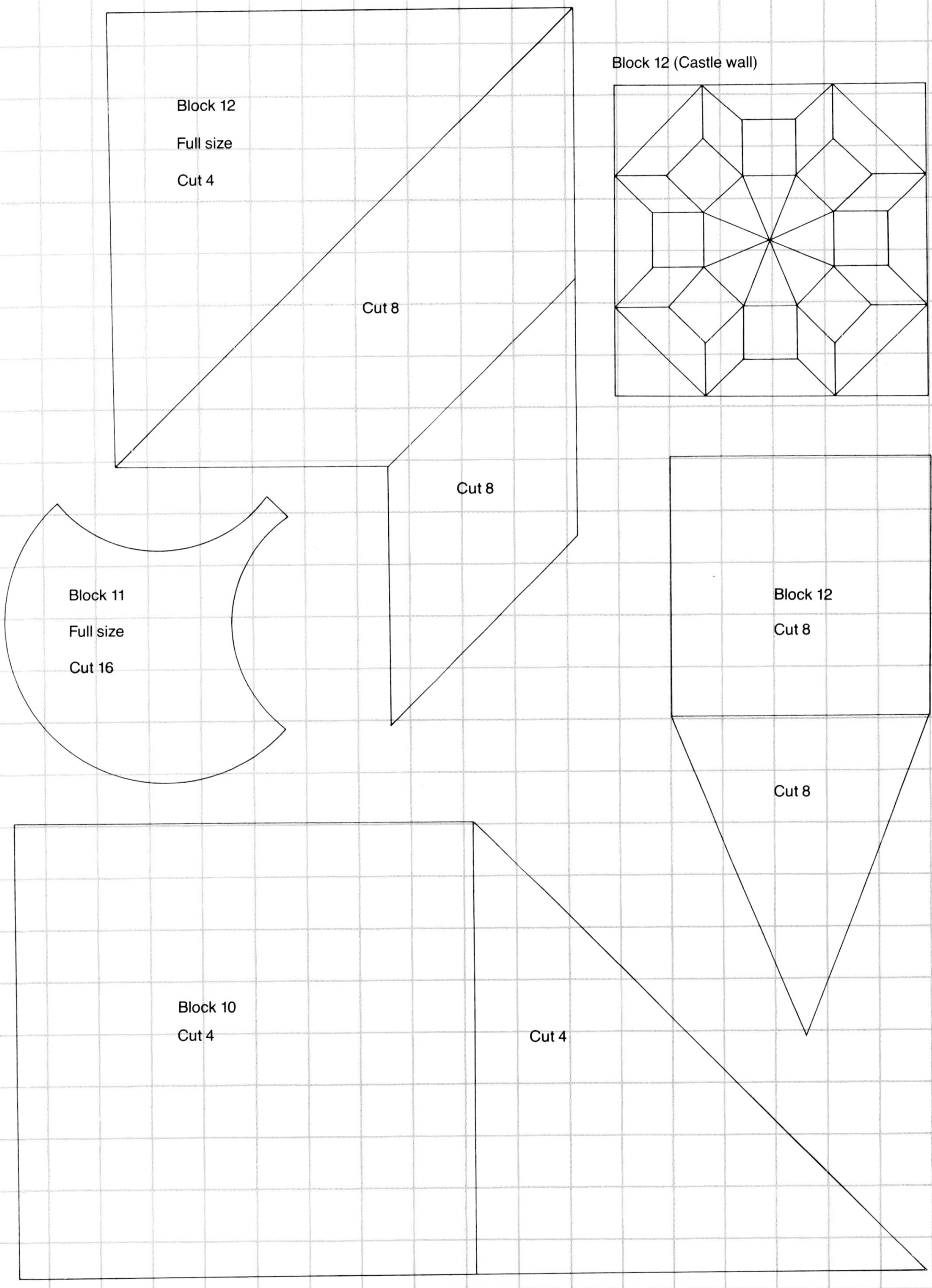

Handbag with strips (side panel) p. 84
Enlarge to 17.5 cm × 20 cm

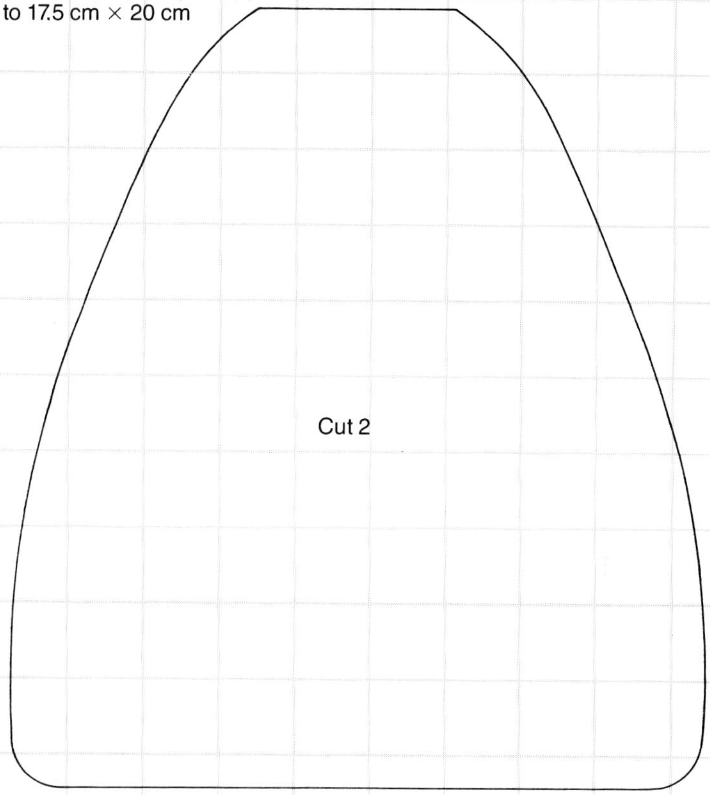

Coaster p. 93
Enlarge to 11 cm × 9.6 cm

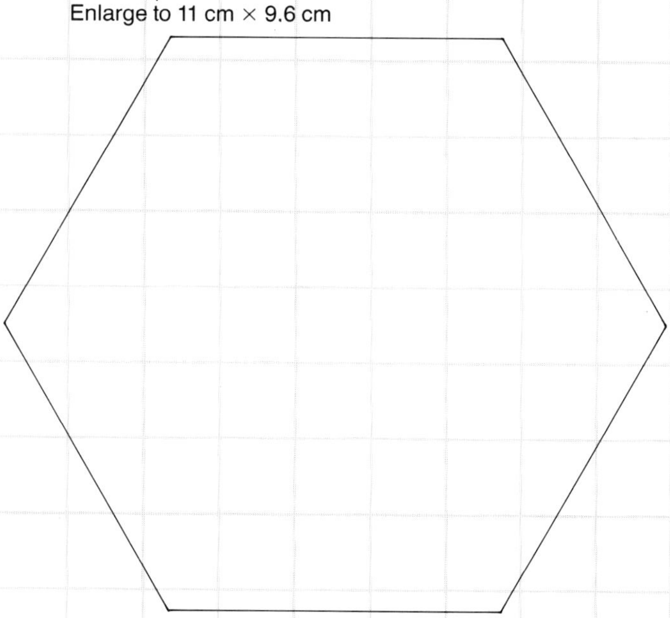

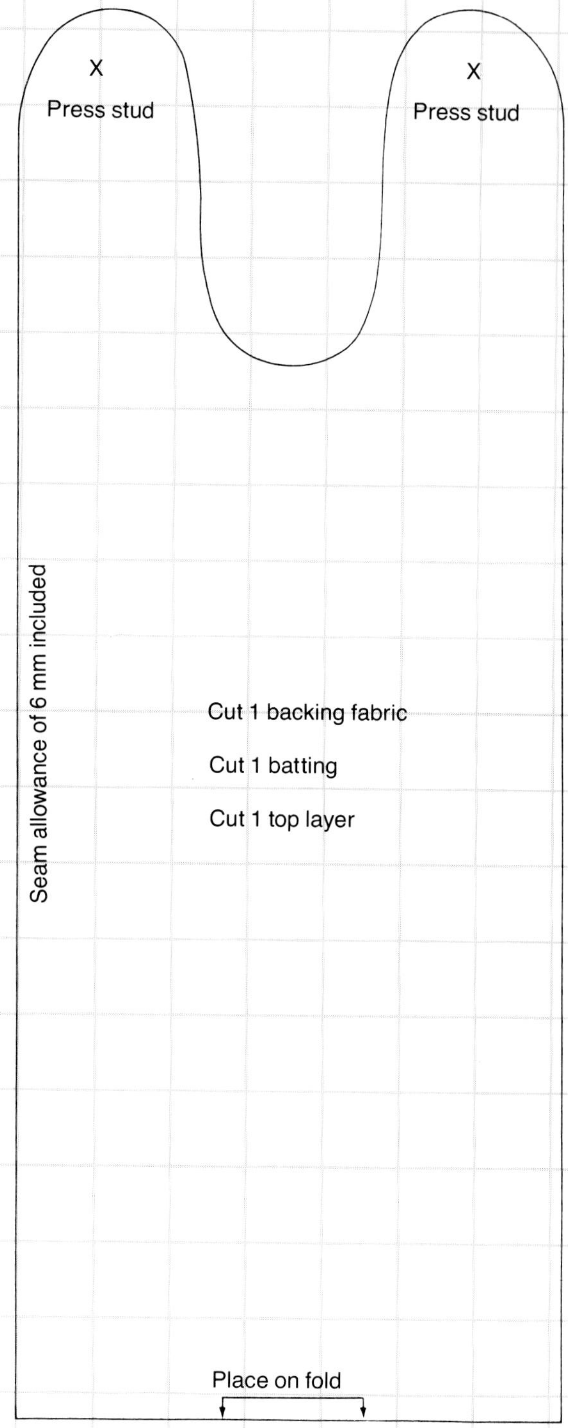

Tissue box container (top and bottom panel) p. 92
Enlarge to 26 cm × 10 cm

Tissue box container (side panel) p. 92
Enlarge to 14 cm × 36.5 cm

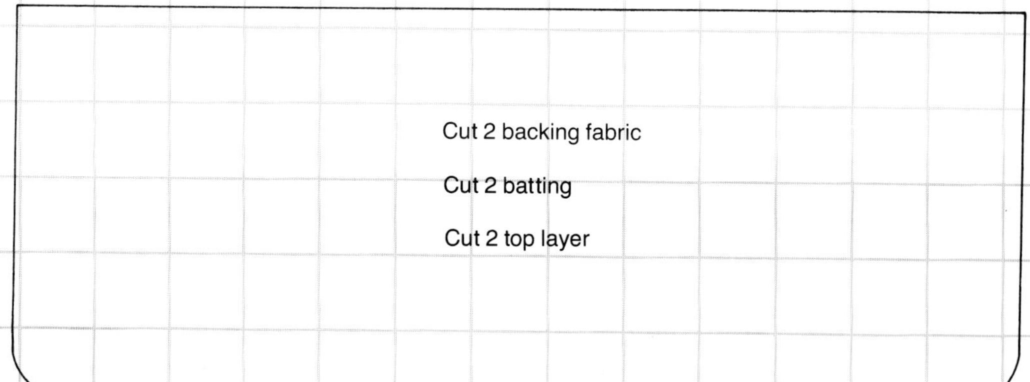

Cosmetics bag (back) p. 93
Enlarge to 22 cm × 24 cm

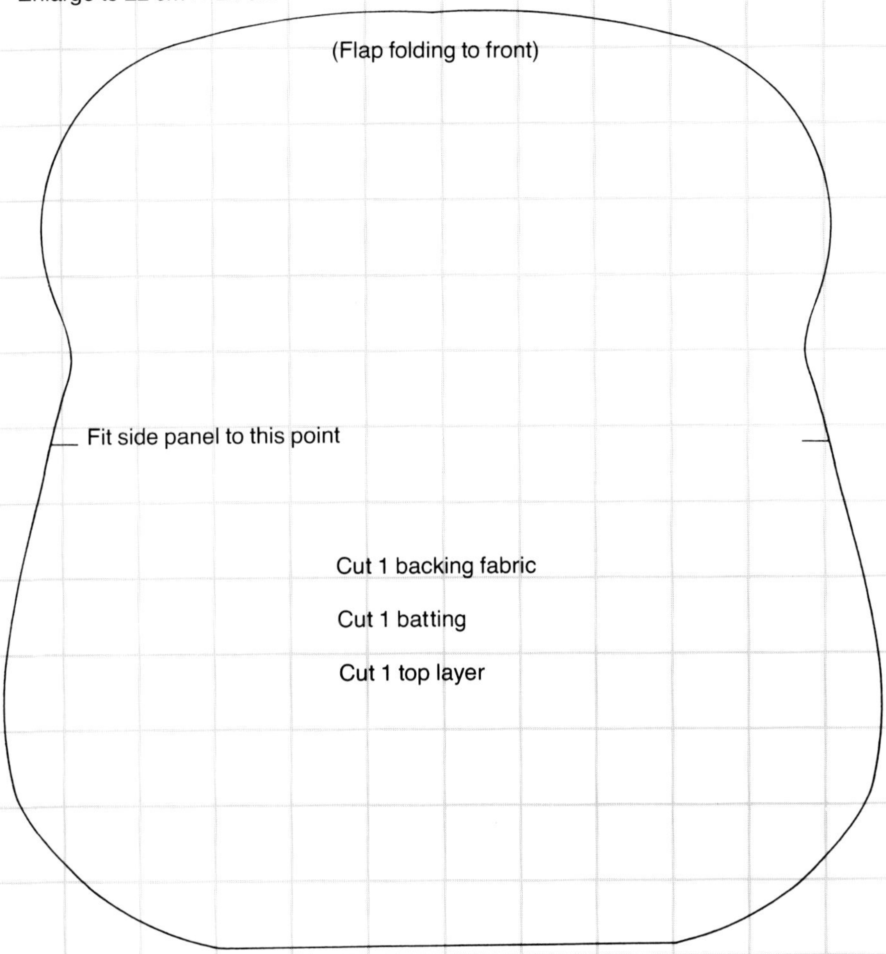

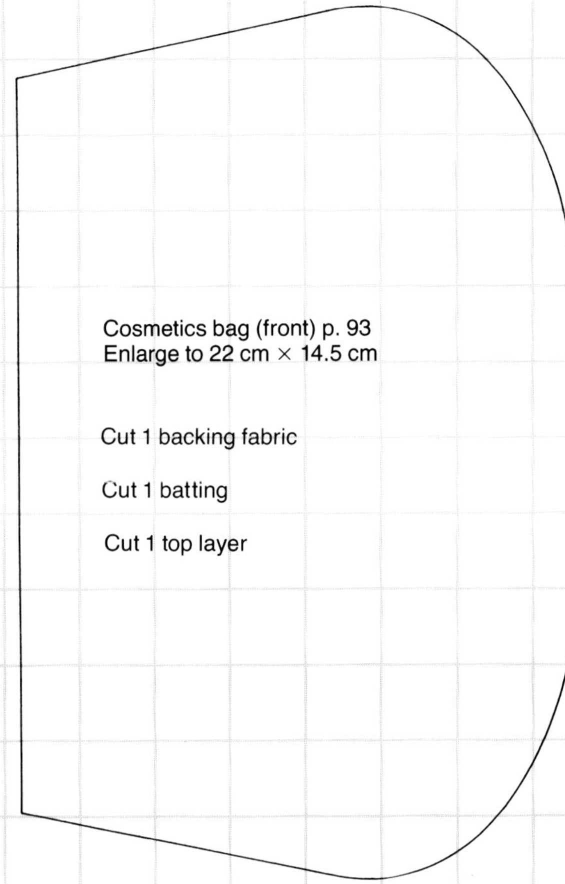

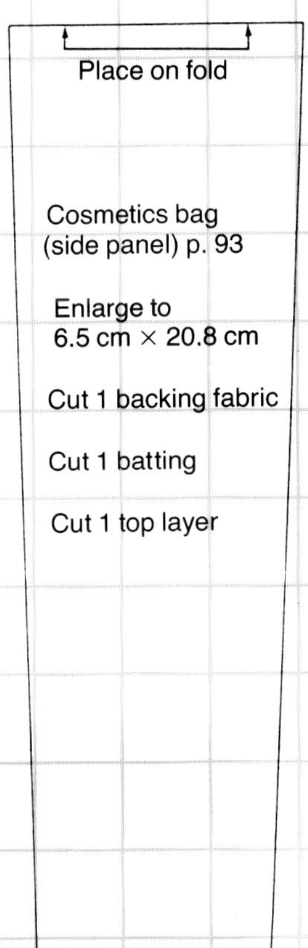

Hawaiian appliqué cushion p. 82
Enlarge to 21 cm × 21 cm and repeat to complete pattern

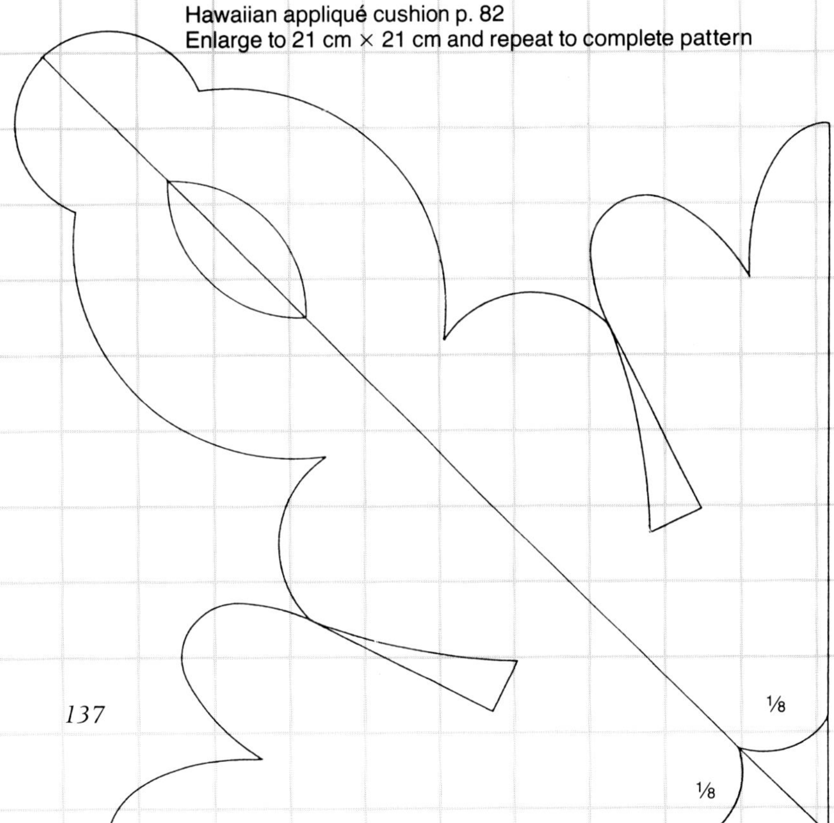

Seminole quilt p. 89
Enlarge to 28 cm × 63 cm

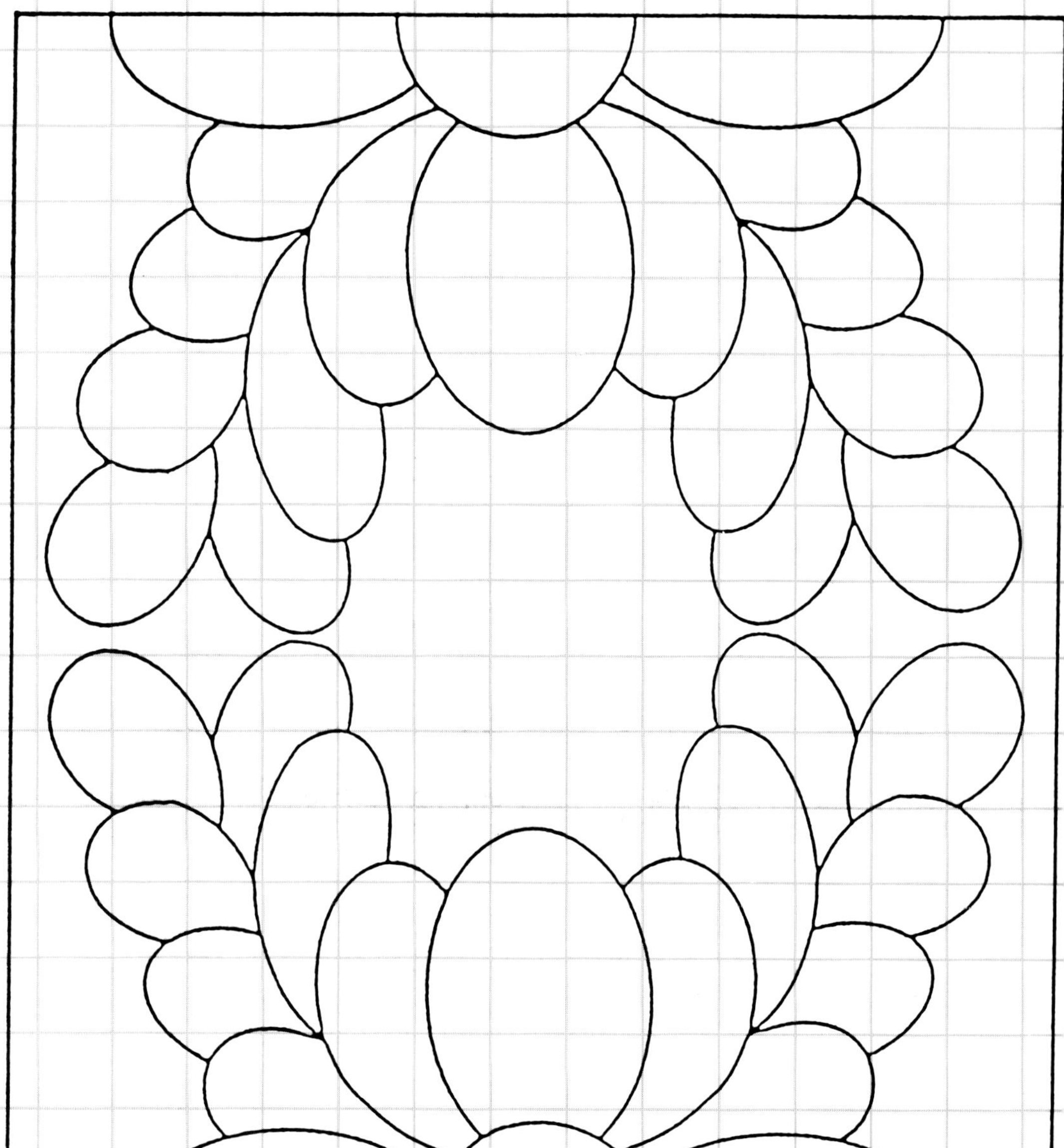

Full-sized extract

Seminole quilt p. 89
Enlarge to 29.5 cm × 138 cm

Full-sized extract

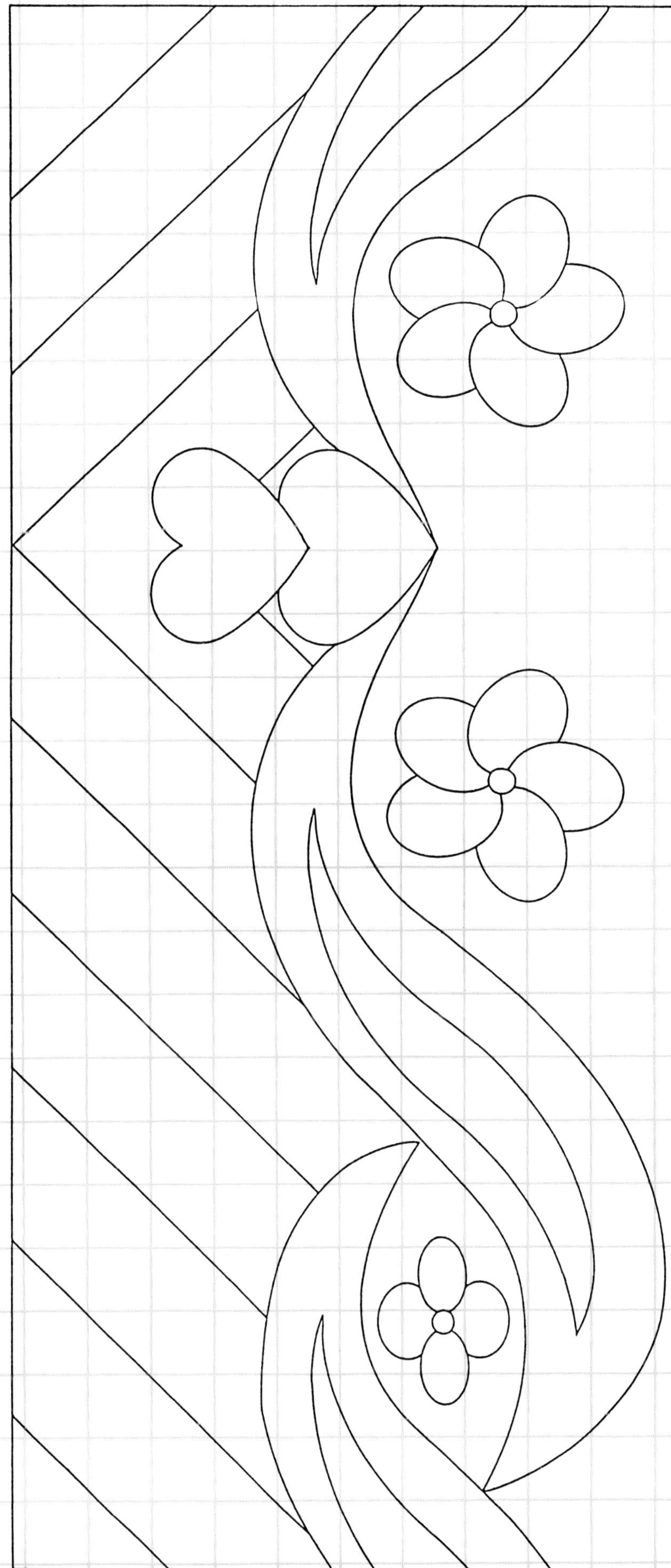

Buffer strip p. 103
Enlarge to 23 cm × 16 cm

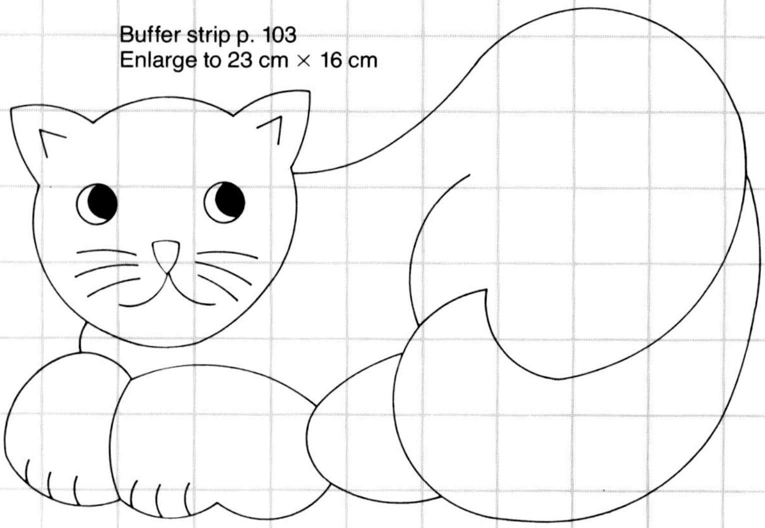

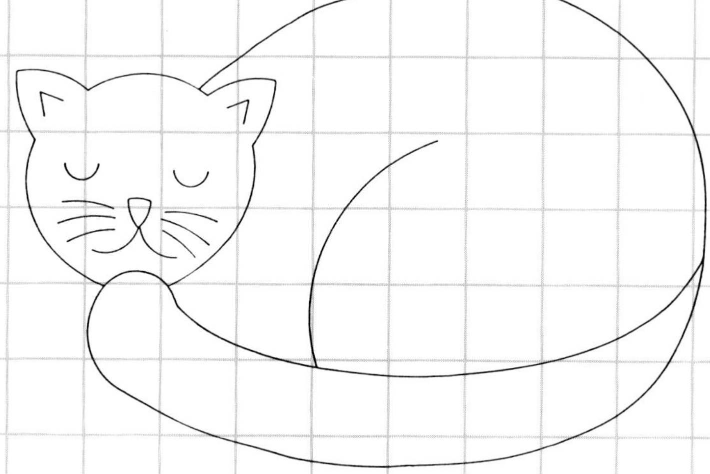

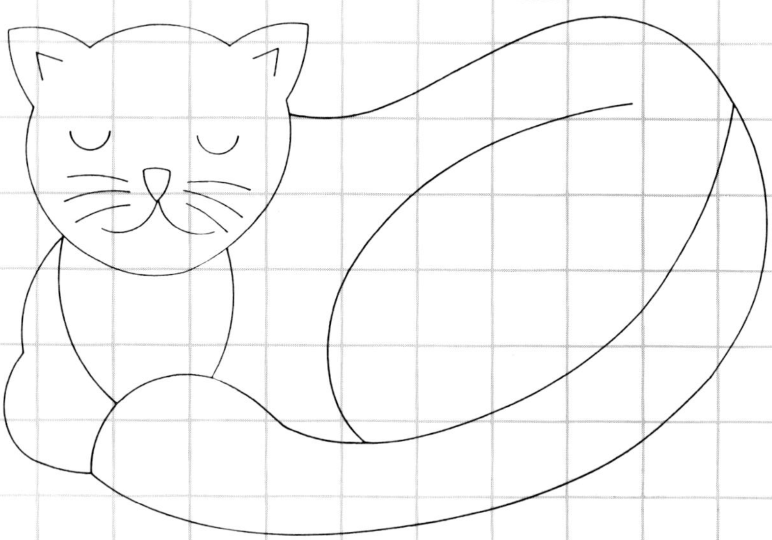

Utility bag p. 102
Enlarge to 14 cm × 5.5 cm

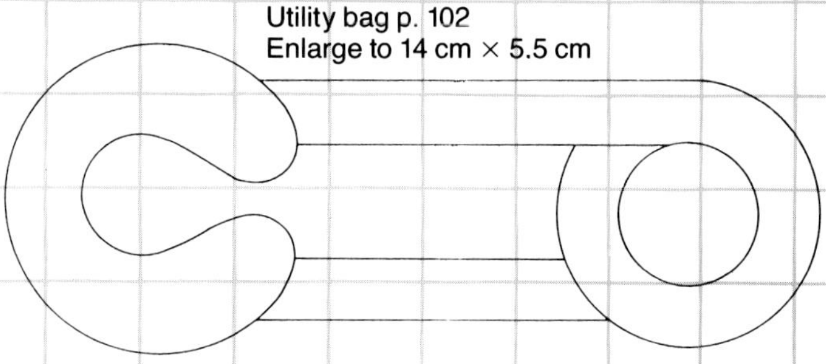

Baby's bib p. 102
Enlarge to 18.5 cm × 24 cm

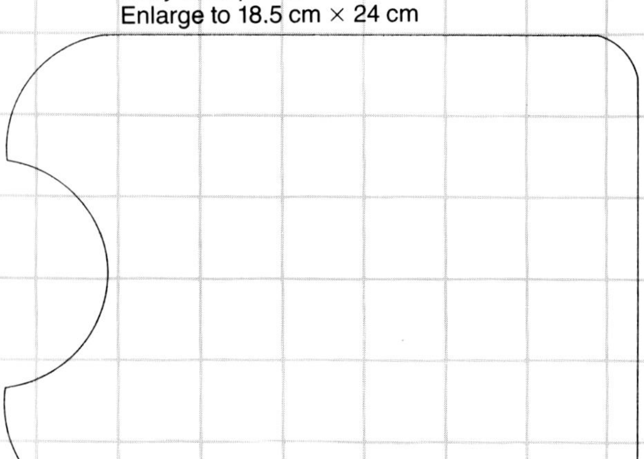

Quilt for a baby's room p. 102
Enlarge to 27 cm × 44 cm
Full size for appliqué motif on baby's bib p. 102

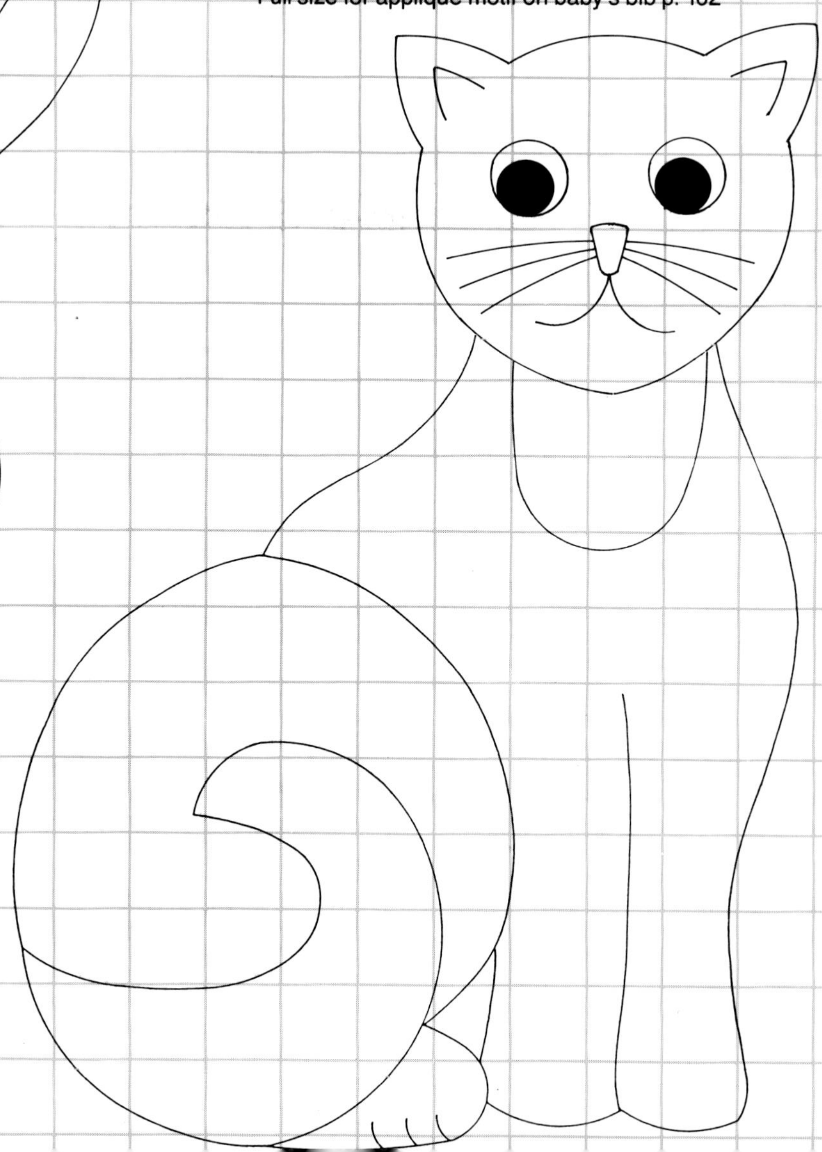

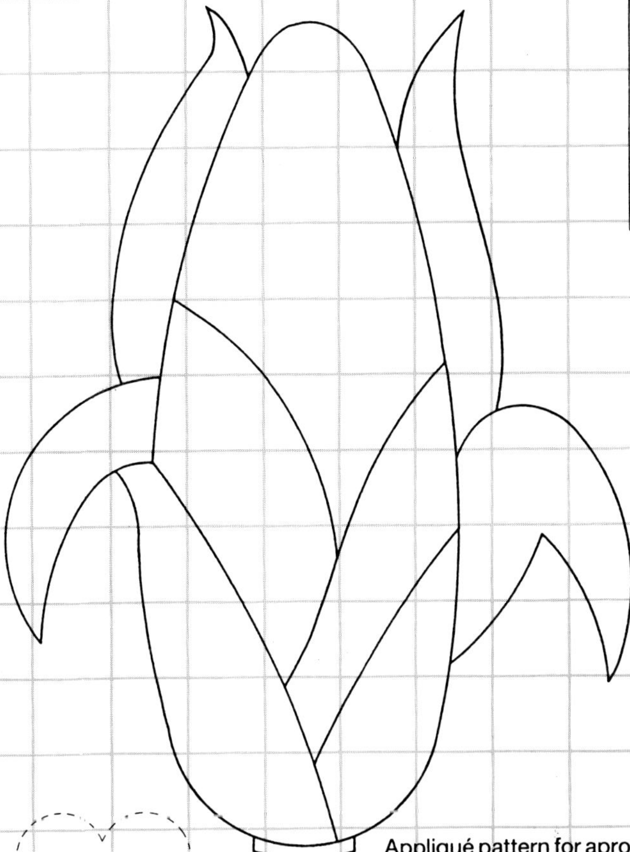

Appliqué pattern for apron and pot holder p. 110
and barbecue utility bag p. 112
Enlarge to 8.5 cm × 11.5 cm

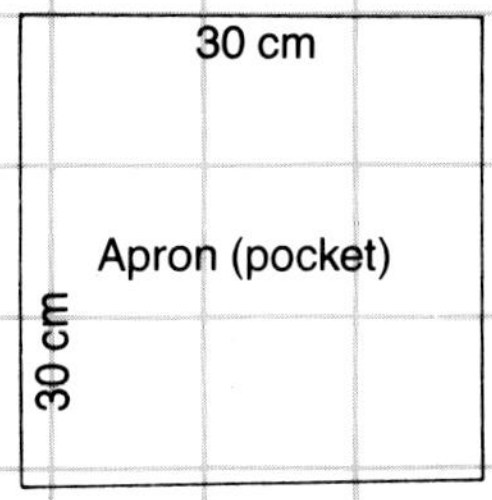

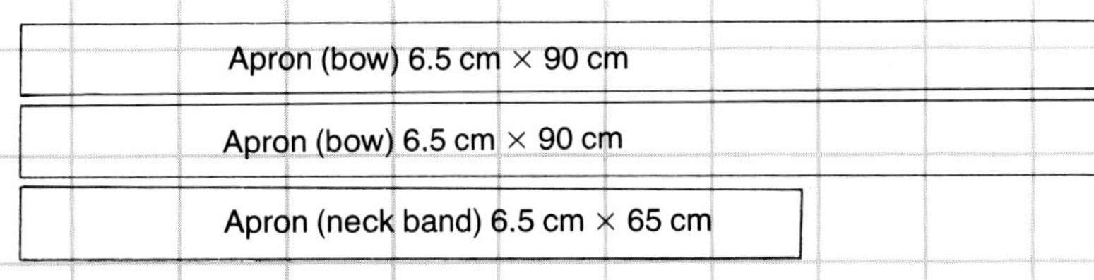

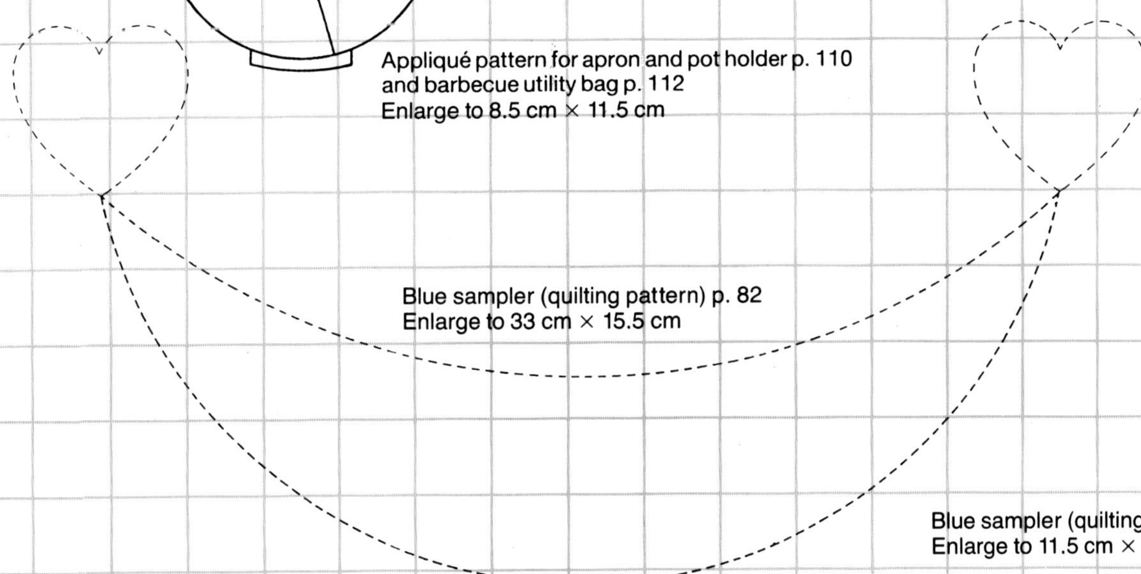

Blue sampler (quilting pattern) p. 82
Enlarge to 33 cm × 15.5 cm

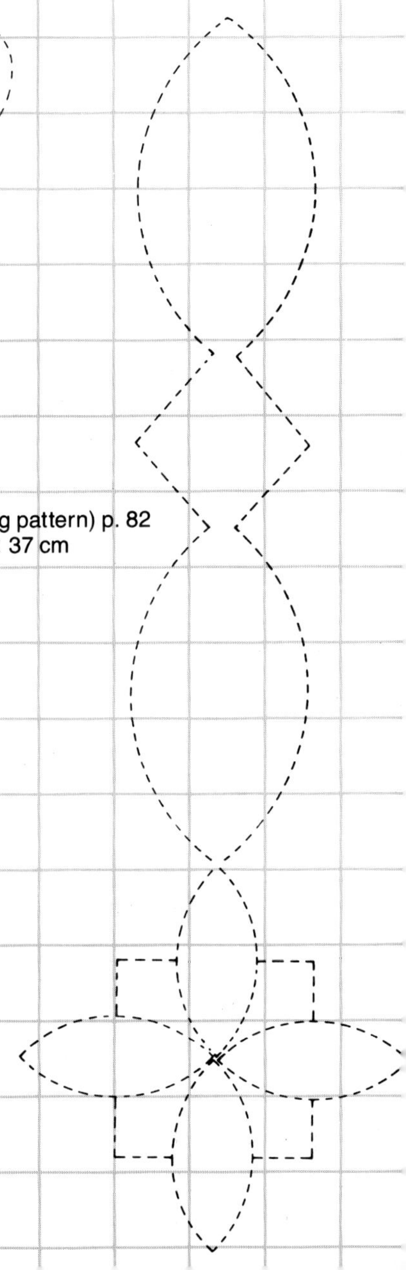

Blue sampler (quilting pattern) p. 82
Enlarge to 11.5 cm × 37 cm

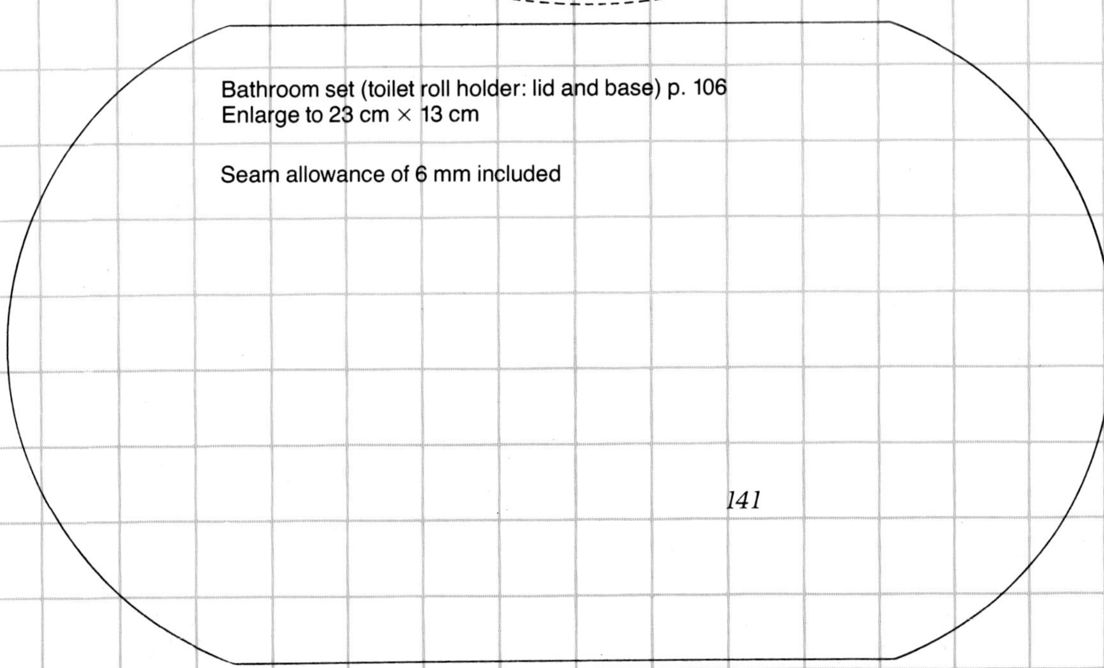

Bathroom set (toilet roll holder: lid and base) p. 106
Enlarge to 23 cm × 13 cm

Seam allowance of 6 mm included

Bathroom set (floor mat) p. 106
Enlarge to 26.5 cm × 55 cm

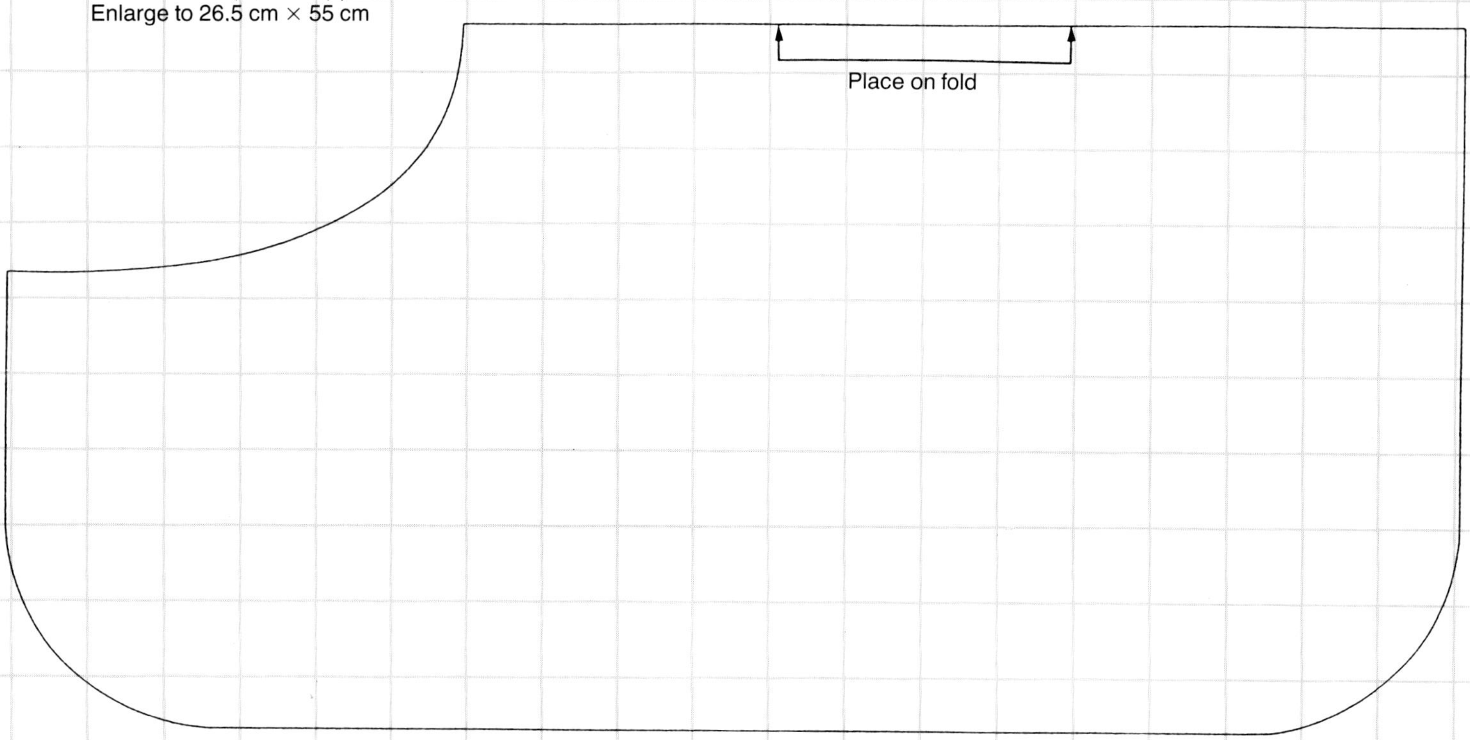

Duck p. 107
Enlarge to 43 cm × 53 cm (1 square = 2.25 cm × 2.25 cm)

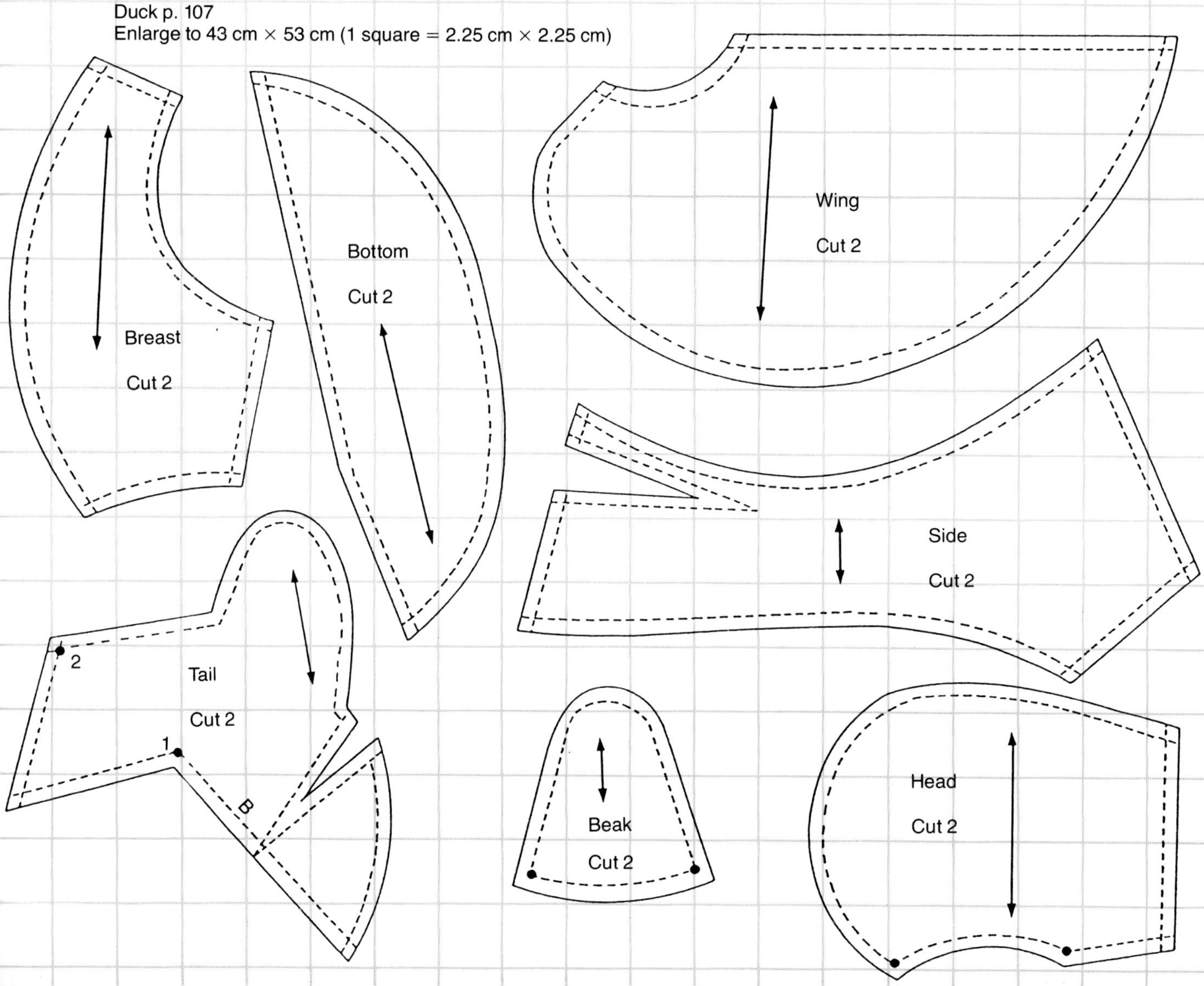

Activity book p. 99

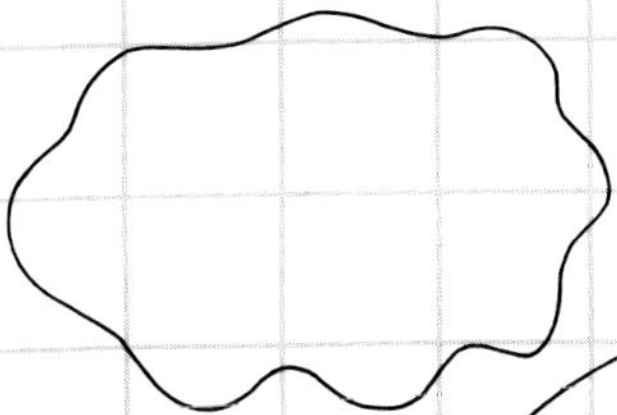

Enlarge to 19 cm × 18.5 cm

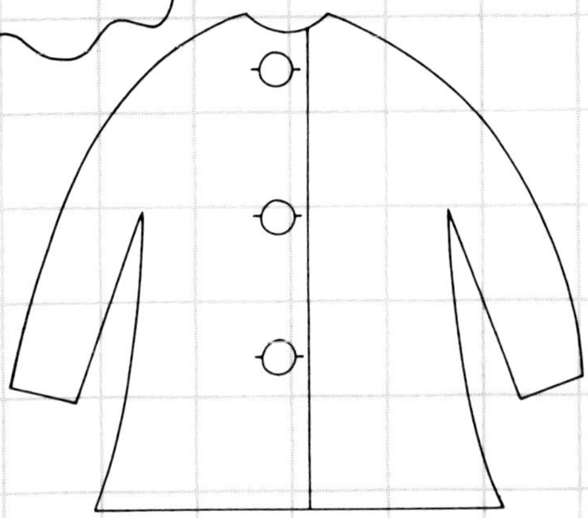

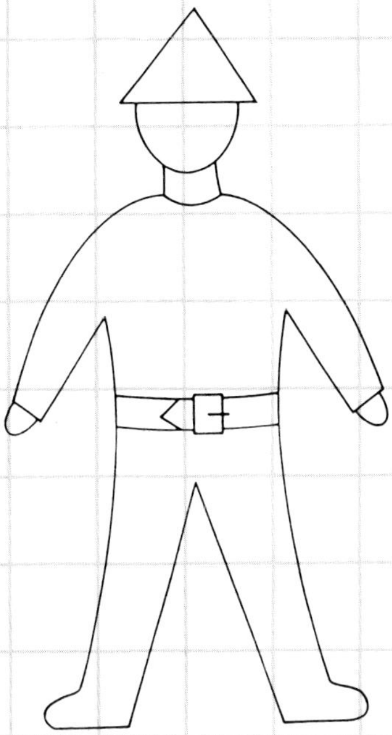

Enlarge to 10 cm × 20 cm

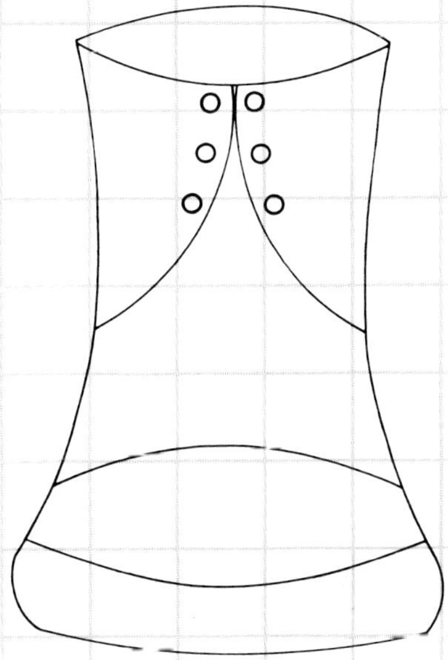

Enlarge to 10.5 cm × 17.5 cm

Enlarge to 16 cm × 19 cm

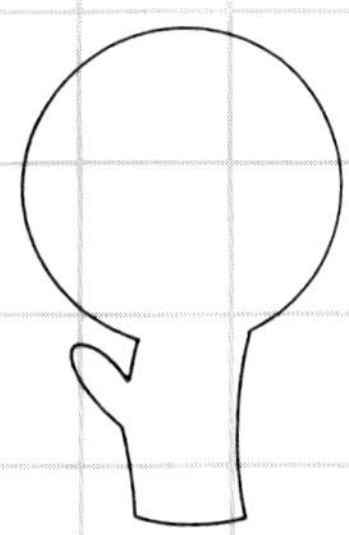

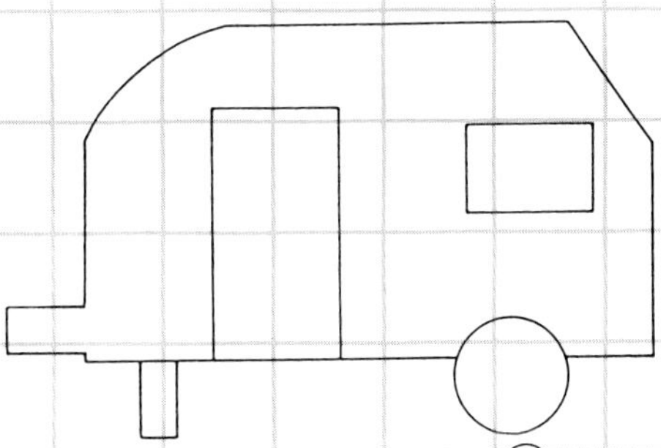

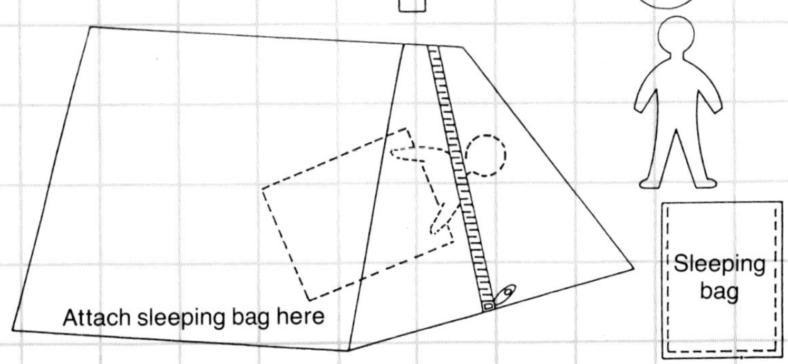

Enlarge to 22 cm × 20 cm

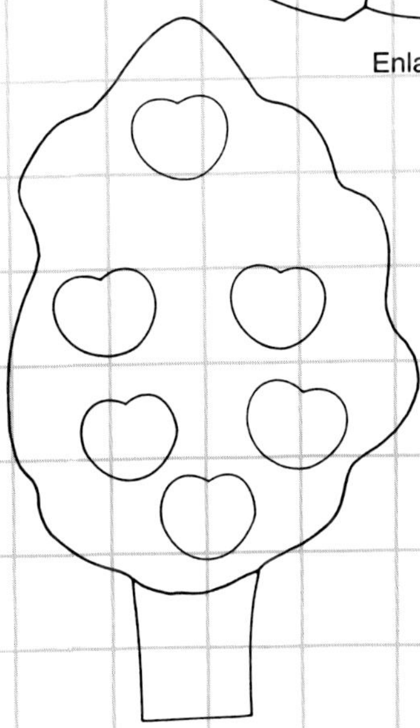

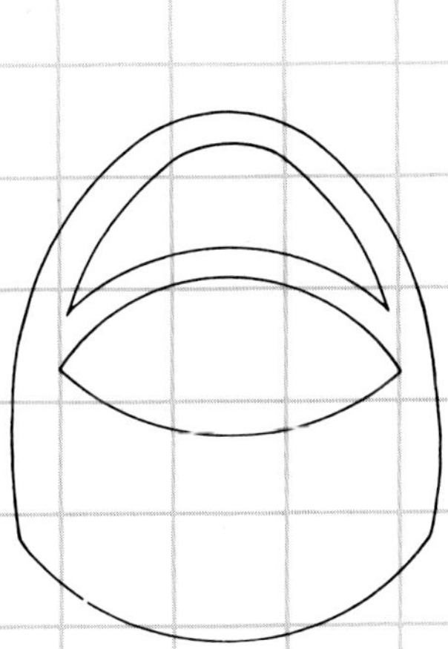

Enlarge to 22 cm × 18 cm

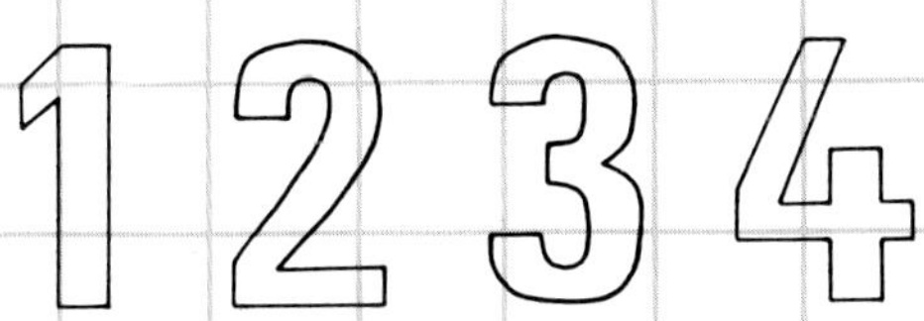

Building blocks p. 96
Enlarge to 4.2 cm × 16 cm

Patchwork jacket p. 84
Enlarge to 57 cm × 72 cm

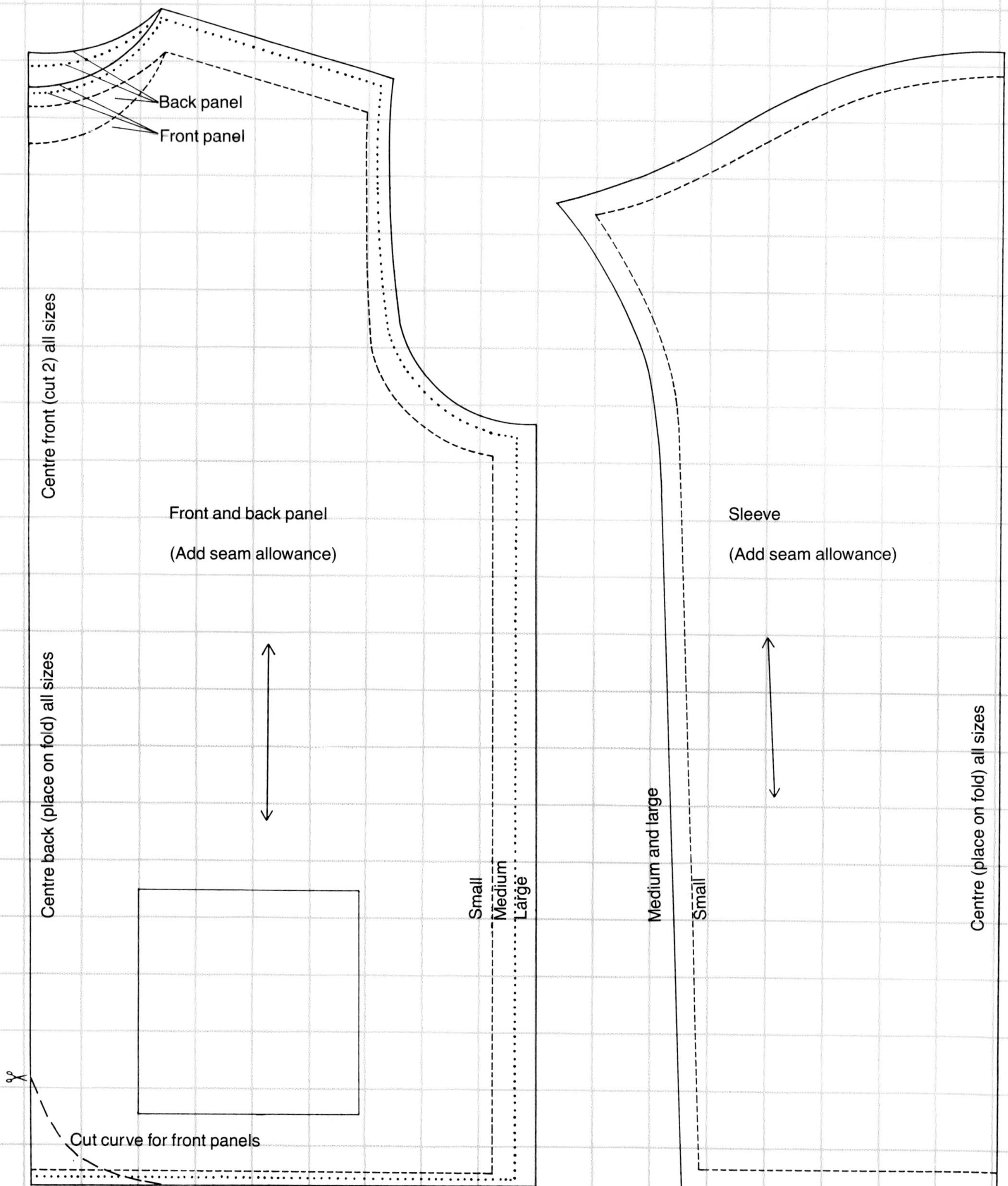